D0853014

LONGMAN

Pocket

IDIOMS
DICTIONARY

PEARSON
Longman

Pearson Education Limited
Edinburgh Gate, Harlow, Essex CM20 2JE, England
and associated companies throughout the world

© Pearson Education Limited 2001

Visit our website: http://www.longman.com/dictionaries

All rights reserved; no part of this publication may be reproduced,
stored in a retrieval system, or transmitted in any form or by any means,
electronic, mechanical, photocopying, recording or otherwise,
without the prior written permission of the Publishers.

First published 2001
008 010 009

Words that the editors have reason to believe constitute
trademarks have been described as such. However, neither the
presence nor the absence of such a description should be
regarded as affecting the legal status of any trademark.

ISBN 978-0-582-77641-8

Set in 7pt MetaPlus Normal by Peter Wray
Printed in China
GCC/07

Contents

ACKNOWLEDGEMENTS

Director	Della Summers
Editorial Director & Publisher	Pierre-Henri Cousin
Editor & Project Manager	Wendy Lee
Lexicographer	Clare Vickers
Illustrator	Chris Simpson
Design	Alex Ingr
Cover design	Abbey Design, Harlow, Essex
Proofreaders	Jane Tait, Ruth Noble

and the Longman Dictionaries team

▶ Using the Dictionary

What are idioms and how are they used?

An idiom is a group of words whose meaning as a group is different from the meaning those words would have if you considered each one separately. Idioms add colour to the language, giving us lively and interesting ways of expressing ourselves. We use them in a wide variety of situations, from friendly conversations and business meetings to more formal written contexts.

The *Longman Pocket Idioms Dictionary* focuses on over 3000 common idioms. It covers expressions whose meanings are fairly easy to understand, such as *put your heads together* and *can't hear yourself think*, as well as some that are less obvious, like *face the music* and *keep your shirt on*. Many compound nouns (nouns made up of more than one word but which have a single meaning), like *wild card* and *acid test*, are also included. So are phrases which you will frequently hear in everyday situations, such as *it's just as well* and *of all things*. Examples show the idiom in a typical context, and give the reader access to real language and natural speech. The *Idiom Activator* (pages 135–145) provides a further tool for language learners, grouping together idioms which have a similar meaning and making it easier to choose the right expression for a particular situation.

How do I find the idiom I am looking for?

Idioms are entered under 'keywords', which are listed in alphabetical order and shown in CAPITAL LETTERS. Many of these keywords are nouns. If the idiom you are looking for contains a noun, or more than one noun, look it up under the first noun in the idiom. For example, *go bananas* is at BANANAS, *cost the earth* is at EARTH, and *piece of cake* is at PIECE. Compound nouns are also found at the first noun. For example, you will find *wild card* under CARD, and *acid test* under ACID.

If there is no noun in the idiom, look under the first word which clearly carries a meaning. This will usually be an adjective or a verb. For example, *thick and fast* is at THICK, *sb has something to prove* is at PROVE, and *where it's at* is at WHERE.

What happens when idioms have different forms?

Very few idioms are fixed in form. This dictionary shows how a phrase can vary in the following ways:

▶ Variations of the main form of the idiom which mean the same thing are shown in italics straight after it:

> **the 64,000 dollar question** *also*
> **the million dollar question**

▶ If part of the expression can be left out, it is shown in brackets:

> **make (all) the right noises**

▶ In idioms such as *a _____ -free zone*, the space with a line under it means that many different words could fill the gap, depending on what you are talking about; for example, a *politics-free zone*, a *humour-free zone*.

▶ Opposites are shown after the main entry and are followed only by an example. Variations which contain the same basic idiom as the main form but take a different standpoint are shown in the same way:

> **fight a losing battle** to keep trying to do something that you cannot succeed in doing ▶ *She was fighting a losing battle against cancer.* **be a losing battle** ▶ *We try to teach our kids to enjoy books, but with TV and pop music it's a losing battle.*

▶ Common adjectives and nouns which are related to the idiom appear at the end of the entry:

> **stab sb in the back** to do something, usually secretly, that harms someone you are working with ▶ *There was a very competitive atmosphere in the marketing department, with everyone stabbing each other in the back.* **a stab in the back** N ▶ *Nielson's decision to leave the party was seen by his comrades as a stab in the back.* **back-stabbing** N ▶ *People work together in local politics; it's not like the back-stabbing that goes on in central government.*

▶ Where there are two versions of the same idiom which contain different nouns, a cross-reference guides you from the less common form to the main entry:

> HAY
> **hit the hay** ▶ hit the SACK
> **hit the sack** *also* **hit the hay** to go to bed and sleep ▶ *I guess we'd better hit the sack – we've got to get going early tomorrow.*

Abbreviations used in this dictionary

ADJ	adjective
etc	etcetera
N	noun
sb	somebody, someone
sth	something
V	verb

Aa

A
the A to Z of sth also **from A to Z** (describing or dealing with) every part of a subject ▶ *'The A to Z of Baby Care'*.

ABOVE
sb is getting above himself/herself someone has begun to think they are better or more important than they really are ▶ *He played once for the local team, and then he started getting above himself.*

ABSENCE
absence makes the heart grow fonder being away from someone you love makes you love them more ▶ *They say that absence makes the heart grow fonder, but relationships can be difficult when you are apart.*

ACCIDENT
an accident waiting to happen a person, thing, or situation that is likely to cause an accident ▶ *All those old bottles of half-finished medicine in your cupboard are an accident waiting to happen!*

ACES
hold all the aces to have all the advantages in a situation ▶ *Don't make the mistake of assuming that the interviewers hold all the aces; they are probably under as much pressure as you.*

> An ace is the playing card that has the highest value, and you keep it to play at the best opportunity.

ACHILLES
the Achilles' heel (of) a weakness in someone's character that causes problems, or the weak part of a plan or argument ▶ *Maria's doing well at school, but science is her Achilles' heel.*

ACID
the acid test something that shows you whether a plan works well, or shows you whether something is true ▶ *Questions about drug use were, at one time, the acid test for political candidates; now nobody cares what they've done in their past lives.*

> Acid is used to test the quality of metals. For example, nitric acid is used to test for gold because it is the only acid that will react with it.

ACQUAINTANCE
have a nodding acquaintance with also **have a passing acquaintance with** to know a person, place, or subject slightly ▶ *The witness said that she had a nodding acquaintance with the man.* ▶ *I've got a good knowledge of PCs but only a passing acquaintance with other types of computer.*

ACT
a balancing act a situation in which someone is trying to do a lot of different things at the same time, especially when this is difficult ▶ *Going out to work and looking after the family can be a difficult balancing act for new parents.*

A

catch sb in the act to see someone doing something, usually something wrong ▶ *I caught the girls in the act of lighting up cigarettes.*

clean up your act to start behaving in a more acceptable way after you have been behaving badly ▶ *Unless the party cleans up its act, we can expect a clear swing to the Opposition in the next election.*

do a vanishing act also *do a disappearing act* to deliberately go away from a place so that nobody can find you ▶ *Bob always does a vanishing act when I want him to help in the garden.*

get in on the act to take part in an activity that someone else has started, in order to get some of the advantages for yourself ▶ *They are the only two countries with military satellites, and they don't want others to get in on the act.*

get your act together to do something in a more organized and effective way than before ▶ *He'll have to get his act together and improve his grades if he wants to study medicine.*

be a hard act to follow also *be a tough act to follow* someone has done something so successful or impressive that it will be difficult for anyone else to be as good ▶ *Shulman's magnificent first novel is an extremely hard act to follow.*

ACTION

a piece of the action also *a slice of the action* an opportunity to be involved in something that is successful or exciting ▶ *Now the band is so successful, everyone in the music business wants a piece of the action.*

ACTIONS

actions speak louder than words what you do is more important than what you say, and people will judge you by the things you do ▶ *Actions speak louder than words, so we have to make sure that we give our customers what we have promised them.*

ADAM

not know sb from Adam not to know someone at all ▶ *A year ago, we didn't know him from Adam – now he's on the front page of every sports section.*

ADMIRATION

a mutual admiration society when two people, groups, or organizations praise each other a lot ▶ *Now we've praised each other's work, let's forget the mutual admiration society and talk about money.*

ADVOCATE

play devil's advocate to pretend to disagree about something so that there will be a discussion about it ▶ *Let me play devil's advocate here and ask 'Why shouldn't we legalize drugs?'*

AGENDA

a hidden agenda the things that you secretly intend to achieve from a plan or action ▶ *He was elected to serve his country, but he had a hidden agenda – all his friends have positions of power now.*

AGREEMENT

a gentleman's agreement an agreement that is not written down, but is made between people who trust each other ▶ *Business in this region has traditionally been conducted by gentleman's agreement – a simple handshake secures a deal.*

AIN'T

it/sb ain't all that something or someone is not as good or special as someone else thinks ▶ *Next time Julie tries to make you feel bad, you just tell her she ain't all that.*

if it ain't broke, don't fix it don't try to change the way something works or is done, when it works well the way it is ▶ *These guys on the board want to change the management structure again. I say, if it ain't broke, don't fix it.*

AIR

clear the air to discuss a problem to try to solve it or get rid of bad feelings ▶ *Mel finally tried to clear the air by asking Carla what was bothering her.*

hot air statements that sound very impressive or exciting but really have no meaning ▶ *Why do our politicians spout so much hot air?*

be in the air if a feeling or idea is in the air, everyone seems to be feeling it or thinking about it ▶ *There was a hint of panic in the air yesterday as the markets fell to their lowest point this month. Divorce may be in the air for Cara and her latest husband.*

be up in the air to be unplanned at the moment ▶ *Everything's up in the air until we hear what's happening in December.*

vanish into thin air also **disappear into thin air** to disappear suddenly in a way that is surprising or difficult to understand ▶ *I don't know, money just seems to disappear into thin air.*

be walking on air to feel extremely happy, often so that you do not notice anything else ▶ *The play just got a great review in New York, so I'm walking on air today.*

AIRS

put on airs also **give yourself airs** when someone is behaving as if they were more important than other people ▶ *I like him – he doesn't put on airs about his famous sister.*

AISLES

be rolling in the aisles laughing a lot while watching or hearing something ▶ *Kevin's jokes still keep audiences rolling in the aisles.*

ALARM

a false alarm something that seems about to happen, but then does not ▶ *I thought I had an ulcer last month, but it was a false alarm.*

ALBATROSS

an albatross (around sb's neck) a problem, often one that is your own fault, that prevents you from succeeding ▶ *The failure of her first film has been something of an albatross round her neck.*

> An albatross is a very large white seabird that sailors (=people who work on ships) think it is very unlucky to kill. In Coleridge's poem, *The Rime of the Ancient Mariner*, a sailor kills an albatross and has to wear it around his neck as a punishment.

ALEC/ALECK

a smart alec also **a smart aleck** someone who is annoying because they think they are very clever, especially saying clever things ▶ *"What are you going to wear tonight?" "Clothes." "Don't be such a smart alec."*

ALIVE

be alive and kicking (of a person) to be still healthy and active; (of an activity) to exist successfully still ▶ *It's nice to know your grandparents are alive and kicking.*

ALL

be all about sth to put all your time and energy into an activity, or be excited about it ▶ *Right now, I'm all about teaching. I've never worked so hard in my life.*

be all dressed up with nowhere to go to be completely ready to do something, but unable to do it ▶ *The crew of the delayed space flight were all dressed up with nowhere to go today, but repairs should only take another 24 hours.*

be all over sb to be kissing and touching another person in a sexual way ▶ *Julia and Dan were all over each other in the back of the car.*

be all over sth to be feeling happy, excited, or confident about doing something ▶ *Man, I was all over that computer course today.*

do sth for all you are worth to do something using all your energy ▶ *She dived into the sea and started swimming towards the beach for all she was worth.*

sb is not all there someone seems rather stupid or is not thinking clearly ▶ *I'm sorry, I was thinking about something else. I'm not all there this morning.*

it's all gone pear-shaped something has gone wrong, or failed, after starting off well ▶ *Internet companies like hers were set to make enormous profits, but it all went pear-shaped when her business partner died.*

ALLEY

a blind alley a course of action that is not succeeding ▶ *In my opinion, medical science is stuck up a blind alley with all this money being spent on genetic modification.*

A blind alley is a road that is closed at one end, so that it is impossible to go anywhere.

be right up sb's alley also **be right up sb's street** to be exactly what someone likes or is good at doing ▶ *Simon's reviewing a travel guide; it's a great job that's right up his alley.*

ALLIANCE

an unholy alliance an association between people who are not normally linked together, and who unite for a bad purpose ▶ *Prices are artificially high because of an unholy alliance of established retailers and big manufacturers.*

ALL-SINGING

all-singing, all-dancing (of a machine, software etc) having many of the newest technical features, enabling it to do a lot of things ▶ *Promotion of* the week is a new all-singing, all-dancing entertainment centre.

ALTAR

be sacrificed on the altar of ___ to be destroyed so that something else can be achieved, especially something you do not approve of ▶ *Essential medical care is being sacrificed on the altar of cost-effectiveness.*

ANGEL

a fallen angel someone who people used to think was successful or morally good, but who is no longer thought of in this way ▶ *Lloyd used to be very popular but since the court case is something of a fallen angel.*

ANIMAL

a different animal very different from another person or thing that you might expect to be similar ▶ *The new X200 model will be a completely different animal from the old X100.*

ANSWER

sb's answer to ___ someone or something supposed to be as good as a well-known person or thing from another group, country etc ▶ *Mel proudly describes the new exhibition as 'the museum world's answer to theme parks'.*

sb won't take no for an answer also **sb refuses to take no for an answer** to keep trying to get or do what you want even though other people will not agree to it ▶ *The guy who refuses to take no for an answer has always been a hero in Hollywood films.*

ANTE

up the ante to increase your demands, the risks that you take, or the amount that you spend, with the aim of gaining more from a situation ▶ *The*

airline upped the ante on its competitors by offering two flights for the price of one.

> The ante is the amount of money that each player gives before starting a game of cards that is being played for money. If the ante is increased or 'upped', there is more risk.

ANTS

have ants in your pants to feel excited or have a lot of energy, so that it is difficult to keep still ▶ *It had been raining all day, and the kids had ants in their pants.*

APE

go ape to become very angry or excited ▶ *If we suggest draining the marsh, the environmentalists will go ape.*

APPETITE

whet sb's appetite to make you want to do something, or have more of something ▶ *His glorious shots of sunlit rice terraces certainly whetted my appetite to visit Bali.*

APPLE

be the apple of sb's eye to be loved very much by someone, especially by an older member of your family ▶ *I became a father late in life, and Geraldine was the apple of my eye.*

a bad apple (in the barrel) also **a rotten apple (in the barrel)** someone dishonest or immoral who has a bad effect on others in a group ▶ *All it takes is one bad apple, and the travel industry loses the trust of its customers.*

APPLECART

upset the applecart also **overturn the**

A

applecart to do something that spoils someone's plans, or spoils a situation that was working well ▶ *Corelli was worried about upsetting the political applecart so close to the election.*

APRON STRINGS

be tied to sb's apron strings to depend too much on your mother, or an organization that behaves like a parent ▶ *In the 1880s, workers were still tied to the apron strings of their companies.* **cut/untie the apron strings** ▶ *Your problem isn't your mother-in-law, it's your husband – he needs to cut the apron strings and start thinking about you.*

AREA

a grey area an area of law, behaviour etc which is not easy to understand or deal with because it does not have clear rules or limits ▶ *Children missing school for no reason falls into the grey area between parental responsibility and the law.*

ARM

chance your arm also *chance your luck* to try to do something that is new or involves a risk, even though you are unlikely to succeed ▶ *You sometimes have to chance your arm if you want to make big profits.*

cost an arm and a leg to be very expensive ▶ *That carpet must have cost an arm and a leg.* **pay/spend an arm and a leg** ▶ *Two years ago we paid an arm and a leg for this printer, and now it's obsolete!*

sb would give his/her right arm to do sth also *sb would give his/her right arm for sth* someone really wants (to do) something very much ▶ *There are many dancers who would have given*

their right arm to star in this sort of show.

the long arm of the law the police, seen as reaching everywhere or into every area of life ▶ *Now the long arm of the law is catching up with criminals who operate across the border.*

twist sb's arm to persuade someone to do something that they do not want to do ▶ *I'll call her and twist her arm a little – I think she'll give us the money.* **arm-twisting** N ▶ *The bill was saved from a major defeat only after intense, last-minute arm-twisting.*

ARMPIT

the armpit of ___ the ugliest place in an area ▶ *This city was once considered the armpit of the East Coast.*

ARMS

be up in arms (about sth) to protest angrily ▶ *Farmers are up in arms about the new tax.*

welcome sb with open arms also *greet sb with open arms* to show that you are very happy to see or greet someone ▶ *He will be welcomed back with open arms by his team-mates.*

ART

have (got) sth down to a fine art to do something very well because you have done it a lot ▶ *I've been on so many business trips lately, I've got packing down to a fine art.*

AS

...as if I really don't think so! ▶ *"I know he's weird, but his party might still be good." "Right, as if!"*

as per usual as usually happens ▶ *When Don came home drunk, as per usual, his wife refused to open the door.*

ASK

don't ask me (why, how etc) I don't know anything about it ▶ *"I'm supposed to copy all these, aren't I?" "Don't ask me. I don't know what he told you to do."*

I ask you! think about this (unreasonable thing) and agree with my disapproval or annoyance ▶ *They wanted me to work on Christmas night without paying me overtime. I ask you!*

sb is asking for it someone is behaving in a way that they know will bring them punishment or problems ▶ *Don's asking for it, going out with Emma when he's supposed to be with Kate!*

ASS

make an ass of yourself to do something which makes people think you are stupid ▶ *The first time I tried playing the game, I made a complete ass of myself.*

ATTENDANCE

dance attendance on sb to do everything possible in order to please or take care of someone ▶ *Some people hate waiters dancing attendance on them all through the meal.*

ATTITUDE

have an attitude (problem) to behave in an angry or threatening way, often with people in authority ▶ *It was the interviewer and not the minister who seemed to have the attitude problem.*

with attitude showing the confidence to do exactly what you want, especially if it annoys or worries other people ▶ *I like what Krista was wearing – it's club fashion with attitude.*

AUNT SALLY

Aunt Sally a person, group, or institution that is often attacked or criticized in public ▶ *It would appear that the team has become the latest Aunt Sally for the British press.*

AUTHORITY

have it on good authority that to know something because someone you can trust has told you about it ▶ *We have it on good authority – from the owner himself – that the horse should run well in tomorrow's race.*

AWAKENING

a rude awakening a sudden realization that something is not true or not as good as you expected ▶ *Anyone who gets married expecting romance for the rest of their life is in for a very rude awakening.*

AXE

get the axe also **be given the axe** (of a person) to be dismissed from your job or (of a plan, service etc) to be ended suddenly  ▶ *Several new teachers may get the axe as the school district tries to save $7 million.*

wield the axe to threaten to get rid of jobs, or to stop something planned, often in order to save money ▶ *The latest company to wield the axe is Hargreaves, who plan to lose 200 jobs by the end of next year.*

sb has an axe to grind someone has a personal aim or strong opinion that may stop them being fair and reasonable ▶ *Selby had an axe to grind, but he did have the courage to stand up for the ordinary taxpayer.*

Bb

B

BABE

a babe in the woods someone who does not know much and can easily be deceived ▶ *He was a babe in the woods when he first came to New York.*

BABY

be sb's baby to be someone's special idea, plan etc ▶ *The training scheme is seen as Morton's baby even though he is no longer running it.*

be left holding the baby also **be left holding the bag** to be left to take care of a situation on your own, without any help from the other people who are responsible for it ▶ *My boss won't take responsibility for the appalling sales figures and yet again I've been left holding the baby.*

sleep like a baby ➤ sleep like a LOG

throw the baby out with the bath water to destroy what is good or important by mistake, while you are trying to get rid of something bad ▶ *There were problems with the old exam system but they threw the baby out with the bath water when they discarded it altogether.*

BACK

at the back of your mind in your thoughts, but not given all your attention ▶ *With the image of glamorous models at the back of her mind, Zoe went on a strict diet.*

the back of beyond somewhere far away from the city and difficult to get to ▶ *My parents live in the back of*

beyond – you never see another car out there.

behind sb's back without telling someone who will be affected by it ▶ *I can't believe that my sister was seeing my boyfriend behind my back.*

break the back of sth to deal with the worst part of a problem ▶ *Rose had broken the back of her assignment by that afternoon.*

break your back to work very hard ▶ *Farming families live there, breaking their backs to make a living from the dry, stony land.* **back-breaking** ADJ ▶ *After years of back-breaking work, they sold the farm.*

cover your back to protect yourself from criticism or blame in the future ▶ *In business we should cover our backs and put it in writing.*

do sth with one hand tied behind your back also **do sth with your hands tied behind your back** to try to do something in spite of a disadvantage ▶ *She is fighting the management's decision with one hand tied behind her back.* ▶ *The foreign students felt they had their hands tied behind their backs because of their language difficulties.*

get off my back! stop criticizing, hurrying, or annoying me ▶ *Get off my back, Charlie. I told her I'm sorry – I can't do anything more.*

get sb's back up also **put sb's back up** to offend or annoy someone ▶ *They kept me waiting, which got my back up.*

get/keep sb off your back to make or continue to make someone stop annoying you ▶ *He paid the newspaper a lot of money to keep its reporters off his back.*

give yourself a pat on the back to feel pleased with yourself because of something you have done ▶ *We'd been patting ourselves on the back for being so careful with money, but we've still spent too much.*

be glad to see the back of to be pleased that someone or something is going away ▶ *Ann Parker was glad to see the back of 2000, the year in which her business collapsed.*

have a broad back to be able to deal with criticism, complaints etc without feeling upset ▶ *I don't care what they say about me – I've got a broad back.*

know sth like the back of your hand to know a place extremely well ▶ *He knew the city like the back of his hand.*

sb is on sb's back someone is criticizing someone else ▶ *The neighbours have been on my back about the broken fence.*

on the back of as a result of; because of ▶ *He came to power on the back of his popularity on television.*

pat sb on the back also **give sb a pat on the back** to praise someone ▶ *I think we should give Fairclough a pat on the back for his performance in the last few games.* **get/receive a pat on the back** ▶ *Students at local schools have received an official pat on the back for collecting so much money.*

put your back into it to work very hard ▶ *They could be leaders in the market if they really put their backs into it.*

say sth behind sb's back to say unpleasant things about someone when that person is not there ▶ *Chris is so polite when he meets me, but apparently he's been saying terrible things about me behind my back.*

stab sb in the back to do something, usually secretly, that harms someone you are working with ▶ *There was a very competitive atmosphere in the marketing department, with everyone stabbing each other in the back.* **a stab in the back** N ▶ *Nielson's decision to leave the party was seen by his comrades as a stab in the back.* **back-stabbing** N ▶ *People work together in local politics; it's not like the back-stabbing that goes on in central government.*

turn your back on to refuse to pay attention to someone or something ▶ *He turned his back on religion when his baby daughter died.*

watch your back be careful because someone may try to cause trouble for you ▶ *She had to watch her back, like any politician.*

(with) your back to the wall in a bad situation in which you are forced to fight ▶ *The New Zealand team always play best with their backs to the wall.*

you scratch my back, I'll scratch yours you help me, I'll help you ▶ *After all, 'You scratch my back, I'll scratch yours' is common practice in the world of business.*

BACKROOM

the backroom boys people who do important work but are not famous or acknowledged ▶ *Local people want to* *build a memorial to the backroom boys who tested the fighter planes.*

BACKWARD

not backward in coming forward not unwilling to ask for what you want ▶ *Please don't be backward in coming forward with ideas and contributions for the magazine.*

BACKYARD

not in my backyard also **Nimby** (about something useful that may be unpleasant or dangerous) not wanted close to where I live ▶ *The Nimby attitude of councillors has prevented the building of a new factory.*

BACON

bring home the bacon
1 to earn money ▶ *They both work, but it's Meg who really brings home the bacon.*

2 to win or do very well in sports ▶ *Berry will be expected to bring home the bacon for the Dragons again this year.*

An old English story says that any man who could say truthfully at the door of a particular church in England that he had not been angry with his wife for 12 months and a day, could take home a large piece of bacon (=pig meat).

This only happened eight times in 500 years.

save sb's bacon to stop someone from failing or being punished ▶ *Farmers had a very dry winter, but the April rains just saved their bacon.*

BAD

sb's got it bad someone is very much in love ▶ *Grant plays an awkward young man who's got it bad for a beautiful girl.*

BAG

be sb's bag to be the kind of thing that someone is interested in or is good at ▶ *If baseball is your bag, this is the book for you.*

bag and baggage with all your possessions ▶ *The next day, she told me to move out, bag and baggage.*

sb's bag of tricks the special skills or methods someone uses in their work ▶ *Computer-generated images have given photography a whole new bag of tricks.*

sth is in the bag success is certain ▶ *The prize hasn't been awarded yet, but McCarthy thinks it's in the bag.*

be left holding the bag ➤ be left holding the BABY

be a mixed bag a group of things or people that are very different from each other ▶ *Their latest CD is a mixed bag of old favourites and ultra-modern songs.*

pack your bags to leave a place ▶ *The managing director should pack his bags and let her deputy take over.*

pull sth out of the bag to do something unexpected that helps you to solve a problem ▶ *The team will have to pull something miraculous out of the bag if they're going to catch up.*

B

use sb as a punching bag ➤ use sb as a PUNCHBAG

BAGS

bags of a large amount or number of something ▶ *I've got bags of time to write the report.*

BAIT

rise to the bait to react to what someone is saying or doing in exactly the way that they want you to ▶ *Helen went in there to argue, but Gita refused to rise to the bait.*

take the bait

1 to accept what someone is offering you to do something ▶ *The survey found that 90% of traffic police took the bait and accepted bribes to 'forget' overloaded trucks.*

2 to react to what someone is saying in exactly the way that they want you to ▶ *"But my sister's so pretty..." she said. "You're as attractive as your sister," he said, taking the bait at once.*

BALANCE

be in the balance also *hang in the balance* to be in an uncertain state because of events that are still happening, or a decision that must be made ▶ *I waited for the meeting to end, knowing that my career was in the balance.*

throw sb off balance also *catch sb off balance* to make someone confused or less certain by surprising them ▶ *Don't let unexpected questions throw you off balance in the interview.*

tip the balance also *swing the balance* to make a difference that decides the result of a situation ▶ *Rising costs tipped the balance against renting an office in the city.*

BALL

a ball and chain someone or something that stops you doing what you want to do ▶ *I hope the prime minister realizes what a ball and chain these taxes could become to small businesses.*

the ball is in sb's court someone must do something before progress can be made in a situation ▶ *You've phoned her twice and left a message, so now the ball's very firmly in her court.*

drop the ball to make a mistake or fail to do something you should ▶ *Someone dropped the ball in getting the safety measures through. The accident should never have happened.*

have a ball to enjoy yourself very much ▶ *They promised themselves they'd have a ball once the exams were over.*

be on the ball to be quick to notice and understand things ▶ *She's over 90 but she's still on the ball.*

pick up the ball and run (with it) to take an idea or opportunity that you have been given and make it successful ▶ *The president was trying to find ways to help industry, but it was up to the leaders to pick up the ball and run with it.*

play ball to work with someone else to achieve a result that is good for both of you ▶ *If his lawyers don't want to play ball, we can't make them.*

start the ball rolling also *set the ball rolling* to start a discussion or an activity ▶ *Geri started the ball rolling by inviting criticism of the education system.*

the whole ball of wax everything, the whole lot ▶ *The police told me how he survived, who helped him, the whole ball of wax.*

B

BALL GAME

it's a (whole) new ball game also **it's a (whole) different ball game** it is a new and different situation ▶ *Kelly would like to go back to work, but it's a whole new ball game now, with the new technology.*

BALLISTIC

go ballistic to become very angry suddenly ▶ *Peter went ballistic when he read the headlines in this morning's newspapers.*

BALLOON

the balloon goes up (a dangerous and difficult situation) starts very suddenly ▶ *On November 5th the balloon went up when 4000 people were forced to leave their homes because of an unexploded bomb.*

a trial balloon something done in order to discover people's opinions about a new idea ▶ *Reports of the chairman's resignation could just be a trial balloon to see how shareholders react.*

⬛ A trial balloon is used to test weather conditions.

sth went down like a lead balloon something that was supposed to be interesting or funny did not get a good reaction ▶ *The song, so successful in Australia, went down like a lead balloon in the UK.*

BALLPARK

a ballpark figure about the right or expected amount ▶ *We think £5000 would be a good ballpark figure.*

be in the same ballpark to be similar to something else, or as expected ▶ *He said it was exciting but it wasn't*

even in the same ballpark as the pressure you feel in the Ryder Cup.

BANANA

banana skin a situation in which someone is embarrassed or made to seem stupid ▶ *There appear to be plenty of banana skins littering the route to the next election.* **slip on a banana skin** ▶ *The minister slipped on a giant banana skin almost as soon as the election was over.*

BANANAS

go bananas to start to behave in an angry, excited, or strange way ▶ *Sheila will go bananas if she finds out you went out with Steve.* ▶ *Excuse the noise, my alarm clock's gone bananas.*

BAND

a one-man band someone who does every part of an activity themselves ▶ *Advertising agencies can be one-man bands, small outfits, or large public companies.*

BANDIT

make out like a bandit to receive a lot of presents or money ▶ *Connie's kids make out like bandits every Christmas.*

BANDWAGON

jump on the bandwagon also **climb on the bandwagon** to start doing something because a lot of other people are doing it ▶ *Yet more wine-growers have climbed on the organic bandwagon.*

BANE

be the bane of sb's existence *also* **be the bane of sb's life** to cause continual trouble or unhappiness for someone ▶ *Income tax, the bane of modern existence, was invented as 'a temporary measure' to raise money for the Napoleonic War.*

▌Bane is an old word meaning poison.

BANG

bang goes ___ that ends (a chance to do or have something) ▶ *If he's lost his job, bang goes the new house.*

go out with a bang to end with a lot of excitement ▶ *The idea of dying didn't worry him, as long as he went out with a bang.*

not with a bang but a whimper (to end) with much less excitement than expected ▶ *The evening ended not with a bang but a whimper when the sound system broke down.*

▌This comes from a line in one of T.S. Eliot's poems called *The Hollow Men*.

BANK

don't bank on it/sth don't depend on it ▶ *"Maybe they have some great job for me." "Don't bank on it."*

sth won't break the bank you can afford it ▶ *The tickets are only £2 each, so they're hardly going to break the bank.*

BANNER

do sth under the banner of ___ to give a particular idea as the reason for doing something ▶ *You could say that feminism marched under the banner of equality, while the sexual revolution marched under that of freedom.*

BAPTISM

baptism of fire a difficult first experience that proves your ability to deal with the situation ▶ *Opening the store a week before Christmas will be a baptism of fire.*

BARGAIN

drive a hard bargain to demand a lot and refuse to give much ▶ *He drives a hard bargain but he only deals in top-quality cars.*

get more than you bargained for to have more problems than you had expected ▶ *Thieves got more than they bargained for when they broke into the flat and found six pet snakes.*

BARGEPOLE

sb wouldn't touch sth/sb with a bargepole someone does not like, trust, or approve of a person or thing ▶ *I wouldn't touch his business ventures with a bargepole.*

BARK

sb's bark is worse than his/her bite someone is not as angry or unpleasant as he/she seems ▶ *Everyone's scared of Mrs Jordan, but her bark's much worse than her bite.*

BARREL

not be (exactly) a barrel of laughs something or someone is not very funny or enjoyable ▶ *Those last few days before the exam weren't exactly a barrel of laughs, you know.*

over a barrel in a position in which someone is forced to do what you want ▶ *She must be working for a pretty powerful organization to have the editor of such an important newspaper over a barrel.* ▶ *I always like doing business with someone who knows he's over a barrel.*

scrape the bottom of the barrel to be forced to use or choose a person or thing that is not very good because there is nothing else ▶ *Two batsmen were injured, so Hearne had to scrape the bottom of the barrel – he came up with Dixon.*

BARRELS

let sb have (it with) both barrels also **give sb both barrels** to criticize someone strongly, angrily, or loudly ▶ *In grand operatic style, she let her husband have it with both barrels, while he went on eating calmly.*

> The barrel is the part of a gun that bullets are shot through.

BASE

get to first base to achieve the first part of something, but no more ▶ *Too often, producers don't even get to first base because they can't find a good scriptwriter.*

> There are many idioms that use the word 'base', which come from the sport of baseball. In this game, there is a base (=a special place with a hard surface) at each corner of the field. A player who has hit the ball must run around all four bases, touching each of them, in order to get a point called a run.

be (way) off base to be completely wrong about something ▶ *You're way off base criticizing Joe for being lazy – he hasn't stopped all day!*

touch base to communicate with someone for a short time to find out what has happened since the last time you spoke to them ▶ *Our sons touch base two or three times a month.*

BASES

cover all the bases to deal with a situation thoroughly ▶ *We have 20 detectives working on this case – we want to make sure we cover all the bases.*

BASH

have a bash (at sth) to try to do something ▶ *Why don't we have a bash at table-tennis this winter?*

BASICS

go back to basics also **get back to basics** to try using simple ideas or methods that have worked in the past ▶ *The police are going back to basics and putting more men on street patrol.* **back-to-basics** ADJ ▶ *The French manufacturers are producing a new back-to-basics model.*

BASKET

a basket case a person or organization that cannot deal with their problems ▶ *Don't believe everything Helen says – she's a basket case.*

BAT

do sth off your own bat to do something because you have decided to do it, and not because someone has told you to ▶ *He applied for early retirement off his own bat when he realized the company was in trouble.*

do sth right off the bat to do something immediately ▶ *We want to*

B

start right off the bat training our dogs not to be aggressive.

go (in) to bat for to support someone who is having problems ▶ *Why not ask Denise to contact them? I'm sure she'd be happy to go in to bat for you.*

In the game of baseball, if one player goes to bat for another one, he hits the ball instead of the other player hitting the ball.

...like a bat out of hell if you leave a place like a bat out of hell, you leave it very fast, often because you are frightened or worried ▶ *She saw a man snatch the bag and take off like a bat out of hell.*

BATH
take a bath to lose a lot of money in business ▶ *The companies were badly managed, and investors have taken a bath.*

take an early bath to be ordered to leave the field in a football game ▶ *He was told to take an early bath for questioning the referee's decision.*

BATON
take up the baton also **pick up the baton** to take the place of someone who stops doing something ▶ *A couple of local singers took up the baton with great success when the band cancelled.* **hand on the baton** ▶ *It is the process of education that allows us to hand on the baton to the next generation.*

A baton is a short stick that is passed from one runner to the next in a relay race (=a race in which a team of runners run one at a time).

BATTERIES
recharge your batteries to have a long rest or a holiday so that you feel better ▶ *The island was a brilliant place to recharge our batteries after the trial.*

BATTLE
the battle lines are drawn the people involved in an argument, competition, election etc are well prepared for the start ▶ *The battle lines were being drawn between Kim and the sales team.*

a battle of wills a struggle between people or groups who have great determination to succeed ▶ *Refusing to eat can become the child's way of winning a battle of wills with her parents.*

a battle of wits a situation in which two people or groups use all their intelligence in order to win ▶ *She plays a murder witness, in a battle of wits with two hitmen who want to kill her before she can testify.*

do battle (with) to argue or struggle (against) ▶ *They are preparing to do battle in the courts over their inheritance.*

fight a losing battle to keep trying to do something that you cannot succeed in doing ▶ *She was fighting a losing battle against cancer.* **be a losing battle** ▶ *We try to teach our kids to enjoy books, but with TV and pop music it's a losing battle.*

sth is half the battle something is an important part of doing something difficult ▶ *If the medicine helps you get a good night's sleep, that's half the battle.*

join battle (with) to start a fight, argument, or competition (with someone) ▶ *PDR is about to join battle with Granville over control of the supermarket chain.*

a running battle a series of related arguments or trouble between two people or groups, that continue for a long time ▶ *I've been fighting a running battle with the water company over my rates these past few months.*

win a battle but lose the war to get one thing you want but fail to achieve the more important overall aim ▶ *They had won the battle for more pay, but they lost the war against poor management, and the factory closed within a year.*

BAY

keep sth at bay also **hold sth at bay** to prevent someone or something from harming you ▶ *He kept the police at bay for two hours and threatened suicide before finally surrendering.*

BE-ALL

not be the be-all and end-all something is not the most important aim (of your life or of a situation) ▶ *In spite of what our society believes, shared interests are not the be-all and end-all of a relationship.*

BEAM

broad in the beam having large hips ▶ *It's a pretty dress, but I'm too broad in the beam for that style.*

off (the) beam wrong or unsuitable ▶ *If you don't listen carefully, your responses may be off beam and people may think you are stupid.*

BEAN

not have a bean to have no money ▶ *I can't buy anything now – I haven't got a bean until payday.*

BEANS

not amount to a hill of beans also **not amount to a row of beans** to be worth very little ▶ *I've been working so hard, and what for? It won't amount to a hill of beans after tax.*

full of beans having a lot of energy ▶ *He's been on holiday and he's come back full of beans and bursting with ideas.*

spill the beans (about) to tell someone a secret ▶ *We're organizing a surprise party for him so don't spill the beans.*

BEAR

be like a bear with a sore head to be angry about everything, and rude to people ▶ *You know how he is when he's had too much whisky – he'll be like a bear with a sore head in the morning.*

BEAT

beat it! go away! ▶ *Just beat it, will you – I'm tired of your whining.*

beat sb hollow to beat someone completely ▶ *Each night we had a game of chess, and he beat me hollow every time.*

(it) beats me also **(it) beats the hell out of me** I don't know ▶ *"What was she talking about?" "Beats me."*

if you can't beat 'em, join 'em if you cannot stop other people from doing something that you do not like, you are going to start doing it yourself ▶ *"If you can't beat 'em, join 'em," I thought, and poured myself another drink.*

B

without missing a beat without showing any surprise or shock, or without pausing ▶ *"I'm going to marry Mark," she announced. "I'm delighted to hear it," he said, without missing a beat.*

you can't beat ___ something is the best of its kind ▶ *You can't beat our colour printers for speed, quality, and reliability.*

BEATING

take a beating also **take a hammering** to be strongly attacked or defeated completely ▶ *She had taken a beating in the press as a result of her decision.*

take a lot of beating also **take some beating** something is better than almost anything else of the same type ▶ *For styling and comfort, this car takes a lot of beating.*

BEAUTY

beauty is in the eye of the beholder people have different opinions about what is beautiful ▶ *Jeff doesn't like it, but I say beauty is in the eye of the beholder – to me it's the loveliest carpet I've ever seen.*

BEAVER

an eager beaver a person who is too keen or excited about doing something

▶ *All the eager beavers were at the meeting, but Joy and I skipped it.* **eager-beaver** ADJ ▶ *There were several eager-beaver young reporters on the case.*

BECK

be at sb's beck and call to be ready to do whatever someone else wants any time they want it ▶ *It's a good job, but you're at the beck and call of the customers at all times of the day.*

BED

sb got out of bed (on) the wrong side also **sb got up on the wrong side of the bed** someone is angry or annoyed without any reason ▶ *Look out for Luke – he got out of bed on the wrong side this morning.*

> This expression probably started as 'get out of bed the wrong way', which comes from the old belief that if you put your left foot on the floor first in the morning, you would have bad luck all day.

sb has made their bed (and they must lie on it) someone has chosen to be in a particular situation, and must accept it even though things have gone wrong ▶ *Everyone told her not to marry him, but she's made her bed and now she must lie on it.*

no bed of roses a difficult, unpleasant situation ▶ *Life is no bed of roses for the trainee teacher.*

put sth to bed to finish dealing with something ▶ *US officials said that the problems regarding compensation had not been put to bed.*

BEDFELLOWS

be strange bedfellows also **make strange bedfellows** two very different people or things are grouped together ▶ *Football and love seem to be strange bedfellows, but they are combined to good effect in this film.*

BEE

a busy bee someone who works hard and is always cheerful ▶ *Tanya's our office busy bee.*

sb has a bee in his/her bonnet (about sth) someone thinks something is more important that it really is ▶ *Many psychologists have had a bee in their bonnets about sex.*

BEELINE

make a beeline for to go quickly and directly towards ▶ *As soon as we got to the hotel we made a beeline for the bar.*

BEEN

been there, done that (seen the movie, bought the T-shirt) I no longer want to do something because I've already done it ▶ *"It would be great to live in London." "Been there, done that. I'm never going to live in a big, smelly city again."*

BEER

be small beer (to sb) to be relatively unimportant to someone ▶ *Doing up an old house is small beer to the Stuarts, who have just rebuilt a ruined castle.*

BEG

beg, borrow, or steal to do everything needed to get something ▶ *You've got to have a hat for the wedding so beg, borrow, or steal one.*

be going begging to be available, because no one else has taken it ▶ *There's more cake going begging – anyone want some?*

BEGGARS

beggars can't be choosers if you really need something, you have to accept whatever is offered, even if you don't like it ▶ *"I can't bear that house!" "Beggars can't be choosers."*

BEGINNING

the beginning of the end a time when something starts to get worse or to end ▶ *In this generation, the children understand Navajo but don't speak it, and that's the beginning of the end.*

BELL

give sb a bell to telephone someone ▶ *It might be worth giving Peter a bell to make sure he's coming.*

sth rings a bell something sounds familiar although you don't remember everything about it ▶ *No, the name doesn't ring a bell – are you sure the call was for me?*

saved by the bell saved from a difficult or embarrassing situation at the last moment ▶ *I was saved by the bell when Harding answered the question instead.*

BELLS

alarm bells ring it suddenly becomes clear that there is a problem with something ▶ *The news that oil prices had shot above $40 a barrel set alarm bells ringing in Brussels.*

bells and whistles extra features added to a product that are not necessary but will make people think that it is special ▶ *If you pay more than that, all you get is extra bells and whistles.* **bells-and-whistles** ADJ

B

B

▶ *It costs a basic $2000, and $2700 for the bells-and-whistles version.*

with bells on completely or in the best way ▶ *"Eating is a celebration,"* he said. *"Enjoy yourself with bells on."*

> This idiom probably comes from a time in the past when people put bells on their horses when they were going to parties, dances, or other kinds of celebrations.

BELLYFUL

I've had a bellyful (of) I have heard about or dealt with something so much that I feel bored and annoyed ▶ *I've had a bellyful of her complaints.*

BELLY-UP

go belly-up (of a company) to fail ▶ *Travel firms that go belly-up are protected by law.*

BELT

be (hitting) below the belt to do or say something unfair or unkind ▶ *I think asking about his ex-wife in front of his girlfriend is a bit below the belt.*

> This idiom comes from boxing (=the sport of fighting by hitting with your hands). Boxers are not allowed to hit each other below the belt.

a belt and braces approach two or more ways of dealing with a problem, to make sure that nothing goes wrong ▶ *The doctors adopted a belt and braces approach to treatment, using both radiotherapy and chemotherapy.*

have sth under your belt to have done something useful or clever ▶ *With over*

70 *films and an Oscar under his belt, he was able to make the films he liked.*

tighten your belt to spend less money ▶ *It was wartime and we all had to tighten our belts.*

BEND

bend over backwards also **lean over backwards** to do as much as you possibly can ▶ *For years we have been leaning over backwards to avoid using sexist language in our textbooks.*

drive sb round the bend also **drive sb round the twist** to annoy someone a lot ▶ *Anyone would agree that a roomful of excited three-year-olds can drive you round the twist.* **go round the bend/twist** ▶ *I think if she hadn't had a break from work she would have gone round the bend.*

BENEFIT

give sb the benefit of the doubt to accept that someone is telling the truth, even though you have doubts about it ▶ *"Do you think she took it?" "I'm not sure, but I'm prepared to give her the benefit of the doubt for now."*

BENT

sb is bent on (doing) sth also **sb is hell-bent on (doing) sth** someone is completely determined to do something ▶ *She tried to interrupt, but he was hell-bent on giving his version of events.*

BERTH

give sb/sth a wide berth to avoid

someone or something ▶ *Directors tend to give 'difficult' actors like him a wide berth.*

A berth is a place near land where a ship can be tied up.

BEST

do your level best to try as hard as you can ▶ *Health authorities are doing their level best to get information out to the public.*

make the best of sth also **make the best of a bad job** to accept something, and do what you can to make it better ▶ *You have to make the best of the body you were born with.*

BET

sth is your/the best bet something is the best thing to do or use ▶ *If you are looking for something low in calories and animal fat, grilled or steamed fish is the best bet.*

be a safe bet to be likely or reasonable ▶ *They asked me where to find Steve, and I said the pub was a safe bet.*

you bet yes, certainly ▶ *"Are you going to take that job in Oslo?" "You bet!"*

BETS

all bets are off (if a situation changes) no one knows what will happen ▶ *The governor looks safe to win again, but if the press gets hold of a scandal, all bets are off.*

hedge your bets to reduce your chances of failure or loss by being sure that you have several choices or possibilities available to you ▶ *Most art dealers are hedging their bets by trading with more than one auction house.*

BETTER

better late than never I'm glad that something is finally being done, although it should have been done before ▶ *"Better late than never," she commented, when told of the proposal to allow women into the club.*

better safe than sorry it is better to be careful now, even if this is inconvenient, so that nothing bad will happen later ▶ *We knew the direct route might be flooded, so we thought, better safe than sorry, and stayed on the motorway.*

get the better of to defeat ▶ *He finally got the better of his opponent, after almost being defeated in the second round.* ▶ *By nine o'clock, my fears had got the better of me, and I left the house to look for my daughter.*

you'd better believe it it's definite! ▶ *"Are you really going to break up with Jane?" "You'd better believe it!"*

BID

make a bid (for) to try to get ▶ *Hargreaves is making a bid for the British Championship tomorrow.*

bid fair to do sth to seem likely to be good or successful ▶ *It bids fair to be an eventful summer.*

BIG

be big on sth to like something very much ▶ *He's big on bargains – he can tell you all about mobile phone deals.*

BIKE

on your bike! go away! ▶ *There's nothing for you here, mate. On your bike, then.*

BILL

fit the bill also **fill the bill** to be exactly what you need ▶ *She was*

B

*looking for a more challenging role,
and Pinter's play filled the bill.*

foot the bill to pay for something
▶ *Taxpayers had to foot the bill for the
repairs to the fountain.*

sb has been sold a bill of goods
somebody has been deceived about
the quality of what they are getting
▶ *I think the Internet is a bill of goods
being sold to a gullible public.*

BIND

a double bind a difficult situation in
which anything you do to try to solve a
problem will cause more problems
▶ *It's a double bind – if we don't
modernize, we lose our competitive
edge and have to cut jobs, and if we
do modernize we have to cut jobs
because we don't need the staff.*

BIRD

a bird brain a stupid person ▶ *He
thinks all women drivers are useless.
What a bird brain!*

the bird has flown a person you were
looking for has escaped ▶ *By the time
the Admiral reached Dunkirk the birds
had flown.*

**a bird in the hand (is worth two in the
bush)** it is better to accept something
that you have, than to try to get
something better that you are not sure
of ▶ *It's not the greatest of jobs, but a
bird in the hand is worth two in the
bush. I can't afford to be out of work.*

an early bird someone who gets up or
arrives somewhere early ▶ *Are you an
early bird, or do you like to sleep late
in the mornings?* **early-bird** ADJ ▶ *They
do a cheap, early-bird dinner, if you
get there before six.*

the early bird catches the worm if you
do something before other people,
you will gain an advantage ▶ *The early*

*bird catches the worm, so order your
phone now – only 100 left in stock!*

a little bird told me I know something
but I am not going to say who told
me ▶ *A little bird told me that you're
expecting a baby.*

BIRDS

the birds and the bees sex (as
explained in a practical way to
children) ▶ *I think it's time we talked
to Simon about the birds and the
bees.*

birds of a feather (flock together)
people who have similar interests tend
to spend time together ▶ *It's easy to
get drugs if you use them – birds of a
feather flock together.*

be (strictly) for the birds (of an idea)
to be silly, useless, or not practical
▶ *This book shows that not all his
scientific projects were for the birds.*

kill two birds with one stone to
achieve two things with one action
▶ *Now we can kill two birds with one
stone – we'll visit Kylie and see if the
house is still for sale.*

BISCUIT

sth takes the biscuit also **sth takes
the cake** something is the worst or
most surprising of its kind ▶ *I've heard
a lot of poor excuses in my time, but
that one takes the cake.*

BIT

be champing at the bit to be impatient
▶ *People were champing at the bit,
waiting to see what I was going to do.*

do your bit to do a fair and reasonable
amount ▶ *Parents like to feel that
they're doing their bit for the school.*

get the bit between your teeth to be
so determined to do something that
no one can stop you ▶ *They got the bit*

between their teeth and gave the opposition a bad time.

it's/that's a bit much something is rather unfair, unreasonable, or rude ► *I think that's a bit much, expecting you to look after her kids while she's out enjoying herself.*

BITE

bite off more than you can chew to try to do more than you can ► *It's a very difficult project and he may find he's bitten off more than he can chew.*

have another bite at the cherry also **have a second bite at the cherry** to get a second chance to do something that you failed to do the first time ► *Her reappointment will please those of us who felt she should have a second bite at the cherry.*

put the bite on sb to create a situation where someone has to spend more money ► *The rise in oil prices continues to put the bite on industrial firms.*

take a bite out of sth to take quite a large amount of money away from something ► *The tax has taken a big bite out of poorer people's incomes.*

that bites (the big one) that is very annoying ► *Damn, I can't park there, it's a tow zone. That bites the big one.*

sb won't bite there is no reason to be afraid of someone ► *Go ahead and ask him if he'll help you – he won't bite.*

BITS

love sb to bits also **love sb to pieces** to love someone very much ► *Mark's*

such a nice man – we all love him to bits.

thrilled to bits also **thrilled to pieces** very excited and pleased that something has happened ► *I've been a fan of the show for years, so I was thrilled to bits when they asked me to be in it.*

BITTEN

once bitten, twice shy if you have failed or been hurt once, you will be very careful next time ► *We're not ignoring the earthquake warning – after all, once bitten, twice shy.*

BLACK AND WHITE

in black and white

1 written down so that everyone can see exactly what it is ► *I looked at the lease and it's there in black and white – we are not allowed to keep pets.*

2 too simple, as if everything or everyone was either completely good or completely bad ► *Star Wars is a film which appeals to children's tendency to see things in black and white.*

black-and-white ADJ ► *The book deals with complex issues in a very black-and-white way.*

be in the black to have money in your bank account ► *The company was still in the black, but it would probably have to make job cuts.*

sb is not as black as he/she is painted someone is not as bad as people think they are ► *I haven't known Neil long but he doesn't seem to be as black as he's painted.*

BLANK

draw a blank

1 to fail to find what you are looking for ► *Police enquiries so far have drawn a blank, but this new evidence*

may help them to find the missing girl.
2 to be unable to answer a question or give information ▶ *If you'd asked me who the president was before the election campaign, I'm sure I would've drawn a complete blank.*

BLANKET
a wet blanket someone who spoils other people's fun ▶ *"I don't think I'll come out tonight." "Oh don't be such a wet blanket."*

BLAST
a blast from the past someone or something that reminds you of a time in the past ▶ *That was a real blast from the past – my old flatmate phoned up.*

BLAZE
go out in a blaze of glory to finish in a successful or impressive way ▶ *He went out in a blaze of glory with two sensational goals in the final match of his career.*

BLEED
bleed sb dry also **bleed sb white** to use up someone's money ▶ *Six years of legal battles have bled the company dry.*

BLESSING
a blessing in disguise something that seems completely bad but which may have good results ▶ *The riots may be a blessing in disguise, if they make the community come together and work on its problems.*

a mixed blessing something good which has some bad things about it ▶ *Owning your home is a mixed blessing, as it means that you are responsible for repairs and maintenance.*

BLESSINGS
count your blessings to think about the good things in your life, not the bad ▶ *Count your blessings – you have a decent house to live in, at a rent that you can afford.*

BLIND
the blind (are) leading the blind people who know very little about what they are doing are advising those who know equally little ▶ *When I got a computer, Jo tried to teach me how to use it, which was a case of the blind leading the blind.*

BLINK
not (even) blink also **do sth without a blink** without showing any surprise or shock, or without pausing ▶ *I told him what I had heard about the job losses, and he didn't even blink.*

in the blink of an eye also **in a blink** very quickly ▶ *Her motorbike goes from a standstill to 60 m.p.h. in the blink of an eye.*

on the blink not working properly ▶ *The video's on the blink again.*

BLITZ
a blitz on sth a great effort or intense period of work ▶ *When we got home, Kath and I had a blitz on the cleaning.*

BLOCK
sb's been around the block (a few times) someone has a lot of experience of life ▶ *You could tell she'd been around the block a few times – too much makeup, hair dyed pink, and a skirt that was way too short.*

knock sb's block off to hit someone very hard ▶ *If you touch my stuff, I'll knock your block off.*

a stumbling block a problem that may stop you from achieving something ▶ *The dialect was a bit of a stumbling block, but people got round it by using their imagination.*

BLOCKS

be off the (starting) blocks to start ▶ *A French company was first off the blocks with a great new product.*

▌ The place where runners begin a race is called the starting blocks.

BLOOD

bad blood (between) anger or unfriendly feelings between people ▶ *Despite a formal settlement, the bad blood between James and his father is not going to disappear overnight.*

be baying for (sb's) blood to be saying loudly or publicly that someone should be punished ▶ *By this time the crowd was baying for the referee's blood.*

blood and thunder exciting and violent action ▶ *He has a huge collection of PC games heavy on blood and thunder, and low on real skill.*
blood-and-thunder ADJ ▶ *Those who thirst for blood-and-thunder politics will support this candidate.*

blood is thicker than water family relationships are stronger and more important than any others ▶ *His friends all have families to think of, and blood is thicker than water.*

sb's blood runs cold someone feels very frightened ▶ *When she heard a man's voice, her blood ran cold.*

blood, sweat, and tears a very great effort ▶ *Outsiders seem to think teaching is easy, but it isn't; it takes blood, sweat, and tears to do it.*

get sb's blood up to make someone very angry and ready to fight ▶ *That's the sort of argument that really gets my blood up.*

have (sb's) blood on your hands to be responsible for someone's death ▶ *These people are terrorists, and have blood on their hands.*

in cold blood deliberately and with no emotion ▶ *Her parents were killed in cold blood by the secret police.*

sth is in your/the blood you enjoy or are good at something, especially when it has been done by your family ▶ *I'm afraid gambling's in my blood – my grandfather lost a fortune on horse races and my mother won a lot of it back.*

be like getting blood out of a stone also **be like getting blood out of a turnip** it is very difficult to get something from someone who is very unwilling to give it ▶ *"It's like getting blood out of a stone," was one pensioner's comment on the 50p-a-week pension increase.*

sth makes your blood boil something makes you very annoyed ▶ *I read the gossip columns every day even though they make my blood boil.*

B

new blood *also* **fresh blood** people who are new to a job, situation etc and bring new ideas and energy ▶ *The company came onto the fashion scene just at the time when it needed fresh blood.*

be out for blood *also* **be after sb's blood** to be very determined to defeat or punish someone ▶ *Didn't we support you when the New York office was out for your blood?*

scent blood to realize that you have a chance to defeat or harm someone, and to be eager to try to do this ▶ *The journalists, scenting blood, tried their hardest to get into the meeting.*

sweat blood to work extremely hard ▶ *People have sweated blood to build up their businesses, and now they feel threatened.*

taste blood to experience some success during a fight, argument etc, which makes you more keen to win ▶ *Hathaway had tasted blood, and went on to score three more goals.*

be too rich for your blood to be too expensive for you ▶ *"This one is priced at $35.88." "Good price, but a little too rich for my blood."*

BLOODY

bloody but unbowed injured or harmed but not wanting to stop fighting ▶ *Hanson emerged bloody but unbowed after yesterday's game.*

BLOUSE

a big girl's blouse a boy or man who is not being brave ▶ *You can't wait for Connie to come and take the spider out of the bath, you big girl's blouse!*

BLOW

blow hot and cold to keep changing your attitude about someone or something ▶ *The government seems to be blowing hot and cold about changing the tax law.*

blow it/that used when you are annoyed with something or someone ▶ *I thought, blow it, I'm not going to hide in a corner to eat my lunch.*

blow sth sky-high to destroy a plan or project, especially by giving away a secret ▶ *It will blow the presidential campaign sky-high if this information becomes public.*

blow sth wide open to make a result much more uncertain, especially because of new information ▶ *All lawyers dream of finding the one vital clue that will blow a case wide open.*

a body blow a serious loss, disappointment, or defeat ▶ *Losing this vote would be a body blow to the government.*

death blow an action or event that makes something fail or end ▶ *The distressing case dealt a death blow to their hopes of a quick settlement.*

deal a blow to to have a bad effect on ▶ *The rise in exchange rates dealt a blow to hopes of a revival in their export market.*

soften the blow *also* **cushion the blow** to try and lessen the bad effect of something ▶ *When the company*  *relocated, he was offered a lump sum to soften the blow.*

strike a blow for to do something to help (a cause or aim) ▸ *We struck a blow for freedom of speech when we gave out those leaflets.* **strike a blow against** ▸ *They sincerely believed that they were striking a blow against tyranny.*

BLOWS

come to blows to start fighting ▸ *The two actors almost came to blows over the size of their dressing-rooms.*

BLUE

out of the blue very unexpectedly ▸ *She got a job offer out of the blue, and by 3.30 she had cleared her desk.*

BLUFF

call sb's bluff to tell someone to do what they are threatening to do, because you do not believe that they will do it ▸ *You can tell your boss that you'll leave unless you get a pay rise, but she may call your bluff. Then you'll be out of a job.*

BLUSHES

spare sb's blushes to avoid embarrassing someone ▸ *It is my privilege to introduce Dr Kataria, and I am not going to spare his blushes – he is a therapist with an international reputation.*

BOARD

above board completely honest and legal ▸ *The union's relationship with the government is completely open and above board.*

across the board in a way that affects everyone or everything ▸ *In those days, companies were cutting jobs across the board.*

go back to the drawing board to start again from the beginning ▸ *He's gone back to the drawing board to revise his strategy for next week's tournament.*

go by the board(s) to disappear or to be stopped ▸ *Some of our services, which we offer to minority groups, will have to go by the board.*

sweep the board to win easily against all the opposition ▸ *If the rebels emerge as a united party, they will sweep the board.*

take sth on board

1 to listen to, understand, and accept something ▸ *I don't think the committee have taken on board the seriousness of this assertion.*

2 to accept ▸ *We can't take on board any new commitments.*

BOARDS

tread the boards to work as an actor ▸ *Yet another star of Australian soap is treading the boards in London this winter.*

BOAT

be in the same boat to be in the same situation ▸ *It wasn't hard being poor as students, since we were all in the same boat.*

miss the boat *also* **miss the bus** to fail to take an opportunity ▸ *Investors may miss the boat if they are still waiting for prices to fall.*

push the boat out to spend more money than you usually do, for something special ▸ *When Barry brought his fiancée to stay, we really pushed the boat out.*

B

rock the boat to spoil a comfortable situation, usually by criticizing it or trying to change it ▶ *Some of the new members want to change the rules of membership, but we advised them not to rock the boat.*

what/whatever floats your boat what/whatever interests or excites you ▶ *This island has noisy night clubs and quiet countryside – it all depends what floats your boat.*

BOB

Bob's your uncle (after that) it will be simple and provide the result you want ▶ *Just put the disk in, click on the icon and Bob's your uncle.*

BODY

body and soul with all your energy and attention ▶ *Matthew threw himself body and soul into the game.*

keep body and soul together to earn just enough money to be able to live ▶ *Although I had a university education, I was working as a waitress just to keep body and soul together.*

over my dead body I will not let it happen if I can avoid it ▶ *"Is Matt*

going to move in with us?" "Over my dead body."

a warm body a person ▶ *We're so used to e-mail and voice mail that we're lucky to be able to speak to a warm body.*

BOIL

go off the boil to become less interested in doing something, so that you are less successful ▶ *It's easy to go off the boil during a long exam, so do the hardest questions first.*

it (all) boils down to ➤ it all COMEs down to

on the boil happening ▶ *He's got several multimedia projects on the boil at the moment.*

BOLT

a bolt from the blue also *a bolt out of the blue* a sudden and surprising event ▶ *We hadn't worked for the store before, and their order came like a bolt from the blue.*

sb has shot his/her bolt someone has done as much as they can and has no more energy or ideas ▶ *The man who'd been shouting at me appeared to have shot his bolt and lapsed into silence.*

BOMB

be the bomb to be extremely good or exciting ▶ *Some skinny girls just think they're the bomb, but I like it when girls have more shape.*

cost a bomb to be very expensive ▶ *You'll have to buy plane tickets, food – it's going to cost a bomb.*

go like a bomb to go very fast, or very well ▶ *The car doesn't look like much, but it goes like a bomb.*

make a bomb to make a lot of money

▶ *Thank you for all your calls – the phone company must have made a bomb last week!*

put a bomb under sb to do something extreme, so as to force someone to change ▶ *Someone should put a bomb under the committee; they are so slow.*

BOMBSHELL

drop a bombshell to shock people by unexpected news ▶ *Just before Christmas the company dropped its bombshell: they would be cutting 400 jobs in the New Year.*

BONE

a bone of contention a subject that people disagree about, especially for a long time ▶ *The cost of the house was still a bone of contention between Richard and Jenny.*

close to the bone also *near to the bone* shocking, embarrassing, or personal ▶ *Some of the book's themes were perhaps too near the bone to be included in a Hollywood movie.*

cut sth to the bone also *pare sth to the bone* to reduce something as much as possible ▶ *Companies have cut costs to the bone in order to remain competitive.*

dry as a bone very dry or completely dry ▶ *The river was now as dry as a bone.*

have a bone to pick with sb to want to talk to someone about a subject you don't agree on ▶ *I have a bone to pick with you – what have you been telling Bill about me?*

This idiom comes from the idea that two dogs with only one bone will fight over it.

BONES

the bare bones (of) the basic structure or elements with no unnecessary parts ▶ *Concentrate on the bare bones of the story – a news report shouldn't have too much detail.* **bare-bones** ADJ ▶ *Even this bare-bones approach will cost $12 million a year.*

feel sth in your bones also *know sth in your bones* to feel very sure of something, although you do not have proof of it ▶ *I felt in my bones that something was very wrong.*

make no bones about sth/it to admit openly ▶ *The service is expensive, we make no bones about it, but it's very good.*

BOOK

bring sb to book to force someone to accept punishment for a bad action ▶ *Companies that pollute the environment should be brought to book and made to pay compensation.*

do sth/play by the book to follow all the rules, or use the accepted methods ▶ *His lawyers don't always play by the book.*

you can't/shouldn't judge a book by its cover you can't know a person just by looking at them ▶ *I think she looks sweet, but you can't judge a book by its cover.*

close the book on sth to accept that a difficult situation is over, and to stop thinking about it ▶ *The company will be happy to close the book on the software piracy case.*

a closed book something that you know nothing about ▶ *What happens inside computers is a closed book to most people who use them every day.*

B

in my book in my opinion ▶ *She's devoting her whole life to her job – in my book nothing is that important.*

an open book a person or thing that is open and honest ▶ *The minister said he had nothing to hide. "My life is an open book," he declared.*

read sb like a book to understand what someone is thinking or feeling ▶ *I know Bob was upset – I can read him like a book.*

it suits sb's book it gives someone a convenient advantage ▶ *He did not cooperate with the union, but he asked them for help when it suited his book.*

throw the book at sb to give someone the worst possible punishment for something they have done wrong ▶ *He was tired of her attitude and the moment she made a mistake, he threw the book at her.*

sb wrote the book on sth someone has special skills or special knowledge about something ▶ *Sam's great – I mean, he wrote the book on how to be a supportive husband.*

BOOKS

cook the books also *fiddle the books* to change (an organization's) records and details dishonestly ▶ *The hospitals were cooking the books by recording simple enquiries as if they were full consultations.*

hit the books also *crack the books* to study very hard ▶ *If you want a scholarship, you'd better start hitting the books now.*

in sb's good books supported or approved of by someone ▶ *She's attending every meeting, hoping to get back in my good books.* **in sb's bad books** ▶ *Gray's are in our bad books at the moment because they lost us a really important order.*

a turn-up for the books also *one for the books* something unusual and surprising ▶ *He's started working for his exam – well, that's a turn-up for the books!*

BOOM

a baby boom a period of years during which a greater number of babies are born than normal ▶ *The post-war baby boom in Europe stretched from 1946 to the early 1960s.* **baby boomer** N ▶ *The president is a baby boomer, and it is his generation who are making policies now.*

lower the boom on to become more strict in dealing with a problem and punishing the people involved ▶ *The government outlined tough measures to lower the boom on non-essential industries.*

BOOT

give sb the boot to get rid of someone, from a job or a relationship ▶ *He promptly gave her the boot when he found a younger girlfriend.*

get the boot ▶ *People in the industry are afraid to complain, in case they get the boot.*

put the boot in to attack someone when they are already in a weak position ▶ *Walter criticized me for my behaviour and then Anna put the boot in by reminding everyone about what happened last year.*

... to boot as well ▶ *The bride was young, pretty, and from a wealthy family to boot.*

BOOTS

die with your boots on to die while you are still working ▶ *The thought of retirement scares the hell out of me. I'd rather die with my boots on.*

sb is/gets too big for their boots someone who is or is getting too proud ▶ *She won't go out with media people – she finds they're too big for their boots.*

lick sb's boots to do your best to please someone in authority in order to get an advantage for yourself ▶ *Luckily he's the sort of boss who hates people licking his boots.* **boot-licking** N ▶ *She was annoyed by all the boot-licking going on.* **boot-licker** N ▶ *He's surrounded by boot-lickers who never say no to him.*

quake in your boots also **shake in your boots** to feel very afraid ▶ *In spite of having a clear conscience, I was shaking in my boots.*

sb is (as) tough as old boots someone is strong and can accept and deal with difficulties ▶ *She's 74, five feet tall, and as tough as old boots.*

BOOTSTRAPS

pull yourself up by your (own) bootstraps to improve your situation by your own efforts ▶ *His business collapsed in 1999 but he pulled himself up by his bootstraps and built up a better one.*

BOSS

show sb who's boss to make another person realize that you have power and authority ▶ *She fired Tom to show the staff who was boss.*

BOTTLE

hit the bottle also **take to the bottle** to start drinking too much alcohol ▶ *He always liked a drink, but after losing his job he hit the bottle in a big way.*

BOTTOM

be at the bottom of sth to be the real cause of something ▶ *I think that lack of communication is at the bottom of many family problems.*

the bottom drops out of your life also **the bottom drops out of your world** your main reason for living suddenly disappears ▶ *The bottom dropped out of our lives when our son died.*

the bottom falls out (of the market) also **the bottom drops out (of the market)** people stop buying something ▶ *On Thursday October 24th, 1929, the bottom fell out of the New York stock market.*

from the bottom of my heart very sincerely ▶ *I would like to say, from the bottom of my heart, how much we all admire you for what you have done.*

get to the bottom of to find the real cause of a problem ▶ *There is so much conflicting evidence, I don't suppose we'll ever get to the bottom of it.*

B

B

hit rock bottom also **reach rock bottom** to get into the worst possible situation, or the lowest level ▶ *After six months of working without visible results, our morale and sense of purpose hit rock bottom.*
be at rock bottom ▶ *He felt he'd been at rock bottom for months.*
rock-bottom ADJ ▶ *All CDs are at rock-bottom prices, for this week only.*

knock the bottom out of to weaken seriously or destroy (a business or market) ▶ *Threats of a new factory have knocked the bottom out of the property market in this lovely old village.*

BOUNCE

be bounced into (doing) sth to be forced to make a decision too quickly, without time to think ▶ *I believe that Britain was bounced into a decision that she will regret later.*

BOUNDS

sth knows no bounds something seems to have no limit ▶ *He had no family of his own and his generosity towards the neighbours' children knew no bounds.*

out of bounds where someone is not allowed to go ▶ *After the bomb scare, the town was declared out of bounds to soldiers and their families.*

BOW

bow and scrape to show too much respect and politeness to someone important ▶ *He hated everyone bowing and scraping, and missed having a normal conversation in the pub.*

take a bow to accept praise and approval, and feel pleased with yourself ▶ *The team can take a bow after this important victory.*

BOX

open (a) Pandora's box to cause a lot of problems because of a lack of knowledge or careful thought ▶ *When he decided to quit, it opened a Pandora's box of resentment and bitterness.*

right out of the box as soon as you start ▶ *I didn't expect to write a hit single right out of the box.*

think outside the box to think in a way that shows imagination ▶ *Computer experts who can think outside the box and come up with creative ideas deserve a good salary.*

BOY

sb's blue-eyed boy the favourite person of someone in authority ▶ *My brother was always the blue-eyed boy of the family; I never could compete.*

boy/girl next door a nice, average person, not having much experience of life ▶ *She was just the girl next door to millions of fans, and few people knew of her battle against drug addiction.* **boy-next-door** ADJ ▶ *Boy bands tend to cultivate a boy-next-door image.*

mother's boy a man or boy whose mother controls or protects him too much ▶ *She thought that, growing up without a father, I was bound to be a mother's boy.*

the old boy network men from the same school, club, etc who give each other jobs or other advantages ▶ *After the spy scandals in the sixties, the head of British Intelligence tried to get rid of the old boy network.*

a/the whipping boy someone or something that is usually blamed instead of the person or group really responsible ▶ *Realizing that I could well end up the whipping boy if things went wrong, I acted very cautiously.*

BOYS

the boys in blue the police ▶ *The documentary followed the boys in blue over nine months.*

boys will be boys it is natural for boys to be thoughtless, noisy, or untidy ▶ *You know how mothers are. They just say, "Oh, well, boys will be boys", and clean up the mess for them.*

be one of the boys to be accepted in a group of men who have typically male interests ▶ *Steve was one of the boys – sport on Saturday afternoon and the pub in the evening.*

BRAIN

the brain drain movement of people to another country or industry to work, because they will be paid more there ▶ *We will set up a Pay Review Body for academic staff in order to halt the brain drain.*

have sth on the brain to keep thinking about something all the time ▶ *I've had that song on the brain all day.*

BRAINS

the brains behind sth the person or people that think of, plan, and develop something ▶ *The brains behind the new system are three Internet addicts from Indonesia.*

blow sb's brains out to shoot someone in the head ▶ *If I believed half the depressing things you say, I'd have blown my brains out by now.*

pick sb's brains to find out everything that someone knows about something by asking them questions ▶ *I want to pick your brains about places to stay in Nepal.*

rack your brains to try very hard to think of something ▶ *I racked my brains trying to think of something sensible to say.*

BRAINSTORM

have a brainstorm also **have a brainwave**

1 to have a sudden good idea ▶ *Phil had a brainwave – he would write about his experiences and sell them to the newspaper.*

2 to behave in a wild or unexpected way for a short time ▶ *I went jogging at 6 this morning – I can't think why, I must have had a brainstorm!*

BRAKES

put the brakes on (sth) to stop or slow down ▶ *We put the brakes on our advertising campaign, but production costs are still rising.*

BRASS

as bold as brass very confident, and sometimes rude ▶ *She walked into his office, as bold as brass, and started questioning him.*

BREACH

step into the breach to help by doing someone else's work when they are unable to do it ▶ *Pat's ready to step into the breach when Jim goes into hospital.*

B

BREAD

sb's bread and butter the activity that brings in most of your money ▶ *Small jobs like oil changes are the garage owner's bread and butter.* **bread-and-butter** ADJ ▶ *Their bread-and-butter product is a database program for small businesses.*

earn your bread also **earn your crust** to earn the money that you need in order to live ▶ *Writing poetry isn't the easiest way of earning your bread.*

sb knows which side his/her bread is buttered (on) someone knows that they must be nice to another person in order to get an advantage ▶ *I nearly told my boss what I thought of her, but I know very well which side my bread is buttered on.*

sb thinks sth is the best thing since sliced bread also **sb thinks sth is the greatest thing since sliced bread** someone thinks that something is extremely good ▶ *They have a computer system which they think is the greatest thing since sliced bread although it seems out of date to me.*

BREADLINE

be on the breadline also **live on the breadline** to be very poor ▶ *After years of living on the breadline, Kay has finally got a good job.*

BREADTH

be/come within a hair's breadth of doing sth to be or come very close to doing something ▶ *He came within a hair's breadth of losing his sight in the crash.*

BREAK

a clean break a clear and definite ending ▶ *After her marriage broke down, Sue wanted a clean break with the past, so she moved to Canada.*

get an even break to be treated as equal to other people ▶ *Many women still don't get an even break in the workplace.*

give me a break! I don't really believe that! ▶ *"It took me almost an hour to finish." "Oh, give me a break, there's no way it took that long."*

give sb a break to stop criticizing or blaming someone ▶ *Give the kid a break, he's doing his best!*

make a break for it to start moving fast in order to escape ▶ *I tried to make a break for it, but one of the boys blocked my way.*

BREAKFAST

eat sb for breakfast also **have sb for breakfast** to defeat someone easily ▶ *You aren't ready to play in competitions yet – they'd eat you for breakfast!*

make a dog's breakfast (out) of sth also **make a dog's dinner (out) of sth** to do something very badly ▶ *Frankly, they made a real dog's breakfast out of the management training course.*

BREAST

make a clean breast of sth to admit that you have done something wrong ▶ *He made a clean breast of it and returned the money.*

BREATH

a breath of fresh air new and interesting ideas or ways of doing things ▶ *Those two new teachers bring a breath of fresh air to the staffroom.*

catch your breath to have time to rest or to think properly ▶ *The city didn't even have time to catch its breath before the next storm hit.*

If you catch your breath when you have been running or doing exercise, you stop for a minute to try to breathe more normally.

don't hold your breath don't expect something to happen soon ► "When will I get the money?" "Don't hold your breath – it can take up to three months."

don't waste your breath also **save your breath** don't say anything, because it will be useless ► Don't waste your breath making excuses – I can see you're drunk.

in the same breath (of two opposite things) said at almost the same time ► The minister called young people lazy and unfeeling, and in the same breath accused them of aggression and violence.

say sth under your breath to say something in a very quiet voice ► "Oh, no, here she comes!" he said under his breath.

take your breath away to be very beautiful, exciting, or surprising ► His first sight of the Grand Canyon took his breath away.

with bated breath feeling anxious about the result of something ► She watched with bated breath as the plane dropped lower and lower.

BREATHE
breathe easier also **breathe easy** to feel safer or more relaxed ► We all breathed easier when she left the company.

BREEZE
be a breeze to be very easy ► He hated the geography exam, but the physics was a breeze.

shoot the breeze to talk in an informal and friendly way ► She enjoyed the meetings – girls sitting around shooting the breeze and getting to know each other.

BRICK
drop sb like a hot brick ➤ drop sb like a hot POTATO

BRIDGE
cross that bridge when you come to it to deal with a problem when it happens and not before ► "What if they don't agree to pay you back for expenses?" "We'll cross that bridge when we come to it."

BRIDGES
build bridges to try to establish a better relationship ► The police want to build bridges with the local community by holding sports events and open days.

burn your bridges to destroy your chances of continuing in a situation ► She couldn't take the exam now – she'd burnt her bridges when she stormed out of the school and swore she'd never go back.

BRIGHT-EYED
bright-eyed and bushy-tailed full of energy and ready to start doing something ► Two hours after her

operation, she was sitting up in bed, bright-eyed and bushy-tailed.

BRING

bring sb up short to surprise someone, so that they stop what they are doing ▶ *The question brought her up short, but after a moment she replied, "Even if I knew the answer to that, I wouldn't tell you."*

BROAD

it's as broad as it's long it's almost the same, without advantage either way ▶ *It's as broad as it's long – it will take you half an hour whichever route you take.*

BROOM

a new broom
a new person in authority who makes changes ▶ *Taylor's been brought in as a new broom, so we're hoping for an improvement in staff relations.*

BROWNIE

get brownie points to do something that impresses someone and makes them like you ▶ *You definitely got lots of brownie points by bringing back his precious golf clubs.*

A 'brownie' is a young girl who is in the lowest level of an international social organization called the Guides or the Girl Scouts which trains girls in practical skills and helps them to develop their character. Brownies get special rewards for doing kind things, which is

where the idea of 'brownie points' comes from.

BRUSH

tar sb with the same brush to criticize someone by connecting them with someone similar ▶ *You can't tar every woman with the same brush just because things didn't go well for you and Jane.*

BRUSH-OFF

give sb the brush-off to show someone that you do not feel friendly or attracted to them ▶ *Look, I'm sorry, I don't want you to think I'm giving you the brush-off, but you can't call me here.* **get the brush-off** ▶ *The film centres around a young executive who gets the brush-off from his female boss.*

BUBBLE

burst the bubble to do something that ends a good situation ▶ *He was quite optimistic after Christmas but the sales figures for January burst the bubble.*

BUCK

the buck stops here/with sb this is the person who is finally responsible ▶ *Julian was a great person to work for. He made it clear that the buck stopped with him and he always supported his staff.*

pass the buck to try to make someone else responsible for a problem ▶ *If a complaint arises, you can be sure that he will pass the buck and his secretary will get the blame.*

BUCKET

kick the bucket to die ▶ *When I finally kick the bucket, I want to be buried at sea.*

BUD

nip sth in the bud to stop something before it can develop ▶ *Nipping bad eating habits in the bud is part of a parent's job.*

BUG

be bitten by the ___ bug *also* **get the ___ bug** to become enthusiastic about a particular activity ▶ *After spending two months in Africa, I've really been bitten by the travel bug.*

BULL

(like) a bull in a china shop *also* **(like) a bull at a gate** behaving in a direct, rude, and careless way ▶ *Larry tends to behave like a bull in a china shop, leaving people hurt and offended.* ▶ *He rushed into the office like a bull at a gate.*

take the bull by the horns to deal with a problem in a direct, confident way ▶ *She took the bull by the horns and asked for a pay rise.*

BULLET

bite the bullet to accept and deal with something unpleasant ▶ *Sandy was the first child to bite the bullet, walking cheerfully into the dentist's surgery.*

BUNDLE

be a bundle of nerves to be extremely worried or frightened ▶ *She was a bundle of nerves before the flight.*

not go a bundle on not to like very much ▶ *My dad doesn't go a bundle on Steve, but Mum thinks he's OK.*

BUNK

do a bunk to leave a place suddenly, often in secret ▶ *It looks as if he's done a bunk, and taken my money with him.*

BURNER

put sth on the back burner to delay dealing with something until later ▶ *We're concentrating on getting out all the Christmas orders, so we've put our work on new products on the back burner.*

BURTON

go for a Burton to be destroyed or killed ▶ *Look out, or that vase will go for a Burton.*

> Burton is a kind of British beer. In the late 1930s, advertisements for the beer showed a group of drinkers with one missing and the sign said 'Gone for a Burton'. During World War II, soldiers used this expression to mean that someone had died.

BUS

miss the bus ➤ miss the BOAT

BUSH

beat about the bush to talk without saying what you mean directly ▶ *Len's been beating about the bush but he means that you will all be on half-pay after Thursday.*

(the) bush telegraph the fast communication of information by people telling each other what is happening ▶ *Everyone seems to have heard about me leaving – the bush telegraph is still as reliable as ever.*

BUSINESS

business is business in business, profit is more important than personal feelings ▶ *If you don't work hard, you're out. Business is business, you know.*

the business end of a ___ the part of a tool or weapon that does the work ▶ *He turned, and found himself looking at the business end of a hand gun.*

funny business also **monkey business** behaviour that is not allowed or approved of ▶ *When they examined his tax returns they saw that there was some funny business going on.*

get down to business to start ▶ *We have a lot to talk about today, so let's get down to business.*

go about your business to do the things that you normally do ▶ *Residents in the area put on their boots and went about their business despite flooded streets.*

sb has no business doing sth someone was wrong to do something ▶ *I want to apologize – I had no business criticizing you like that.*

in business ready to start an activity ▶ *You've got the paint – I'll get the brushes. OK, now we're in business.*

sb is not in the business of doing sth someone is not doing what they are being criticized for ▶ *We're not in the business of increasing government spending; we just want to ensure that taxpayers get value for money.*

sth is the business something is very good or works well ▶ *This computer really is the business – it's so fast.*

it's business as usual something is working normally in difficult circumstances ▶ *It's business as usual today at Pat's Café after yesterday's fire.*

like nobody's business very much or very fast ▶ *Tickets went like nobody's business – the show was sold out in a day.*

sb means business someone is determined to do something ▶ *If a new teacher starts off strict, enforcing the rules, her class will know she means business.*

mind your own business I refuse to involve you in something that does not concern you ▶ *"Mind your own business," the old man warned him. "And stay right away from this street."*

sb was minding his/her own business someone was acting normally, not expecting what happened ▶ *He was just driving along, minding his own business, when a drunk driver slammed into him on the wrong side of the road.*

none of your business You do not have a right to know! ▶ *"Have you got a boyfriend, Kate?" "None of your business!"*

BUTS

no buts (about it) you really mean what you are saying ▶ *We are in the business of uniting Europe – no buts about it.*

BUTTER

butter wouldn't melt in his/her mouth also **butter wouldn't melt** someone seems very good and moral ▶ *You'd think butter wouldn't melt in his mouth, but you have to watch out for him.*

BUTTERFLIES

have butter-flies (in your stomach) to feel very nervous before doing something

▶ He always has butterflies before he goes on stage, but it makes him give a better performance.

BUTTERFLY

break a butterfly on a wheel to give a severe punishment to someone who has not done anything very bad ▶ Stopping Anna from seeing her friends just because she was late home once seems to be breaking a butterfly on a wheel.

BUTTON

(right) on the button

1 exactly right ▶ Captain James Cook was right on the button when he named this place 'The Friendly Islands'.

2 on time ▶ Jack was there to meet the plane at 11 on the button.

BUTTONS

push (sb's) buttons also **push the right buttons** to know what to do to get the reaction you want ▶ He always manages to push Mum's buttons by saying "a woman's place is in the home".

BUZZ

get a buzz (from) to get a strong feeling of pleasure ▶ She gets a buzz from cooking new dishes and trying them out on other people.

BY

by and large generally ▶ By and large, the more questions you ask in a survey, the less polite people will be.

BYGONES

let bygones be bygones you should try to forget something bad that someone has done and forgive them ▶ I'm willing to let bygones be bygones, but my sister still won't talk to me.

Cc

CAGE
rattle sb's cage to annoy or frighten someone ► *"I think they'll throw me out of the team." "Boy, you must have really rattled their cage."*

CAHOOTS
be in cahoots (with) to be working secretly together (with) ► *He's convinced the jury that his client wasn't in cahoots with the burglars.*

CAKE
sth takes the cake ➤ sth takes the BISCUIT

you can't have your cake and eat it (too) you cannot have the advantages of something without the bad effects ► *I wish I could enjoy the kids' company without having to clean up after them, but you can't have your cake and eat it too.*

CALL
call of nature going to the toilet ► *"Where's Sam?" "He was here but he left – call of nature, I think."*

a close call also *a close shave* a situation in which something bad nearly happened ► *My brother had a close shave when he fell in front of a bus.*

there is/you have no call to do sth there is/you have no reason to ► *My sons are good boys and you have no call to complain about them that way.*

a wake-up call an event that makes people realize that a situation is very bad ► *The Oregon game was our*

wake-up call. We knew we'd never get to the final if we kept losing like that.

CAN
a can of worms a lot of problems connected with the original one ► *Then we come to the question of insurance, which opens a whole new can of worms.*

carry the can to accept responsibility or blame ► *When the suppliers fail to deliver, it's always the shopkeepers who carry the can.*

in the can (of films) made and ready to show ► *We've got six half-hour episodes already in the can.*

CANDLE
burn the candle at both ends to be extremely busy, especially going to bed late and waking early ► *Many young people tend to burn the candle at both ends, to prove that they are successful and interesting.*

sb/sth can't hold a candle to one thing is not nearly the equal of another ► *None of the other singers could hold a candle to her.*

CANDY
like taking candy from a baby very easy ► *"I'll get Ray to agree," he said confidently. "Persuading him is like taking candy from a baby."*

CANNON
cannon fodder ordinary soldiers during a war who are likely to be killed or hurt ► *We're the cannon fodder,*

mate. They're sending us in to make sure the area's cleared.

a loose cannon someone who might do something unexpected ➤ *He doesn't care whether he keeps the job or not and that makes him a loose cannon.*

> A cannon is a large, heavy gun on wheels, used in the past. It was very dangerous if one of the cannons came loose (=untied) on a ship, because it rolled around with the motion of the waves and was very difficult to control.

CANOE

paddle your own canoe to do things in your own way ➤ *I prefer to paddle my own canoe, and my boss trusts me to work without supervision.*

CAP

go cap in hand (to sb) to ask for money or help in a respectful way ➤ *Elderly people should receive a heating allowance every winter, instead of having to go cap in hand to the government.*

if the cap fits (wear it) if you feel the critical remark describes you, accept it ➤ *"So you think I'm mean with my money." "Well, if the cap fits...."*

to cap it all last and worst of all ➤ *There was no bedding or hot water, and to cap it all, the phones didn't work.*

CAPITAL

___ with a capital ___ an extreme example of something ➤ *I was in trouble with a capital T.*

CARBON

be a carbon copy to be very similar ➤ *That second goal was a carbon copy of his first.*

CARD

play your last card to try one last thing in an effort to achieve something ➤ *Eve played her last card. Two huge tears rolled down her cheeks. "Please don't hate me," she said.*

a wild card a person or thing that could behave in a strange or dangerous way ➤ *He was a bit of a wild card, my grandfather – rather too fond of strong drink.*

CARDS

the cards are stacked against sb ➤ the ODDS are stacked against sb

hold all/most of the cards to have all or most of the advantages ➤ *She knew she would lose the argument since Don held most of the cards.*

if sb plays his/her cards right if someone deals with a situation in an intelligent way ➤ *If you play your cards right, you might even get him to give you more money.*

sth is on the cards something will probably happen ➤ *Nobody seems to like the building but pulling it down isn't on the cards.*

play your cards close to your chest also **keep your cards close to your chest** to keep your plans or thoughts secret ➤ *Our reporters could not get a commitment from the mayor; he's playing his cards close to his chest.*

put (all) your cards on the table also **lay (all) your cards on the table** to tell people honestly what your plans or feelings are ➤ *I've laid all my cards on the table and told you everything. Now it's your turn.*

CARPET

roll out the red carpet (for sb) to give a lot of special attention to someone ➤ *They decided to roll out the red* carpet for their American visitors last week.

sweep sth under the carpet to pretend a problem does not exist ▶ *The poor quality of teaching staff at the university has been swept under the carpet.*

CARRIED

get carried away to lose your self-control ▶ *Mum got carried away and put half a bottle of brandy in the sauce.*

CARROT

(the) carrot and (the) stick reward and punishment ▶ *Most managers use both carrot and stick to make sure that the work gets done.*

CART

put the cart before the horse to do things in the wrong order ▶ *I feel we're putting the cart before the horse, planning our advertising campaign before we have anything good to sell.*

CARTE BLANCHE

give sb carte blanche to give someone complete authority ▶ *He gave him carte blanche to edit his own part of the film.*

CASE

be a case in point to be a good example ▶ *Some restaurants suit small gatherings better than large groups, and The Rose Garden is a case in point.*

get off my case! stop annoying or criticizing me ▶ *Why don't you get off my case and think about your own problems?*

I rest my case I need not say any more to prove my argument ▶ *"He's always criticizing." "I've just had a letter of complaint from him." "I rest my case."*

> In the US, when lawyers have finished trying to prove their case in a court of law, they often say "the defence rests" or "the prosecution rests".

an open and shut case a legal case that is easy to prove, and will not take long in a court of law ▶ *We thought it was an open and shut case, but the jury took several days to decide.*

CASH

cash in hand (paid in) coins and notes, not through a bank ▶ *Tony was working illegally without a visa, being paid cash in hand.*

cash on the barrel also **cash on the nail** all the money in coins and notes, not paid through a bank ▶ *If I give you cash on the nail, what's your best price for the car?*

CASTLES

castles in the air plans or hopes that are not likely to become real ▶ *Don's ideas of starting a school were just castles in the air – he was too impractical to actually do it.*

CAT

(has the) cat got your tongue? you aren't talking – why not? ▶ *"Did she like it?" "Mm." "Did you speak to her?" "Mm." "Cat got your tongue?" "No!"*

fat cat someone who is rich and powerful ▶ *Fat cats from overseas are behind the deal to buy up the land.*

let the cat out of the bag to let people know something secret ▶ *With one careless sentence he let the cat out of the bag about the new legislation.*

like a cat on hot bricks also **like a cat on a hot tin roof** acting in a nervous or anxious way ▶ *What's the matter? You've been like a cat on hot bricks all night.*

like the cat that got the cream also **like the cat that got the canary** very pleased ▶ *He's like the cat that got the cream tonight – he won thousands at the races!*

sb looks like something the cat dragged in someone looks untidy and unattractive ▶ *You must have had a rough night – you look like something the cat dragged in!*

play cat and mouse (with sb) also **play a cat and mouse game**
1 one person is trying to find the other one, and the other is trying not to be found ▶ *Police spent the weekend playing cat and mouse with protesters on the site of the proposed new dam.*
2 to let someone think they are

getting what they want, and then stop them from getting it ▶ *She seems to be playing a cat and mouse game with Will; does she really like him or is she just teasing him?*

put the cat among the pigeons to cause trouble in a group by something you do ▶ *Your fax about staff redundancies put the cat among the pigeons.*

there's not enough room to swing a cat also **you could not swing a cat** the room or house is very small ▶ *We squeezed a bed and a cupboard in but then there wasn't enough room to swing a cat.*

when the cat's away (the mice will play) when someone in authority is not there, people can do what they want ▶ *Our boss was off sick so we had a lazy day – when the cat's away, you know!*

CATCH

a Catch 22 (situation) a situation in which you cannot do one thing until you do another, but you cannot do that thing until you have done the first one, with the result that you can do neither ▶ *It's a Catch 22 – she can't get a job in town without a car, but she'll never be able to buy one on the wages she's getting here.*

> This idiom comes from the title of a book about World War II by Joseph Heller. The main character is very frightened of being killed, and wishes he could persuade military officials that he is crazy so that he would not have to fly in raids (=attacks) against the enemy. However, the officials know that anyone who is so frightened cannot be crazy, and

therefore he is forced to fly again and again. This is the Catch 22 situation.

catch sb redhanded to see someone at the moment when they are doing something wrong ► *The terrorist was caught redhanded, actually planting the bomb.*

be caught napping not to be prepared for something ► *Experts on the region*

admit that they were caught napping by the changes of 1989.

be caught short

1 to be without something when you really need it ► *Here, take £20 – you don't want to be caught short.*

2 to be unable to get to a toilet when you really need it ► *Don't have anything else to drink – you don't want to be caught short on the bus!*

CATS

it's raining cats and dogs it is raining hard ► *You can't go home now – it's raining cats and dogs.*

CAUSE

a lost cause something that has no chance of succeeding ► *Dad's still a*

member of the party, but I think it's a lost cause – they'll never win.

CAUTION

err on the side of caution to choose the safest way of doing something ► *Because the law is unclear, doctors tend to err on the side of caution when treating dying patients.*

throw caution to the winds to stop being careful and do something involving a risk ► *Throwing caution to the winds, I decided to join her in a hang-gliding lesson.*

CAVE

an Aladdin's cave of sth a place that contains a lot of interesting or unusual things ► *Her home became an Aladdin's cave of art treasures.*

CEILING

go through the ceiling ➤ go through the ROOF

CENT

not a red cent no money at all ► *The article went into the magazine, but I never got a red cent for it.*

CENTS

not have two cents to rub together to have very little money ► *In those days my family didn't have two cents to rub together.*

CENTURY

drag sb into the 21st century to make people more modern in their ideas ► *Computer companies are hoping to drag my parents' generation kicking and screaming into the 21st century.*

CEREMONY

not to stand on ceremony not to worry about the rules of polite behaviour ► *Help yourself to drinks – we don't stand on ceremony in this house.*

CERT
a dead cert something that is certain to happen or succeed ▶ *He says the horse is a dead cert for the 3 o'clock race.*

CHALICE
a poisoned chalice an important job or opportunity that seems good but will cause someone a lot of problems ▶ *He is still delighted at being chosen, but the job may prove to be a poisoned chalice.*

CHALK
(not) by a long chalk not at all, not in any way ▶ *I haven't finished what I want to say, not by a long chalk.*

be (like) chalk and cheese to be completely different from each other ▶ *Although I love my sister dearly, we're like chalk and cheese.*

CHANCE
blow the/your chance to miss an important opportunity ▶ *He was hoping for a record score but he blew his chance early in the game.*

chance would be a fine thing it would be good to have the opportunity ▶ *"Maybe you'll meet a millionairess!" "Chance would be a fine thing! Where could I possibly meet someone like that?"*

fat chance it's not likely! ▶ *He says Kim will go out with him, but I say fat chance.*

given half a chance also *if you give sb half a chance* if someone has the opportunity ▶ *I don't blame you for asking – I'd have done the same thing, given half a chance.*

have a fighting chance also *stand a fighting chance* to be able to succeed, but only by trying very hard ▶ *I believe we still have a fighting chance of retaining the title.*

be in with a chance to have the possibility of winning or succeeding ▶ *Two British skaters are still in with a chance.*

CHANCES
(the) chances are (that) it is likely (that) ▶ *If you like the house, chances are that other people will too, so you have to put your offer in today.*

fancy someone's chances to think that someone will be successful ▶ *I don't fancy our chances of getting tickets this late.*

CHANGE
a change of heart a complete change in the way you feel ▶ *I used to think I hated exercise, but I've had a change of heart since I learnt to ski!*

it/that makes a change something is pleasantly different from usual ▶ *"She was on time for work this morning." "That makes a change!"*

CHAPTER
chapter and verse all of the information in detail ▶ *After accusing her of theft, he followed up with chapter and verse.*

a chapter of accidents a set of unlucky events, happening one after the other ▶ *The chapter of accidents began when we missed the plane in Geneva.*

CHARM
work like a charm to have exactly the right effect ▶ *I told the boys, "You can stay up as long as you like if you read one of your school books." It worked like a charm – they were both asleep by 9 o'clock.*

CHASE

cut to the chase to move on to the most important part of something ▶ *Let's not waste time talking – it's time we cut to the chase and had a look at your presentation.*

a wild goose chase a long time searching for something without finding it ▶ *She went everywhere to find one like mine, but it was a wild goose chase; they've stopped making them.*

CHEEK

cheek by jowl (with) very close together (with) ▶ *Refugees from the flood were having to live cheek by jowl with the farm animals.*

CHEER

a Bronx cheer a rude sound made by putting your tongue between your lips and blowing ▶ *The referee got a Bronx cheer from one of the angry fans.*

CHEESE

a/the big cheese also **a/the big wheel** an important or powerful person ▶ *During* the conference, big cheeses from the medical profession stayed at this hotel.

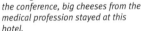

CHEESED OFF

be cheesed off to feel annoyed ▶ *Tom's been a bit cheesed off since his bike was stolen.*

CHEQUE

a blank cheque permission to do what you want ▶ *You treated your contract as a blank cheque to go off on trips at our expense.*

CHERRY

the cherry on the cake also **the cherry on top** a pleasant addition to something good ▶ *It's an excellent little car and the cherry on the cake is the low price.*

CHESTNUT

the/an old chestnut a boring story or subject of conversation that everyone has heard many times before ▶ *The conversation inevitably turned to education, an old chestnut that teachers dread at parties.*

CHICKEN

a chicken and egg situation the question of which of two situations causes the other ▶ *I was facing the classic chicken and egg situation: did I fail to get a job because I wasn't confident, or did my lack of confidence come from not getting a job?*

no spring chicken someone who is no longer young ▶ *Nobody knows her exact age, but she's certainly no spring chicken.*

play chicken to do something dangerous to see who gets frightened first ▶ *Yet another teenager has died playing chicken on the railway line.*

CHICKENS

the chickens (have) come home to roost the bad results of something are starting to be noticed ▶ *Too little has been spent on education, and now the chickens have come home to roost – more people than ever cannot read.*

don't count your chickens (before they're hatched) don't be too sure that you will get what you are expecting ▶ *"We'll buy a new car when I get a pay rise." "Don't count your chickens – you may be stuck on that salary for years."*

CHIEFS
too many chiefs and not enough Indians too many people saying what should be done, and not enough people doing the work ▶ *There are too many chiefs and not enough Indians on this particular committee.*

CHILDHOOD
second childhood when an older adult behaves like a child ▶ *Poor old Grandma seems to be in her second childhood – she's always talking to imaginary friends.*

CHILL
send a chill down your spine to make you feel frightened ▶ *I read the document, and it sent a chill down my spine. These people have no regard for human life.*

CHIN
take sth on the chin to accept criticism or a difficulty without becoming upset ▶ *He took our complaints on the chin, promising he would produce better work in future.*

CHINK
a chink in sb's armour a weakness that makes a person or group easy to attack ▶ *Their product looked good, but during the demonstration the chinks in their technological armour began to show.*
a chink of light a small amount of hope ▶ *After days of battling for the baby's life, we saw a chink of light yesterday – he started to breathe on his own.*

CHIP
be a chip off the old block to be very like one of your parents ▶ *Jim argues just like his father – he's a real chip off the old block.*

have a chip on your shoulder to be easily offended or angry about something ▶ *He had a huge chip on his shoulder because he had not been to university.*

CHIPS
cash in your chips to die ▶ *When my granddad cashed in his chips we sold the house.*

have had your chips to have lost every chance of succeeding in what you are trying to do ▶ *I've really had my chips now – I completely messed up the last exam.*

CHOICE
Hobson's choice a situation in which there is only one thing you can do or have, unless you do nothing ▶ *It's Hobson's choice – we have to accept the service that the bank chooses to offer.*

CHOP
chop and change to keep changing your mind or the way you do something, especially in an annoying way ▶ *In the old days you went into a job at 16 and you stayed there for life – you didn't chop and change like they do nowadays.*

get the chop *also **be given the chop*** to be dismissed from your job ▶ *In the motor industry hundreds of workers have been given the chop.*

sb is for the chop ▶ *There are rumours that the sales manager is for the chop.*

sb is licking his/her chops ➤ sb is licking his/her LIPS

CHORD

strike a chord (with sb) *also **touch a chord (with sb)*** to have meaning for someone because they are reminded of their own experiences ▶ *The film's depiction of the early sixties strikes a nostalgic chord.*

CIRCLE

come full circle *also **go full circle*** something, such as an idea, fashion, or way of life, has changed many times but has finally come back to where it was or what it was like at first ▶ *I think this discussion has come full circle, as we seem to be back with our original idea.*

square the circle to solve a problem which seems impossible to solve ▶ *This car tries to square the circle of being powerful as well as environmentally acceptable.*

a vicious circle when one problem causes others, which make the first problem worse, so that the process is repeated again and again ▶ *Peter was in a vicious circle: he got ill, and then worrying about his health made him so stressed that his illness got worse.* ▶ *People with bulimia eat huge amounts of food, then force themselves to vomit, so a vicious circle develops.*

CIRCLES

be going around in circles *also **be running around in circles*** to fail to move forward because nothing you do seems to solve the basic problem

▶ *I felt I was going around in circles, talking to different people at the bank and getting different advice from everyone.*

CIRCUS

a three-ring circus a place of confusion and noise ▶ *The ticket hall turned into a three-ring circus when the main computer broke down.*

CLAIM

a claim to fame something that makes a person or place special ▶ *Until she published her best-seller, her main claim to fame was an academic paper on 12th century abbeys.*

CLANGER

drop a clanger to make an embarrassing mistake ▶ *I dropped a real clanger at the party when I mentioned Tom's wife – I didn't realize she'd left him.*

CLAPPERS

go/work like the clappers to go/work extremely fast ▶ *Be careful, everyone goes like the clappers along this bit of road.*

CLASS

a class act a person or group that

performs in an excellent way ▶ *The DataWise Group is definitely a class act that deserves its position in the market.*

CLASSES
the chattering classes educated people in a society who are always giving their opinions ▶ *The chattering classes are travelling on the new trains and telling everyone how good they are.*

CLEANERS
take sb to the cleaners to take all of someone's money ▶ *She's going to divorce him and I hope she takes him to the cleaners!*

CLOCK
do sth against the clock to work fast to get something done in a specific time ▶ *It took us three days to paint the house, working against the clock before the new owners moved in.*
do sth round the clock to do something all day and all night ▶ *This service allows you to pay your bills and check your bank balance round the clock.*

CLOCKWORK
go like clockwork to work as it is supposed to, without any problems ▶ *All that summer the bottling process went like clockwork.*

CLOGS
pop your clogs to die ▶ *If I pop my clogs before I retire, you'll get £50,000.*

CLOSET
out of the closet
1 openly admitting to people that you have feelings (such as being attracted to the same sex), beliefs, or habits that you have kept secret ▶ *There is a great feeling of relief that comes when you're out of the closet.*
2 openly discussed for the first time ▶ *In the last few years, mental illness has come out of the closet but sadly there is often a feeling of shame attached to it.*

CLOTH
be cut from the same cloth to be very similar ▶ *Don't assume that all women are cut from the same cloth. Jill won't necessarily react like me.*

cut your coat according to your cloth also *cut your cloth* to spend only as much money as you can afford ▶ *Anyone who's had to control a household budget knows that you have to cut your coat according to your cloth.*

CLOTHES
the emperor's (new) clothes a situation when everyone pretends to admire something that is not really sensible or special because they think they will look stupid if they do not ▶ *I don't believe anyone really likes modern music – it's just the emperor's new clothes.*

CLOUD
a cloud on the/your horizon something bad that is likely to happen ▶ *The darkest cloud on our horizon is not revolution, it is too much state control.*

be on cloud nine to be extremely happy ▶ *After he rang and asked me out, I was on cloud nine.*

(every cloud has) a silver lining every bad situation has some good points ▶ *Every cloud tends to have its silver lining, and if this tax forces us to use our cars less it will be good for the environment.*

under a cloud suspected of doing something wrong ▶ *He left his last job under a cloud, and it has never been satisfactorily explained.*

CLUB

join the club also **welcome to the club** I am in the same situation ▶ *"My trouble is, I'm scared of flying." "Join the club – I always take the train."*

CLUE

not have a clue not to know (anything) ▶ *I wouldn't have a clue how to get to the restaurant.* ▶ *John wanders around, looking as if he hasn't a clue, but he's a brilliant artist.*

CLUED UP

be clued up (on sth) also **be clued up (about sth)** to know all the facts about something ▶ *Choosing the right bottle can be a problem, if you're not clued up on wine.*

CLUTCHES

in sb's clutches to be under somebody's control ▶ *Once a moneylender has you in his clutches, you'll never get out of debt.*

COALS

haul sb over the coals to criticize someone severely ▶ *The politician was hauled over the coals by the media because of inefficiency in his department.*

taking coals to Newcastle taking something to a place where there is already plenty of it ▶ *You don't need to buy T-shirts before you go travelling in Asia – that would be taking coals to Newcastle.*

> This idiom comes from the time when there was a lot of coal in Newcastle, a town in NE England, so it was not necessary to take coal there

COAST

the coast is clear it is safe to do something without being seen or caught ▶ *The thief waited until the coast was clear, then slipped quietly out of the building.*

COBWEBS

blow away the cobwebs also **clear away the cobwebs** to make you feel

less tired or bored ▶ *I need a good long walk to blow away the cobwebs.*

COCK

a cock-and-bull story an excuse that does not seem to be true ▶ *Nobody believes that cock-and-bull story about the bank keeping his credit card – he's just being mean.*

COG

a cog in the machine someone who does a small and possibly unimportant job in a large organization ▶ *I'm just a small cog in the company machine, and I don't have much control.*

COIN

be coining it (in) to be earning a lot of money ▸ *It was hot, and they were coining it in at the ice-cream stall.*

COLD

come in from the cold to be accepted into a group that has previously not wanted you ▸ *Since it came in from the cold, South Africa has greatly increased its wine exports.*

COLLAR

be/get hot under the collar to be or become angry ▸ *He got very hot under the collar when his proposals were criticized.*

COLOUR

see the colour of sb's money to make sure that someone has enough money to pay ▸ *Most small businesses want to see the colour of their client's money before they provide services.*

COLOURS

nail your colours to the mast to say what you think, publicly and definitely ▸ *He had courage, and usually nailed his colours to the mast by saying what he thought.*

> Ships use flags or colours to show other ships who they are and where they come from. The colours were raised at the start of a battle to show that the ship intended to fight. If colours were nailed to the mast (=the pole that the sails hang from) they could not be taken down to admit defeat.

pass with flying colours to pass with great success ▸ *Sheila took her final*

exams this summer, and passed with flying colours.

show (yourself in) your true colours to let people see your true opinions after you have been hiding them ▸ *At this point I must show myself in my true colours, as an old-fashioned moralist.*

COMB

go through sth with a fine-tooth comb to examine very carefully ▸ *The police went through the whole area with a fine-tooth comb, but they never found the body.*

COME

come clean to tell the truth, especially after lying ▸ *If politicians would come clean and admit their mistakes, they'd earn a lot more respect.*

come down hard on sb to criticize or punish someone severely ▸ *Jones promised to come down hard on people who abused the system.*

come off it! don't be silly! Don't lie! ▸ *Come off it, Lynn, I don't believe you aren't interested in him!*

come on strong to show by your behaviour that you think someone is sexually attractive ▸ *I always come on too strong with men and scare them away.*

come to pass to happen ▸ *We were promised improvements that have never come to pass.*

come to think of it now that I consider the facts ▸ *No, I probably won't see Jessie till Saturday, come to think of it.*

come unglued also **come unstuck** to fail ▸ *They think they can go into the exam without doing any work, but they'll come unstuck later.*

don't come it with me! don't criticize or argue with me ▸ *Don't come it with*

C

me, young lady! I know exactly where you've been.

don't come the ___ with sb don't pretend to be (what is stated) ▶ *Don't come the innocent with me – you knew perfectly well what was going on.*

it (all) comes down to also **it (all) boils down to** the most important point is ▶ *There are all sorts of tips for successful management, but basically it comes down to good organization.*

___'s coming home a team from your own country or area is going to win (in a particular sport) ▶ *Tennis isn't coming home yet, but it may be on its way.*

when it comes (right) down to it also **when you get (right) down to it** when we are thinking about the most important thing ▶ *I'm going to get a job that I enjoy. When it comes down to it, money isn't everything, is it?*

COMEUPPANCE

sb gets his/her comeuppance a punishment someone receives is what they deserve ▶ *Violent football fan Huggins finally got his comeuppance yesterday with a fine of £500.*

COMFORT

sth is cold comfort a good piece of news does not make a bad situation seem any better ▶ *When your computer breaks down, it is cold comfort to be told that they are becoming more reliable.*

COMPANY

get into bad company also **fall into bad company** to spend time with people who do bad things ▶ *He's basically a good boy who got into bad company at school.*

sb is in good company someone should not feel embarrassed about something they have done because many good or famous people have done the same ▶ *Addicts of the show are in good company this week, as several college lecturers have admitted to liking it.*

present company excepted (of course) not including the people you are with ▶ *Most of the accountants I've met, present company excepted of course, are rather dull.*

two's company (three's a crowd) a third person would not be welcome, as two people want to be by themselves ▶ *"Why don't you stay for supper, Jill?" "No, I'll leave you two alone – two's company, three's a crowd."*

COMPLIMENT

a back-handed compliment something that someone says to you that is both pleasant and unpleasant at the same time ▶ *"You're a very good listener." "That's a back-handed compliment – you mean I don't contribute to the conversation."*

CONDITION

in mint condition in perfect condition ▶ *I've seen a 1950 coin like this advertised for twice the price, but it was in mint condition.*

CONSPIRACY

a conspiracy of silence an agreement to keep important information secret ▶ *Instead of admitting their mistake, the managers took part in a conspiracy of silence which lasted for a year.*

CONTENT

do sth to your heart's content to do something as much as you want ▶ *You*

can listen to your music to your heart's
content – just keep the volume down
so you're not disturbing people.

CONVERSATION
a conversation piece an unusual thing
that gives people something to talk
about ▶ *A huge Victorian statue made
an ugly but interesting conversation
piece.*

CONVERTED
be preaching to the converted to be
wasting time persuading people who
already have the same opinions as you
▶ *Candidates for election spend a lot
of their time preaching to the
converted at party meetings.*

COOKIE
sb is a smart/tough cookie someone
is clever/determined to succeed
▶ *Self-confident, positive, and almost
bossy, she's a tough cookie.*

COOKS
too many cooks (spoil the broth) too
many people are trying to do the same
job at the same time, so that it is done
badly ▶ *The newsletter is a jumble of
different styles and topics – too many
cooks, I reckon.*

COOL
cool, calm, and collected not nervous,
upset, or embarrassed ▶ *Our school
secretary always kept cool, calm, and
collected in any crisis.*

keep your cool to remain calm in a
bad situation ▶ *Try to keep your cool
and don't let Jordan annoy you.*

lose your cool also **blow your cool** to
become angry suddenly ▶ *He started
getting confused and contradicting
himself, until eventually he blew his
cool and shouted at her.*

COOP
fly the coop to leave the place where
you live or work ▶ *Jay flew the coop as
soon as he could and got a job in
London.*

COP
cop (a load of) this look at or listen to
this ▶ *Cop this, the car's been stolen!*

cop it to be punished ▶ *You'll cop it
from your Mum when she finds out!*

it's a fair cop I admit it, and it is fair to
accuse me ▶ *OK, OK, it's a fair cop, I
did break the window.*

not much cop not very good ▶ *The
trouble with old bands making
comebacks is that you realize they
weren't much cop in the first place.*

COPYBOOK
**blot your
copybook** to
do something
wrong that
changes
people's good
opinion of
you
▶ *Andrews
blotted his copybook after 20 years in
the police force when he was caught
drinking on duty.*

CORD
cut the (umbilical) cord to stop relying
on your parents for help or money
▶ *He keeps saying he wants to cut the
cord, but he's asked his father for the
plane fare home.*

> The umbilical cord is the tube
> that attaches a baby to its mother
> before it is born.

CORNER
to back sb into a corner also **to paint**

sb into a corner to put someone into a situation which it is very difficult to get out of ▶ *He comes up with some brilliant excuses when he's backed into a corner.*

fight your/sb's corner to try very hard to defend yourself or someone else ▶ *He will always fight his corner if he thinks something's important.*

turn the corner to start to get better ▶ *We knew Dad had turned the corner when he started complaining about the hospital food.* ▶ *Stock prices turned the corner towards the end of the week, to everyone's relief.*

CORNERS

cut corners not to do certain things in a process in order to save time, money, or energy ▶ *If you cut corners when you're building, it'll probably go wrong.*

from/to the four corners of the earth also **from/to the four corners of the globe** from or to all the parts of the world ▶ *Spain is hosting a conference of ecologists from the four corners of the globe.*

CORRIDORS

the corridors of power the place where important government decisions are made ▶ *The message from the corridors of power is that interest rates will be one of the most important subjects at next week's talks.*

COTTON WOOL

wrap sb in cotton wool to treat someone more carefully than is necessary ▶ *Some parents tend to wrap their children in cotton wool, instead of letting them learn by their mistakes.*

COUCH POTATO

couch potato someone who spends their free time sitting down, doing things like watching television, playing computer games or eating ▶ *Doctors are worried that too many young people are turning into couch potatoes.*

COUNSEL

keep your own counsel to keep your plans or opinions secret ▶ *If you don't want an argument with Terry, it's best to keep your own counsel when the subject of housework comes up.*

COUNT

be out for the count to sleep deeply ▶ *After that big dinner, I was out for the count, and I didn't hear the doorbell.*

COUNTER

under the counter secretly, because it is illegal ▶ *Those magazines are banned, but are still available under the counter.* **under-the-counter** ADJ ▶ *He admitted he made under-the-counter cash payments to football players.*

COURAGE

Dutch courage courage or confidence that you get by drinking alcohol ▶ *I'll need some Dutch courage before I go on stage tonight.*

have the courage of your convictions to be brave enough to do what you think is right ▶ *If you think he's making a mistake, you should say something – you* *must have the courage of your convictions.*

COURSE

be on course to be doing the right things to help you succeed ▶ *We're still on course to hold the conference in October.*

stay the course to continue with something even though it is difficult ▶ *The problem with diets is that most people fail to stay the course.*

steer a middle course to follow a course of action that is between two extreme things ▶ *The government wants to steer a middle course between state control of the economy and free-market capitalism.*

COURT

hold court to be the centre of a crowd of people who listen to you and admire you ▶ *He sits at his big*

mahogany desk, holding court with loyal supporters who laugh at his jokes.

be laughed out of court to be so silly or unlikely that nobody believes it ▶ *Fifty years ago the idea that women should have equal rights in the workplace would have been laughed out of court.*

pay court to sb to pay a lot of attention to someone and try to please them ▶ *The politicians are paying court to the voters but they won't keep their promises.*

> In the past if a man paid court to a woman, he showed that he loved her or wanted to marry her by visiting her often, giving her lots of attention, praising her good qualities etc.

COUSIN

a country cousin someone considered less fashionable or less well-informed because they do not live in a city ▶ *Sam felt like a country cousin when she went to the reception in her old dress and last year's shoes.*

COVENTRY

send sb to Coventry to stop speaking to someone you disapprove of ▶ *The other kids in Adam's class sent him to Coventry because he never shares his sweets.*

COVER

blow sb's cover to make public who someone really is, or what is planned ▶ *Lawyers argued that the book put secret agents in danger by blowing their cover.*

COW

a sacred cow something that is generally considered too important to criticize or change ▶ *The TV company has been criticized for getting rid of the 10 o'clock News, a sacred cow.*

COWS

till the cows come home for a very long time ▶ *You can argue until the cows come home. I'll never agree with you.*

CRACK

a fair crack of the whip a reasonable chance to succeed or be heard ▶ *Local newspapers should make sure that everyone gets a fair crack of the whip.*

get cracking to start now ▶ *Now we're all here, let's get cracking with the first question.*

have a crack at sth to have an attempt or opportunity to do something ▶ *Dave's going to have a crack at scuba-diving next month.*

sth is not all it's cracked up to be also **sth is not everything it's cracked up to be** something is not as good as people say it is ▶ *It's a nice hotel, but it's not everything it's cracked up to be.*

CRACKS

fall through the cracks to be ignored, especially because two or more people in authority have failed to work together ▶ *Sales opportunities have fallen through the cracks because the heads of marketing and design weren't talking to each other.*

paper over the cracks to hide the effects of a problem without improving the situation ▶ *Their marriage has finally broken up, though they managed to paper over the cracks until their children left home.*

CRADLE

from the cradle to the grave from the beginning to the end of someone's life ▶ *Church records used to mark an individual's progress from the cradle to the grave.*

CRAZY

like crazy a lot, or with a lot of energy ▶ *The cat was fighting like crazy to get free, but Phil held on to it.*

CREAM

cream of the crop used about someone or something that is the best of its kind ▶ *All the skin cleansers were good, but the cream of the crop was a Japanese product made of seaweed.*

CREATURE

creature comforts the things that make life pleasant and comfortable, such as good food, a warm house, and modern equipment ▶ *I don't mind camping, but after about three weeks I start missing my creature comforts.*

a creature of habit someone who always does the same things in the same way ▶ *Under Taurus it says "you are a creature of habit and like a comfortable home".*

CREDIT

do sb/sth credit also **do credit to sb/sth**

1 to be a reason to admire someone or something ▶ *Your actions do you credit – it would have been easy to walk away from the problem but you dealt with it bravely.*

2 to give something the right amount of attention ▶ *At last I had time to sit down and do credit to his wonderful cooking.*

give sb credit (for sth) also **give credit where credit's due** to praise someone or to show them some respect ▶ *I think Jeff's a lot more honest than we give him credit for.* ▶ *I don't agree with their policy, but we should give credit where credit is due – they have done what they promised in the election.*

CREEK

be up the creek (without a paddle)
to be in a very difficult situation ▶ *Bill*

crashed the car yesterday – now he's up the creek, with no money to buy a new one.

CREEPS

give sb the creeps to frighten someone ▶ *These old houses give you the creeps, don't they?*

CRÈME

the crème de la crème the very best ▶ *They are proud to welcome the crème de la crème to perform at their concert hall.*

CREST

be riding (on) the crest of a wave to be very successful at this time ▶ *House prices were rising fast and estate agents were riding the crest of this wave.*

CROCODILE

shed crocodile tears to pretend that you feel sad or sorry ▶ *It's time the government stopped shedding crocodile tears over child poverty, and tackled the cause of the problem.*

CROPPER

come a cropper
1 to fail in something ▶ *The business*

came a cropper when her hard-working partner moved to Canada.
2 to fall over ▶ *She came a cropper on the icy pavement.*

CROSS

a heavy cross to bear a serious problem that troubles someone for a long time ▶ *Her husband's illness had been a heavy cross to bear.*

> The cross in this idiom is two pieces of wood in the shape of a 'T' which were used as a structure on which to crucify someone (=kill someone by nailing them to a cross as a punishment). The person being crucified often had to carry or 'bear' their own cross to the place where they would die.

CROSSFIRE

get caught in the crossfire to be affected by an argument between other people ▶ *Poor Michelle got caught in the crossfire when her parents split up.*

CROSSROADS

come to a crossroads also **be at a crossroads** to have to make a decision that will affect your future ▶ *After losing his job he was at a crossroads, and Joe's offer of a partnership came at just the right time.*

CROW

as the crow flies if you travel in a straight line ▶ *It's only 15 miles to central London as the crow flies, but it takes over an hour to get there by car.*

eat crow to be forced to admit that you are wrong ▶ *Critics who laughed at the Internet when it first appeared* *were forced to eat crow as it spread around the world.*

CROWD

follow the crowd to do the same thing as other people ► *Young people tend to follow the crowd, liking the same music, sports, and film stars.*

stand out from the crowd to be different and easily noticed ► *She dresses and moves with an elegance that makes her stand out from the crowd.*

CRUEL

be cruel to be kind to do something that may upset someone but will help them in another way ► *It's embarrassing telling someone that they have bad breath, but sometimes you have to be cruel to be kind.*

CRUNCH

when/if it comes to the crunch when/if an important decision has to be made ► *When it came to the crunch, I couldn't marry Anna, although I liked her very much.*

CRUST

earn your crust ➤ earn your BREAD

the upper crust people in the highest social class ► *The novelist made fun of the behaviour of the upper crust.*

upper-crust ADJ ► *She's from a very upper-crust family, you know.*

CRY

be a far cry from to be very different from ► *The noisy atmosphere at Ray's Bar was a far cry from the quiet elegance of the Grand Hotel.*

in full cry putting all your energy into chasing someone or making a noise ► *I came down to London with the police in full cry after me.* ► *If you have*

never heard the orchestra in full cry, go and buy this CD.

CRYING

for crying out loud used to emphasize anger or a complaint ► *Be quiet, for crying out loud, I'm trying to work!*

CRYSTAL BALL

a crystal ball something that shows you the future ► *Without a crystal ball, it's impossible to foresee who'll win.*

> A crystal ball is a glass ball that fortune tellers (=people who can tell what will happen in the future) look into to find out what will happen.

CUD

chew the cud to have a long talk ► *After the meeting, buy the team lunch, so you can chew the cud for an hour or so.*

CUDGELS

take up the cudgels to fight or argue for someone or something ► *Mark took up the cudgels on behalf of his son, and wrote a strong letter of complaint.*

CUE

take your cue from to copy what someone does ► *Taking its cue from the airline industry, the company announced that it would ban smoking on its buses.*

CUFF

off the cuff without preparing what you are going to say ► *I can't give you an answer off the cuff – I'll look it up at home.* **off-the-cuff** ADJ ► *Morris's off-the-cuff remarks about politicians have got him into trouble on many occasions.*

CUP

not sb's cup of tea something you do not like very much ▶ *Well, jazz isn't really my cup of tea, but I'll come to your concert.*

CUPBOARD

cupboard love pretended love, especially as shown by animals or children to people who give

them things they want ▶ *"The cat likes me best." "Yes, but it's only cupboard love – you're the one who feeds him."*

CURRENT

go against the current *also* **swim against the current** to have a different opinion from most people ▶ *Italian designer Brazzi is going against the current with his new collection.*

CURTAIN

the curtain falls on sth the end of something comes ▶ *Too many public figures have seen the curtain fall on their careers because of gossip that is reported as news.*

a curtain raiser the first event of many ▶ *Short pieces by young composers were played as curtain raisers for last year's festival.*

CURTAINS

it is curtains for *also* **it means curtains for** someone will leave, or die, or something will end ▶ *If the company reorganizes, it will probably mean curtains for my division and me too.*

CURVE

throw sb a curve to surprise and confuse someone by doing something that they do not expect ▶ *Sometimes life throws you a curve that turns out to be lucky, although you don't realize it at the time.*

This idiom comes from the game of baseball. A curve ball is a way of throwing the ball so that it suddenly and unexpectedly curves away from the batter (=person hitting the ball) just as it gets to him or her.

CUT

sb can't cut it not to be able to do a job or activity ▶ *Jason just couldn't cut it as a waiter.*

be a cut above to be better than ▶ *These new wines are a cut above the average supermarket red.*

be cut and dried to be certain and simple to deal with ▶ *My parents prefer to have everything cut and dried, sorted out, tidied away – changes upset them.* **cut-and-dried** ADJ ▶ *This seems like a cut-and-dried case of robbery.*

cut and run to leave a situation suddenly when it becomes too difficult ▶ *Tim faces a long lawsuit, but he is not the type of man to cut and run.*

the cut and thrust of sth the active, exciting, dangerous part of something ▶ *These academics can't operate in the cut and thrust of the real world, can they?*

cut sb dead to ignore someone deliberately when you meet them ▶ *I called to her and she cut me dead – turned her back and started talking to Keith.*

cut sth fine *also **cut sth close*** to leave yourself very little time to do something ▶ *You're cutting it fine, aren't you? The play starts in five minutes.*

cut it out! stop it! ▶ *Rob's mum thumped on the wall and shouted "Cut it out, lads, go to sleep!"*

not be cut out to be sth/for sth not to be suitable for a particular job or life ▶ *I decided that I wasn't cut out to be a teacher.* ▶ *Many fair-skinned people are not cut out for the strong Egyptian sunshine.*

cut up rough to react in an angry or violent way ▶ *Joe cut up rough when he was asked to leave.*

CYLINDERS

be firing on all cylinders to be completely awake and mentally active ▶ *Sorry, I'm not firing on all cylinders today. Can you repeat the question?*

Dd

DAGGERS

be at daggers drawn to be very angry with each other ▶ *Those two are both in love with Fran, so they are at daggers drawn.*

look daggers (at sb) to look at someone very angrily ▶ *Wendy overheard your remarks, that's why she's looking daggers at you.*

DAISIES

be pushing up (the) daisies to be dead ▶ *His uncle's been pushing up the daisies for at least ten years.*

DAMNED

damned if you do, damned if you don't whatever you do, you will be criticized ▶ *If I invite Mike, Lee will be angry, and if I don't, Mike will be hurt – I'm damned if I do and damned if I don't.*

DAMPER

put a damper on to take the fun or enthusiasm out of something ▶ *Complaints from the neighbours put a damper on the party.*

DANCE

lead sb a (merry) dance to cause trouble for someone because they do not know what you will do next ▶ *Pam led him a merry dance before she finally agreed to marry him.*

DARK

keep sth dark to keep something secret ▶ *They're keeping the engagement dark at the moment.*

keep sb in the dark *also* ***leave sb in the dark*** to give someone no information about something important

▶ *For 50 years people have been kept in the dark about the dangers of nuclear waste.*

whistling in the dark seeming more confident about a situation than you really are ▶ *She says it's a temporary separation, but she's whistling in the dark – he's never coming back.*

DASH

cut a dash to look impressive and attractive ▶ *Rod cuts quite a dash in his naval uniform.*

DATE

a blind date a romantic meeting arranged between two people who have not met each other before ▶ *They married six weeks after meeting on a blind date.*

be past his/her/its sell-by date to be no longer young, useful, attractive, fashionable etc ▶ *Isn't traditional school uniform well past its sell-by date?*

DAWN

a false dawn an improvement which is only temporary ▶ *The ceasefire turned out to be a false dawn, and fighting started again within a few days.*

D

DAY

call it a day to decide to stop doing something ▶ *We've been working non-stop and I think it's time to call it a day.*

carry the day also **win the day** to win an argument or competition ▶ *Bob is quiet, but his suggestions always win the day.*

day in, day out also **week in, week out** or **month in, month out** or **year in, year out** all the time, with no variety ▶ *I was sick of doing the same old job day in, day out.*

day of reckoning a time when you are judged and maybe punished ▶ *I hadn't done any work for weeks, and the day of reckoning was getting closer.*

> According to many religions the day of reckoning is the day you die when you are judged by God.

early in the day too soon to make a judgment ▶ *It's a bit early in the day to say that the company's failed.*

from/since day one from/since the beginning ▶ *Ian's been part of the family from day one – my parents love him!*

give me (a) ___ any day (of the week) also **I'd rather have (a) ___ any day (of the week)** I like something much more ▶ *Nowadays everyone has a car, but give me a bike any day of the week.*

sb has had his/her day also **sth has had its day** he/she/it is no longer needed, useful, fashionable etc ▶ *Landline phones have had their day, and mobiles are the future.*

it's not my day/week/year etc it's an unlucky day/week/year etc when unpleasant things have happened

▶ *I missed my bus and I left my lunch at home – it just hasn't been my day.*

live to fight another day to survive, so that you can try again after losing or failing ▶ *Frank didn't make it to the final, but he's lived to fight another day.*

make a day of it to make something more enjoyable by spending a whole day doing it ▶ *Instead of just going into town to shop, we could see a film and make a day of it.*

make sb's day to make someone very happy ▶ *I bought John a plant, and he said it had made his day.*

a rainy day a time when you will need money ▶ *If I won the lottery, I'd save most of it for a rainy day.*

a red-letter day a very exciting or important day ▶ *The opening of the theatre was a red-letter day in the history of British opera.*

rue the day to wish that you had not done something ▶ *We may rue the day that we bought such an old house.*

save the day to do something that makes a bad situation end in success ▶ *We were losing 3-2, and then Brown saved the day by scoring in the last five minutes.*

that'll be the day! that is very unlikely! ▶ *"Is he married?" "That'll be the day!"*

DAYLIGHT

in broad daylight in the daytime, so that everyone can see ▶ *I saw them kissing in broad daylight!*

see daylight

1 to begin to understand ▶ *I think I'm beginning to see daylight – it was you who took the money.*

2 to be published or noticed ▶ *His diaries are unlikely ever to see daylight.*

DAYLIGHTS

beat the (living) daylights out of sb to hit someone a lot ▶ *He beat the living daylights out of Rigby, who ended up in hospital.*

frighten the living daylights out of sb also ***scare the living daylights out of sb*** to frighten someone very much ▶ *Don't jump out at people – you scared the living daylights out of me!*

DAYS

sb's/sth's days are numbered someone or something will not continue or exist for long ▶ *The days of the single-phone family are numbered as more young people buy mobile phones.*

the good old days the past when it is seen as better than the present ▶ *My grandparents talk a lot about the good old days.*

halcyon days a time in the past that was better than the present ▶ *Some modern bands are producing music that recalls the halcyon days of 1960s rock.*

> The word 'halcyon' comes from the Greek word for a bird called a kingfisher. In ancient times it was believed that the kingfisher sat on its eggs on the surface of the sea for 14 days in the middle of winter, during which time the sea was always calm.

sth has seen better days something is old and in bad condition ▶ *Mum drove a battered van that had seen better days.*

it's early days (yet) it is too soon to judge the result of something ▶ *We have to be cautious – I know we're doing very well but it's early days yet.*

the old days the past ▶ *In the old days we could park free wherever we wanted.*

one of those days a day when everything seems to be going wrong ▶ *Please excuse the mess – it's been one of those days.*

DEAD

dead set very determined ▶ *She is dead set on buying the house even though it's falling to pieces.*

sb wouldn't be seen dead also ***sb wouldn't be caught dead*** someone would be too embarrassed or ashamed to do or wear something ▶ *Adam loves riding his bike but he wouldn't be seen dead in cycling shorts!*

DEAF

fall on deaf ears not to be listened to, to be ignored ▶ *All her pleas for help fell on deaf ears.*

DEAL

big deal! I don't think it's very important, impressive, or special ▶ *So your dad's annoyed – big deal! I think we can cope with that.*

get a raw deal to be treated unfairly ▶ *Women often get a raw deal when it comes to working conditions.*

sth is a done deal something is an arrangement that is going ahead and cannot be changed ▶ *It's a done deal – the merger is going ahead.*

no big deal it doesn't matter ▶ *Look, it's no big deal to me if we don't go. I've got other things to do.*

DEATH

be dicing with death to do something extremely dangerous ▶ *Young people are dicing with death if they try these drugs.*

D

die the death to become completely unfashionable or unpopular ▶ *She thinks men's suits should have died the death in the sixties.*

hold on like grim death *also* **hang on like grim death** to keep holding something very tightly ▶ *Val's horse nearly fell, but she held on like grim death until the finishing line.*

to death very much or strongly ▶ *I was bored to death at the concert.* ▶ *She loves that kitten to death.*

DECK

hit the deck to fall to the ground deliberately ▶ *He hit the deck a moment before the grenade exploded.*

DECKS

clear the decks to clear everything away, deal with unfinished work etc ▶ *I want to clear the decks before Liz comes so I can relax and talk to her.*

DEGREE

give sb the third degree to question someone in a very severe or cruel way ▶ *The secret police gave her the third degree about the messages she'd been passing on.*

to the nth degree to the highest level ▶ *In the army you learn teamwork to the nth degree – your life could depend upon it.*

DENT

make a dent in sth to reduce by a large amount ▶ *The new taxes have hardly made a dent in their income.*

DEPTH

be out of your depth to be unable to deal with a situation that you do not understand, or a subject that you do not know enough about ▶ *I was soon out of my depth, as the conversation turned to economics.*

DEPTHS

sink to the depths to be able to do very bad things ▶ *I can't believe he could sink to the depths of stealing from his own family.*

DESIGNS

have designs on to want, and be ready to get, in a secret or dishonest way ▶ *I was sorry for the old man, that's all – did you think I had designs on his money?*

DEVICES

be left to your own devices to be left alone with no care or help ▶ *Nobody cares about the new students – they're just left to their own devices.*

DEVIL

be a devil! do something brave! ▶ *Be a devil and ask Gerry to dance!*

better the devil you know (than the devil you don't) it is better to continue in a situation you know than try a new one ▶ *I've decided not to change jobs, even though this one isn't great – better the devil you know.*

between the devil and the deep blue sea in a situation in which either choice you make will be bad ▶ *The voters here feel they are caught between the devil and the deep blue sea, and many won't vote at all.*

give the devil his due to admit there are some good qualities in a bad person ▶ *Harry is very annoying but he's generous, to give the devil his due.*

talk of the devil also *speak of the devil* here's the person we are talking about!

▶ *Dad's bound to find out we're here – oh, talk of the devil, here he comes!*

DIAMOND

a rough diamond a good person who is not very polite or well educated ▶ *Charlie's a real rough diamond – he drinks too much and swears a lot, but he'd never let you down.*

DICE

the dice are loaded (against sb) a situation is unfair, because someone is at a disadvantage ▶ *The dice were loaded against our team, as two of our players were ill.*

DIE

the die is cast an important thing has happened which cannot be changed ▶ *The book is published, the die is cast, and I must accept the judgment of my readers.*

I almost died also *I nearly died* I felt very surprised, amused, or embarrassed ▶ *I came on stage and forgot my words – I almost died.*

to die for very good, attractive, or desirable ▶ *Diana's got hair to die for – long, thick, and naturally blonde.*

sb would rather die (than do sth) someone really does not want to (do something) ▶ *He's getting old, and he needs you. But he'd rather die than admit it.*

DIFFERENCE

a ___ with a difference this may be the thing or person you expect, but it is better than you expect ▶ *Most people own a camera, but this is a camera with a difference.*

same difference two things are about the same ▶ *"Where shall we sit – here or by the window?" "It doesn't matter – same difference."*

DIFFERENCES

bury your differences to stop thinking or arguing about things you disagree about ▶ *We've agreed to bury our differences and concentrate on winning the next election.*

DIME

be a dime a dozen to be very common or easy to find ▶ *Fish recipes are a dime a dozen, but this one's really good.*

DINE

dine out on sth to use a personal story to amuse or interest people ▶ *In years to come I would be able to dine out on the experience of being arrested, but at the time it wasn't much fun.*

DINNER

be dressed up like a dog's dinner to look silly because the clothes you are wearing are very formal ▶ *I'd enjoy weddings more if I*

didn't have to be dressed up like a dog's dinner.

D

make a dog's dinner (out) of sth
➤ make a dog's BREAKFAST (out) of sth

DINNERS

sb's had more ___ than you've had hot dinners someone has had a lot of what you are talking about
▸ *Michelle's had more jobs than I've had hot dinners – when is she going to settle down?*

DIRECTION

point sb in the right direction to advise someone on what they should do ▸ *I didn't know where to start with my essay but my teacher pointed me in the right direction.*

DIRT

dig up dirt *also* **dig for dirt** to discover something that may harm a person ▸ *Journalists are trying to dig up dirt on her private life, but she appears to have no dark secrets.*

dish the dirt to talk or write about other people's private lives ▸ *Tom got a lot of money for dishing the dirt on the famous people he has known.*

treat sb like dirt to treat someone unkindly and without respect ▸ *His children treat him like dirt, and his wife is only interested in his money.*

DIRTY

do the dirty on sb to do something bad, especially to someone who trusts you ▸ *Don't go and work for that man – he did the dirty on his sales staff.*

DISCRETION

discretion is the better part of valour it is better to be careful than to take unnecessary risks ▸ *There are times when it's good to be open with the press but sometimes discretion is the better part of valour.*

DISH

sb can dish it out but they can't take it someone likes to criticize other people, but does not like being criticized by anyone else ▸ *TV critics can dish it out but often they can't take it.*

DISTANCE

go the (full) distance to finish what you have to do ▸ *I was exhausted, but determined to go the distance even if it meant working all night.*

within striking distance (of sth) *also* **within spitting distance (of sth)** very near ▸ *Sam's within striking distance of getting her degree.* ▸ *We lived within spitting distance of the Eiffel Tower.*

DIVIDENDS

pay dividends the time or effort given to something is bringing advantages ▸ *A bit of research into your holiday area pays dividends in terms of enjoyment.*

DO

can/could do without would be happier without ▸ *We can do without your critical comments, thanks.* ▸ *I could do without Ben coming round for a chat every evening.*

could do with need(s) or would like ▸ *This room could do with a coat of paint.* ▸ *I could do with a drink.*

couldn't do without not to be able to continue normal life without ▸ *I couldn't do without my computer.*

do a ___ to behave like (someone) by doing something they are known for ▸ *I wish I could do a Gauguin and move to Tahiti.*

be done for *also* **be done in** to be finished, very tired, or in a bad situation ▶ *Mick was pretty well done for after completing 70 laps.* ▶ *The electric car was done in by falling oil prices.*

do sb proud to make someone feel proud or happy ▶ *The George Hotel does its customers proud with a wonderful menu.*

DOCTOR

just what the doctor ordered exactly what you need ▶ *After six losses, our victory on Saturday was just what the doctor ordered.*

DOG

dog days
1 a dull period of time when there is little action ▶ *The team's dog days ended last week with a brilliant game against Vale Park.*
2 very hot, still days in the summer ▶ *Then came the dog days when the wind dropped and the yacht made little progress.*

> The ancient Romans called these hot days 'dog days' because a star called the dog star rises and goes down at the same time as the sun during the hottest weeks of the year.

dog eat dog people doing nasty things to competitors in order to succeed ▶ *Small shops find it hard to compete with supermarkets. It's dog eat dog out there!*

(be) a dog in the manger someone who will not let other people have

something that they cannot use or enjoy themselves ▶ *Andy doesn't want the house, but he won't sell it to me – he's just a dog in the manger.*

every dog has its day even an unimportant person has a time in their life when they are successful or important ▶ *The best performance was by 87-year-old Gerry Menzies, proving that every dog has its day.*

a shaggy dog story a long story told as a joke, that ends in a silly or unexpected way ▶ *Bill was usually in the bar, telling shaggy dog stories to anyone who'd listen.*

top dog the winner, or most successful person ▶ *Alex has beaten everyone at chess and billiards, so he's definitely top dog.*

you can't teach an old dog new tricks it is difficult to make people learn new ways of doing things ▶ *"Who says you can't teach an old dog new tricks?" said his grandmother. "I've just learnt how to use the Internet."*

DOGHOUSE

in the doghouse (with sb) not liked (by someone) at the moment because you have done something wrong ▶ *Stan forgot their wedding anniversary, so he's in the doghouse with Cathy.*

DOGS

sth is going to the dogs a country, organization etc is not as good as it was, and is getting worse ▶ *Schoolchildren are taking drugs and* *carrying guns – the whole country's going to the dogs.*

let sleeping dogs lie to avoid mentioning a subject or problem ▶ *Would it really help if you told her about your past? Why not let sleeping dogs lie?*

throw sb to the dogs to allow someone else to be criticized instead of you ▶ *The manager had been thrown to the dogs by the hotel owners.*

DOLLAR

the 64,000 dollar question *also* **the million dollar question** a difficult but important question ▶ *"Will she marry you?" "Ah, that's the 64,000 dollar question."*

This idiom comes from the name of a game show on television in the US in the 1950s called *The $64,000 Question* in which the amount of money offered for the final question was $64,000.

you can bet your bottom dollar you can be sure (that) ▶ *You can bet your bottom dollar she'll be the first to leave.*

DOLLARS

look (like) a million dollars looking very attractive and well ▶ *She looked like a million dollars in her new silk dress.*

DOMINO

a/the domino effect a situation in which one event causes several other similar events, one after the other ▶ *When one country's economy becomes unstable it seems to have a domino effect on others in the region.*

A domino is a small block of wood with white dots on it, used in the game of dominoes. This idiom comes from the idea that if you stand many of these blocks up on end in a line and push the first one, the rest of the dominoes in the line will fall down one after the other.

DONKEY

(the) donkey work the hard and boring part of a piece of work ▶ *After we've done the donkey work and entered our clients on the database, we can start our marketing campaign.*

DOOM

be all doom and gloom to give no hope for the future ▶ *Sure, we've lost a couple of games, but it's not all doom and gloom.*

DOOR

at death's door very ill and likely to die ▶ *She's only got a cold – she's hardly at death's door.*

do sth by the back door to achieve something indirectly or secretly ▶ *I started as a designer and got into fashion journalism by the back door.*

be knocking at the door of sth to be trying to join an organization, group etc ▶ *He's knocking at the door of the 'A' team but he needs more practice.*

lay sth at sb's door to blame someone for something ▶ *I'm not sure how much of this mess we can lay at Don's door.*

show sb the door to say clearly and in an unfriendly way that you want someone to leave ▶ *I expected him to show me the door when I told him I was from the local paper, but he agreed to talk.*

DOORS

behind closed doors privately or secretly ▶ *Interviews for new staff have been going on behind closed doors.*

open (the) doors for to give someone opportunities that they did not have before ▶ *Their television appearance opened doors everywhere, and now they're in great demand.*

DOS

the dos and don'ts things you should and should not do ▶ *There's an article on the dos and don'ts of foreign travel.*

DOSE

go through sth like a dose of salts to finish dealing with something very quickly ▶ *She brought me some books to read, and I went through them like a dose of salts.*

DOSES

in small doses taking only a small amount at one time ▶ *Computer games are all right – in small doses.*

DOT

dot (all) the i's and cross (all) the t's to complete something carefully, paying attention to detail ▶ *The ideas in this report are good, but you must dot the i's and cross the t's before you give it to Mr Evans.*

on the dot (of seven etc) exactly (at a particular time) ▶ *On her first day she arrived on the dot of nine.*

DOUBLE

at the double very quickly ▶ *Come on boys, at the double! We're already late.*

DOWN

be down and out to have no job, no money, and nowhere to live ▶ *He lost*

his job last year and now he's down and out. **down-and-out** N ▶ *She was virtually a down-and-out by the time she died.*

down under in or to Australia or New Zealand ▶ *Visit your family down under on one of our new cut-price flights.*

have a down on sb also **have a downer on sb** to dislike someone, and think that everything they do is wrong ▶ *He's had a down on me ever since I lost his briefcase.*

it's/that's down to (sb or sth) it's the responsibility or fault of someone ▶ *The police don't decide whether you go to prison; that's down to the judge.*

DOWNER

have a downer on sb ▶ have a DOWN on sb

DOWNHILL

be downhill (all the way) from here also **be downhill (all the way) from now on** to be easy to do, because the hard part is finished ▶ *We've convinced the committee, so it should be downhill all the way from now on.*

go downhill to become worse ▶ *I'm afraid the business has gone downhill fast since Dad's illness.*

DOZEN

(it's) six of one, half a dozen of the other there is not much difference between two possible choices (half a dozen = six) ▶ *I don't mind whether we take the bus or walk – it's six of one, half a dozen of the other.*

D

talk nineteen to the dozen to talk a lot, very quickly, without stopping ▶ *Meg and Nick went off together, talking nineteen to the dozen.*

DRAG

be a drag to be boring or difficult ▶ *The history lectures are a real drag, but the ones on politics are brilliant.*

be a drag on sth to make progress difficult for something ▶ *High rates of tax continue to be a drag on expanding businesses.*

drag sb kicking and screaming to force someone to do something they do not want to do ▶ *She's dragging the sales department kicking and screaming into the 21st century.*

DRAIN

go down the drain *also* **go down the tubes**

1 to become worse or fail completely ▶ *Yet another brilliant idea down the tubes!*

2 to be completely wasted ▶ *I paid £2000 for that useless car – it's just money down the drain.*

laugh like a drain to laugh noisily without being able to stop ▶ *I asked her for a pay rise, and she just laughed like a drain.*

DRAW

be quick on the draw to understand a situation and react to it quickly ▶ *Anna was quick on the draw and gave them the answers they needed.*

DRAWER

out of the top drawer at the highest or best level ▶ *Her performance, as usual, was out of the top drawer.*

DREAM

the American dream the belief that everyone in the US can be rich and successful if they work hard enough ▶ *Rick's success is proof that the great American dream can still come true.*

dream on! that isn't going to happen! ▶ *"The computers should be fixed today, right?" "Dream on!"*

dream ticket a combination of people who you think are very likely to succeed ▶ *Ian and Joe proved to be a dream ticket for women voters.*

live in a dream world to have very unrealistic plans, ideas, or opinions ▶ *Kids today are living in a dream world if they think success comes without hard work.*

run/go like a dream to run or go perfectly ▶ *Except for the odd problem our old car's still running like a dream.*

sb wouldn't dream of doing sth someone would never do something, because they know it is wrong or stupid ▶ *I wouldn't dream of suggesting that men can't understand women's problems.*

DREAMS

in your dreams that isn't going to happen! ▶ *"I think Monica wants to go out with me." "In your dreams!"*

not in my wildest dreams *also* **never in my wildest dreams** never, not at all ▶ *I didn't think I'd get top marks, not in my wildest dreams.*

the ___ of sb's dreams the thing or person someone would like most ▶ *You have to accept that you're never going to find the job of your dreams in this town.*

DRESSED

dressed to kill
wearing expensive, exciting, or beautiful clothes ▶ *I turned up in jeans and found Jean was dressed to kill – velvet dress, high heels, the lot.*

DRIBS

in dribs and drabs a few at a time, not all at once ▶ *Reactions to the news have been coming in dribs and drabs all week.*

DRIFT

get the/sb's drift also **catch the/sb's drift** to understand the general meaning ▶ *You didn't finish what you were saying, but I got the drift.* ▶ *I catch your drift – I'm not wanted.*

DRIVE

drive sb crazy also **drive sb mad** to annoy someone a lot ▶ *Living with his mother was driving them both mad.*

DROP

do sth at the drop of a hat
1 to do something every time there is an opportunity to do it ▶ *He brings out those pictures of his grandchildren at the drop of a hat.*
2 to do something very quickly ▶ *It wasn't easy to replace our top scorer at the drop of a hat.*
drop dead! stop talking about that and leave me alone! ▶ *"You've never been very good at this game, have you?" "Drop dead!"*

drop-dead gorgeous very beautiful and sexually attractive ▶ *She was looking drop-dead gorgeous in her new swimsuit.*
a drop in the ocean also **a drop in the bucket** a very small amount of something compared with the amount that you need or want ▶ *We need 130 and we've collected 15 – just a drop in the ocean.*
drop sb in it also **land sb in it** to cause someone to be blamed or criticized for something ▶ *I'm sorry if I dropped you in it, but she asked me why you weren't here.*

DRUM

bang the drum (for) also **beat the drum (for)** to support or advertise something with lots of energy ▶ *The TV programme helped bang the drum for health education.*

DUCK

a dead duck a person or thing that is too old, unsuccessful, or useless ▶ *The audiotape will soon be a dead duck.* ▶ *Politically, he was a dead duck by 2001.*
a lame duck
an elected official, government etc lacking power because their time in office will soon end ▶ *Johnson has been a lame duck since he was defeated in the Republican primary.* **lame-duck** ADJ ▶ *The lame-duck government dragged on for another six months.*

D

a sitting duck a person whose position makes it easy to treat them badly ► *Car drivers are sitting ducks for the tax department.*

take to sth like a duck to water to learn how to do something very easily and naturally ► *Nobody in my family likes boats, but I took to sailing like a duck to water.*

DUCKLING

an ugly duckling an unattractive or unsuccessful young person who becomes beautiful and successful later ► *It's hard to believe, but she was always considered the ugly duckling of her family.*

DUCKS

play ducks and drakes (with) to treat in a careless way that causes harm and waste ► *Why should governments be able to play ducks and drakes with people's lives?*

DUDGEON

in high dudgeon coldly angry because of bad treatment ► *She slapped his face and left in high dudgeon.*

DUE

give sb his/her due to be fair, praising as well as criticizing ► *To give the creep his due, he was a hard worker and never wasted time.*

DUES

pay your dues to work hard and learn what is required before becoming successful ► *The hotel manager had paid his dues, working his way up from kitchen assistant.*

DUMPS

be down in the dumps
1 to feel very sad ► *He rang me on*
Christmas Day, down in the dumps because he was on his own.
2 (in business) not to be active or successful ► *The coffee market is down in the dumps at the moment.*

DUST

bite the dust to die or fail ► *Hundreds of small businesses are biting the dust every day.*

(when) the dust settles a time when people stop being upset, excited, or confused ► *When the dust settles, he'll realize that this was the right decision.* ► *Wait for the dust to settle before you make your move.*

gather dust to be no longer used or thought about ► *Last year's best-sellers are now gathering dust in publishers' warehouses.*

be like gold dust to be very valuable and difficult to find ► *Tickets for the match are like gold dust.*

not see sb for dust someone is leaving very quickly, often in order to avoid something ► *If I won the lottery you wouldn't see me for dust – I'd be off round the world!*

shake the dust (of sth) from your feet to leave or forget about a difficult situation ► *It had taken Mary three years to shake the dust of her failed marriage from her feet.*

DUTCH

go Dutch (with sb) to share the cost of a meal, film etc with someone ► *No, you shouldn't pay – let's go Dutch.*

sth is double Dutch (to you) you cannot understand something that someone is saying or has written ► *These instructions are double Dutch to me. Can you understand them?*

Ee

EAR

bend sb's ear to talk a lot, or too much, to someone about a particular subject ▶ *He's been bending my ear about his problems at work.*

an ear (for sth) the ability to learn and understand a spoken language, music etc easily ▶ *She has a good ear for languages but her spelling's terrible.*

sth goes in one ear and out the other when you tell someone something, they do not listen or remember it ▶ *I explained exactly what I wanted, but obviously it all went in one ear and out the other.*

be grinning from ear to ear to have a big smile on your face ▶ *The artist was photographed with her prize, grinning from ear to ear.*

have the ear of to be listened to by someone in a powerful position ▶ *You have to get the ear of the President if you want anything done.*

keep an ear out for sth to listen carefully so you do not miss something ▶ *Can you keep an ear out for the postman while I'm shopping?*

keep your ear to the ground also **keep an ear to the ground** to be sure that you find out what people are saying and thinking ▶ *I want to know if anyone's thinking of selling their*

house – keep your ear to the ground, will you?

lend an ear to listen ▶ *An important part of a family doctor's job is to lend a sympathetic ear to lonely patients.*

listen with half an ear to listen while thinking about something else ▶ *I was eating breakfast, listening with half an ear to the radio news.*

make a pig's ear (of sth) to do a piece of work so badly that it is useless ▶ *Last time I tried to cut someone's hair I made a complete pig's ear of it.*

be out on your ear to be forced to leave a job, an organization, or your home ▶ *Teachers would be out on their ear if they slapped a pupil.*

play sth by ear to react to a situation as it happens ▶ *We'll listen to her presentation, and then play it by ear.*

turn a deaf ear (to sth) to refuse to listen to what someone is asking or telling you ▶ *Local councillors have turned a deaf ear to complaints about the new road.*

EARFUL

get an earful to have to listen to someone who is complaining ▶ *I agreed to have lunch with him, and promptly got an earful about his family problems.* **give sb an earful** ▶ *I rang the insurance company and gave them an earful about the premiums going up.*

EARS

be all ears to be eager to hear what is being said ▶ *"Do you want to know what happened with Jo?" "Yes, go on, I'm all ears."*

sb's ears are burning also **are your ears burning?** people have been talking about you (your ears are supposed to feel hot when people talk

about you when you are not there)
▶ *Your ears must have been burning this morning – Helen's been telling us how wonderful you are.*

sb's ears are flapping someone is eager to listen to your private conversation ▶ *"Phone me later – the kids are here with their ears flapping."*

fall on deaf ears to be ignored completely ▶ *All our complaints to the management have fallen on deaf ears.*

have sth coming out of your ears to have eaten, drunk, studied etc too much of something ▶ *If you eat any more, you'll have chocolate coming out of your ears.*

pin back your ears also **keep your ears pinned back** to listen very carefully ▶ *Pin back your ears and I'll run through our plan again.*

prick up your ears to start to be interested in what someone is saying ▶ *Adams pricked up his ears as soon as I mentioned money.*

be up to your ears (in sth) also **be up to your eyes (in sth)** to have more of something than you want or can deal with ▶ *I can't come this weekend – I'm up to my ears in work.* ▶ *Jo's up to her eyes – don't disturb her now.*

wet behind the ears young and without much experience in life ▶ *Some of the team play jokes on the new players who are still wet behind the ears.*

EARTH

bring sb (back) down to earth (with a bump) to force someone who is enjoying themselves to think about ordinary, practical things ▶ *When her letter arrived at my hotel, it brought me down to earth with a bump.* **come (back) down to earth (with a bump)**

▶ *It took us a few weeks to come back down to earth after our holiday.*

cost the earth to be extremely expensive ▶ *Clothes don't have to cost the earth to look good.*

sb is down to earth someone is practical, direct, and sensible ▶ *He writes about cancer in a style that is down to earth yet sympathetic.* **down-to-earth** ADJ ▶ *He's attracted to straightforward, down-to-earth women.*

like nothing on earth, very bad or ill ▶ *The orchestra is good but the choir sounds like nothing on earth.* ▶ *Whenever I drink wine I feel like nothing on earth next morning.*

promise sb the earth also **promise sb the moon** to promise to give someone something impossibly good ▶ *Beware of hotels that promise you the moon, and advertise what they can't deliver.*

run sb/sth to earth also **run sb/sth to ground** to find someone or something after searching for a long time ▶ *After several weeks the police finally ran him to ground in Glasgow.*

EASIER

that's/it's easier said than done it would be difficult to do (what someone has suggested) ▶ *"Try to forget him, Fiona." "Yes, well, that's easier said than done."*

EASY

easy come, easy go something that is easily obtained is easily got rid of or used ▶ *"Has she got another boyfriend already?" "Oh, you know Mandy, easy come, easy go."* ▶ *He spent all his winnings on presents for everyone – you know, easy come, easy go.*

easy does it do something slowly or gently ▶ *Pull the table over this way –*

easy does it, don't scratch the paint.
I'm easy I don't mind ▶ *"Shall we eat before or after the film?" "I'm easy."*

EAT

eat sb alive
1 to defeat or destroy someone easily ▶ *The lawyers would eat him alive if he made a statement like that in court.*

2 (of insects) to bite someone a lot ▶ *We sat outside, and got eaten alive by the mosquitoes.*

EBB

be at a low ebb to be at a low level or in a bad condition ▶ *Recent surveys show that the president's popularity is at a low ebb.*

> When the tide is at low ebb, the water in the sea is at its lowest level of the day.

ECONOMY

a false economy something that saves you money now but will cost more later ▶ *Tools are expensive, but it's a false economy to go for the cheapest.*

EDGE

be on the cutting edge of sth also **be at the cutting edge of sth** to have the advantage over competitors because of new methods, style, or equipment ▶ *The research skills we have developed put us on the cutting edge of the drug industry.* **cutting-edge** ADJ ▶ *Cutting-edge technology doesn't come cheap; this system will cost around £3000.*

go over the edge to become so afraid or unhappy that you stop behaving in a reasonable way ▶ *Our aim is to help depressed people before they go over the edge.* **push sb over the edge** ▶ *It was the pressure of exams that finally pushed him over the edge.*

be on a knife edge also **be on a razor edge** to be in a difficult situation where a wrong decision could be dangerous ▶ *The future of the company is on a knife edge while we wait for the result of the vote.*

have/gain the edge on also **have/ gain the edge over** to have or get an advantage over someone ▶ *At the beginning of the month, ABC still had the edge over the other taxi companies.*

lose your edge to become less good at what you do ▶ *The company lost its edge when we failed to invest in new technology.*

be on edge to be nervous ▶ *We're all a bit on edge about the test results.*

be on the edge (of sth) also **be close to the edge**
1 to be in a situation in which something bad or dangerous could easily happen ▶ *At the time, we all believed we were on the edge of a nuclear war.*
2 to be in a situation in which you are so upset, tired etc that you could easily have mental problems ▶ *I was close to the edge after my mother died.*

on the edge of your seat very eager to know what will happen next ▶ *His action films usually keep the kids on the edge of their seats.*

take the edge off sth to make something less powerful, good, bad, etc ▶ *Advertisements claimed a new*

pill would take the edge off hunger.
▶ *The rain took the edge off our picnic.*

EDGES

fray at the edges to start to collapse or be destroyed ▶ *After a morning's wait, our sense of humour was somewhat frayed at the edges.*

have rough edges to have faults and imperfections that can be corrected ▶ *Interviewers are trained to overlook a candidate's rough edges.* ▶ *The orchestra's performance had too many rough edges.*

EEL

(as) slippery as an eel used to describe someone whom you cannot trust, because they are not direct or honest ▶ *Make sure he agrees to do it by the weekend – he's as slippery as an eel.*

EFFECT

have a knock-on effect (of an action or problem) to affect other things ▶ *Economic growth in Asia is bound to have a knock-on effect in Europe.*

EGG

a/the curate's egg something partly good and partly bad ▶ *Unfortunately, his latest book is a bit of a curate's egg.*

> This idiom comes from a joke in the magazine, *Punch,* in which a curate (=a priest of the lowest rank) is eating breakfast with the Bishop (=a priest of the highest rank) at the Bishop's house. When the Bishop asks him if he has a bad egg, he says, "Oh, no, my Lord, I assure you! Parts of it are excellent!" (Vol 109; November 1895)

end up with egg on your face also **have egg on your face** to seem silly and be embarrassed ▶ *The scheme was a failure and the committee ended up with egg on its face.*

EGGS

put all your eggs in one basket to depend completely on one thing or action ▶ *Don't put all your eggs in one basket – it's better to invest in several types of company.*

EGGSHELLS

walk on eggshells also **tread on eggshells** to be very careful not to say or do the wrong thing ▶ *Janet's got such a short temper that we all walk on eggshells when she's here.*

ELBOW

elbow grease hard physical effort ▶ *Come on, put some elbow grease into that polishing!*

give sb the elbow to dismiss someone from work, or finish a relationship with them ▶ *They've finally given old Bill the elbow.*

ELEMENT

be in your element to be in a situation that you enjoy and that suits you ▶ *From the moment we arrived at the racecourse I was really in my element.*

ELEMENTS

brave the elements to go out when the weather is bad ▶ *Tom didn't feel like braving the elements so I took the dog for a walk.*

ELEPHANT

a white elephant something that is useless but expensive ▶ *This shopping centre has become a white elephant, with 20 shops still empty.* **white-elephant stall** N ▶ *I gave that horrible vase to the white-elephant stall at the charity fair, and Mrs Granger actually bought it.*

EMPEROR

the emperor's (new) clothes a situation when everyone pretends to admire something because they think they will seem stupid if they do not ▶ *I don't believe anyone really likes modern music – it's just the emperor's new clothes.*

END

at the end of the day when you consider everything in a situation ▶ *We give advice but, at the end of the day, people must make their own decisions.*

be at the end of your tether to feel that you cannot deal with a difficult situation any longer ▶ *After so much unpleasantness, I was really at the end of my tether and just had to get away.*

be at a loose end to be bored because you have nothing to do ▶ *Why don't you stay for dinner if you're at a loose end?*

be at the sharp end (of sth) (in an organization) to deal directly with the public ▶ *Before setting up his own business he had worked at the sharp end, as a salesman.*

at your wits' end very worried, not knowing how to solve a problem ▶ *I don't want to cause a family row, but I'm at my wits' end trying to decide what to do.*

come to a bad end also **come to a sticky end** to die or be defeated in an unpleasant way ▶ *My grandmother was convinced that Joe would come to a bad end.*

a dead end a situation in which progress is no longer possible ▶ *The idea's still discussed at scientific conferences, but most biologists feel it's a dead end.*

> A dead end is a road which is closed at one end.

the end of the road the point at which a process or activity cannot continue ▶ *Even if I refuse this job, it won't be the end of the road for my career.*

get the wrong end of the stick to have a completely wrong idea about something ▶ *People who think we're encouraging drug use have got the wrong end of the stick.*

go off the deep end to suddenly become very angry or upset ▶ *Even little things send me right off the deep end these days.*

I'll never hear the end of it people will continue to criticize or make jokes about something you have done ▶ *I knew that if I left the pub early I'd never hear the end of it.*

it's not the end of the world it is a less serious problem than you think ▶ *If you don't get it done by Friday it's not the end of the world, but I would like it as soon as possible.*

keep your end up to do the part of an activity that you are supposed to do, even though it is difficult ▶ *I was terribly nervous talking to the directors, but I think I kept my end up.*

be on the receiving end (of sth) to be the person receiving something unpleasant ▶ *She always seems to be*

E

on the receiving end of his critical remarks.

the thin end of the wedge a small change that is the beginning of a bigger change that you do not want ▸ *If you allow people to buy guns for self-defence it may be the thin end of a very dangerous wedge.*

be thrown in at the deep end to have to start doing a difficult job without

being prepared for it ▸ *She was thrown in at the deep end when her boss was taken ill.*

the ___ to end all ___s something that is the most extreme of its kind ▸ *We're going to have the party to end all parties on Tony's birthday.*

> This idiom comes from the phrase 'the war to end all wars' which was used to describe World War I.

ENDS

go to the ends of the earth to do everything you can ▸ *If someone's been mistreated, he'll go to the ends of the earth to help them.*

make ends meet to have just enough money to buy what you need ▸ *Most students can only make ends meet if they take part-time jobs.*

tie up loose ends to complete the last small details ▸ *We decided on our overall strategy last week and now we're just tying up some loose ends.*

ENVY

green with envy very annoyed because you want what someone else has ▸ *Modern spy technology would make even James Bond green with envy.*

ESCAPE

have a narrow escape to only just avoid something unpleasant or dangerous ▸ *A couple had a narrow escape when their tent was hit by lightning.*

EVILS

the lesser of two evils the less unpleasant of two unpleasant choices ▸ *She disliked the interviewer so much that she thought being unemployed might be the lesser of two evils.*

EXPENSE

do sth at sb's expense also **do sth at the expense of sb/sth** to cause harm or disadvantage to somebody or something ▸ *She had a good laugh at my expense.* ▸ *Employers are cutting production costs at the expense of their workers' safety.*

EXPERIENCE

put it/sth down to experience to deal with something unpleasant by learning something useful from it ▸ *Going sailing with two seasick children was awful, but we put it down to experience.*

EYE

at the eye of the storm central to a situation that people are shocked, angry, or arguing about ▸ *The young* *doctor found himself at the eye of a storm of complaints.*

not (even) bat an eye ➤ not (even) bat an EYELID

cast an eye over sth to read or look at something quickly ▶ *Do you have time to cast an eye over these accounts?* ▶ *Gavin has agreed to cast an expert eye over our programme.*

catch sb's eye

1 to be noticed by someone ▶ *I bought a pair of red sandals that caught my eye.* ▶ *I tried to catch the waiter's eye, but he ignored me.*

2 to look at someone at the same time as they are looking at you ▶ *I caught Luke's eye in the mirror, and he winked at me.*

easy on the eye very pleasant to look at ▶ *His latest film's a bit boring, but he's very easy on the eye.*

an eye for an eye (a tooth for a tooth) a system of punishment in which you hurt someone in the same way as they hurt someone else ▶ *On the principle of an eye for an eye, murderers used to be put to death.*

get your eye in to practise something such as a ball game ▶ *I tried a few practice shots to get my eye in.*

give sb the eye

1 to look at someone as if you think they are sexually attractive ▶ *He kept giving me the eye when his friends weren't looking.*

2 to look at someone as if you are angry with them ▶ *It was time to go – Dave was tired and I was sure the nurse was giving me the eye.*

have an eye for sth also **have a good eye for sth** to be good at noticing things of a particular kind ▶ *Vicky has*

always had an eye for a bargain – just look at this lamp.

have an eye to the main chance also **have your eye on the main chance** to keep looking for ways to get an advantage ▶ *A businessman has to have an eye to the main chance.*

have your eye on sth to want to get something ▶ *I had my eye on a bigger house in the next road.*

in your mind's eye in your imagination or memory ▶ *In my mind's eye I could see my mother's garden on a spring morning.*

sth is one in the eye for sb something will upset or shame someone you don't like or don't agree with ▶ *I passed the exam, which was one in the eye for the teachers who said I'd fail.*

keep an eagle eye on to watch very carefully ▶ *While the children were playing on the beach, I was keeping an eagle eye on the weather.*

keep an eye out for also **keep your eyes open for** to be sure to notice

▶ *Keep an eye out for somewhere to eat – I'm starving.*

not see eye to eye to disagree ▶ *My English teacher and I never saw eye to eye.* ▶ *She doesn't see eye to eye with her mother about bringing up children.*

there's more to sb/sth than meets the eye someone or something is better, more interesting, or more complicated than they appear ▶ *Andy is very quiet but there's more to him than meets the eye.*

E

there wasn't a dry eye in the house an event or statement made everyone feel very sad or sympathetic ▶ *During the last 20 minutes of the film, there wasn't a dry eye in the house.*

turn a blind eye (to sth) to ignore something ▶ *Parking here is illegal, but the police tend to turn a blind eye to it.*

with an eye to
1 with the aim of ▶ *The town is holding a music festival, with an eye to making more money from tourism.*
2 paying special attention to ▶ *The house had been furnished with an eye to light and space.*

sb would give his/her eye teeth to also *sb would give his/her eyeteeth to* someone very much wants to ▶ *I'd give my eye teeth to be able to travel for a year.*

EYEBALL
eyeball to eyeball face to face, usually for a serious or angry discussion ▶ *Can he keep his temper when he's eyeball to eyeball with an angry customer?*

EYEBROWS
raise eyebrows to surprise or shock people ▶ *The appointment of such a young conductor has raised eyebrows in the music world.*

EYELID
not (even) bat an eyelid also *not (even) bat an eye* not to seem at all shocked, surprised, or embarrassed ▶ *My kids will sit through horror films without batting an eyelid.*

EYES
all eyes are on everyone is paying attention to ▶ *All eyes were on the mayor at the presentation yesterday.*

do sth with your eyes shut also *do sth with your eyes closed* to do something very easily because you have done it often ▶ *I could drive to the hospital with my eyes shut.*

sb's eyes are bigger than his/her stomach someone has taken more food than they can eat ▶ *Can't you finish that? Your eyes were bigger than your stomach, weren't they?*

sb's eyes are popping (out of his/her head) also *sb's eyes are out on stalks* someone is very surprised, excited, or shocked by what they are looking at ▶ *The girls are wearing tiny bikinis and Dave's eyes were popping out of his head.* ▶ *They were having an argument in the street and the neighbours' eyes were out on stalks.*

feast your eyes on sb/sth to look at someone or something with enjoyment and pleasure ▶ *The children were feasting their eyes on the huge display of toys.*

go into sth with your eyes open to know what the problems in a situation might be ▶ *I went into that job with my eyes open, prepared for a 50-hour week.*

have eyes in the back of your head to be able to notice everything that is happening around you ▶ *You need to have eyes in the back of your head when you're looking after three-year-olds.*

keep your eyes glued to sth to watch something steadily ▶ *He was sitting on the sofa with his eyes glued to the TV screen.*

keep your eyes open to notice carefully what is happening around you ▶ *Keep your eyes open and learn from experience.*

keep your eyes peeled (for sth) *also* ***keep your eyes skinned (for sth)*** to keep looking out for something ▶ *We were keeping our eyes peeled for a place to eat.*

only have eyes for sb to only be interested in or love one person ▶ *Jane's stunningly beautiful, but Bill only had eyes for me.*

open your eyes to sth to realize something about a situation ▶ *It's time you opened your eyes to what's really happening.* **open sb's eyes (to sth)** ▶ *Our frightening experience opened my eyes to the power of the sea.*

set eyes on *also* ***clap eyes on*** to see ▶ *I've never set eyes on this house you're talking about.* ▶ *He hasn't clapped eyes on Laura since she left him.*

be up to your eyes (in sth) ➤ be up to your EARS (in sth)

EYETEETH

sb would give his/her eyeteeth to ➤ sb would give his/her EYE teeth to

E

Ff

FACE

blow up in your face to cause a lot of trouble suddenly ▶ *We knew the peace negotiations could easily blow up in our face.*

come face to face with
1 to meet someone ▶ *I turned the corner and came face to face with a huge cop.*
2 to have to deal with something ▶ *When people come face to face with the poverty in this city they are often shocked.* **face-to-face** ADJ ▶ *Dan wanted the financial issues to be dealt with in face-to-face discussion.*

couldn't/wouldn't show your face to feel too ashamed or embarrassed to meet people ▶ *I knew I couldn't show my face in the pub if I hadn't scored a goal.*

sb's face doesn't fit someone is not suitable for an organization because they are different from other people there ▶ *It doesn't matter what your qualifications are; if your face doesn't fit, they won't employ you.*

fall flat on your face to fail, often in a way that is embarrassing ▶ *She started three businesses in a year, and ended up falling flat on her face.*

fly in the face of to be completely different from, or opposed to ▶ *This new evidence about breast cancer flies in the face of traditional views.*

in the face of sth having to deal with (something bad) ▶ *Teachers went on strike in the face of harsh criticism from the public.*

in your face also **in-your-face** expressing ideas that are not the socially accepted ones, in a very direct way that is often shocking ▶ *The band's style is aggressive and in your face but they're very popular.*

sb is not just a pretty face someone is intelligent or good at their job ▶ *"That's a great idea!" "Well, I'm not just a pretty face, you know."*

sth is written all over sb's face also **sb has sth written all over his/her face** someone's expression shows very clearly what they are thinking ▶ *She doesn't actually say anything to me, but her disapproval is written all over her face.*

keep a straight face to continue to look serious even though you want to laugh ▶ *Jan tried to keep a straight face as her brother picked up the broken chair.*

a long face a sad or disappointed expression on your face ▶ *The Eagles lost the match, so there were long faces all round.*

lose face to be embarrassed or lose people's respect ▶ *Try to offer criticism in a way that does not make your student lose face or feel less confident.* **loss of face** N ▶ *We can't withdraw from the negotiations without a serious loss of face.*

on the face of it looking at something in a simple way without knowing what lies below the surface ▶ *On the face of it, this is a respectable suburban street, but it is actually a centre of organized crime.*

put on a brave face also **put a brave face on it** to try not to show that you are afraid, worried, or upset ▶ *When the results came out, several students had to put on a brave face.* ▶ *Mum*

was unhappy about my engagement, but she put a brave face on it.

save (sb's) face to make people continue to respect someone ▶ *Richard supported me for once, which saved my face with my boss.*

face-saving ADJ ▶ *Public opinion forced the government to find a face-saving formula for abandoning the project.*

set your face against sth to be very determined that you will not do or allow something ▶ *The mayor has set his face against banning traffic from the High Street.*

show your face

1 to be seen at a place where you are supposed to be, usually for a short time, even though you may not want to go ▶ *I thought I'd show my face at the meeting so that people wouldn't forget to keep me informed.*

2 to be seen at a place, especially when you should not ▶ *Don't show your face here again, you're not welcome!*

shut your face stop talking! ▶ *"Give me that or I'll tell your Mum!" "Shut your face!"*

be staring sb in the face

1 to be very clear and easy to

recognize ▶ *I puzzled over the problem for hours and all the time the answer was staring me in the face.*

2 (of a bad or difficult situation) to be very likely to happen ▶ *We had very little food left, and starvation was staring us in the face.*

stuff your face to eat a lot ▶ *He sat there stuffing his face as if he hadn't eaten in weeks.*

take sth at face value to accept something without looking for any hidden meaning ▶ *If we take her remarks at face value, she's not worried but her son says she is.*

> The face value of a note (=piece of paper money) or a coin is the amount that is printed on it. However, its value may actually be more or less than that amount.

throw sth back in sb's face

1 to refuse advice or help in an angry way ▶ *I don't like having offers thrown back in my face like that.*

2 to attack someone by using something positive they have said against them ▶ *When he got elected, they threw his idealism back in his face.*

vanish off the face of the earth also **disappear off the face of the earth** to disappear suddenly ▶ *"Where's Rob?" "I haven't a clue, he's just vanished off the face of the earth."*

you can do sth till you're blue in the face you can do something a great deal but you won't achieve anything ▶ *You can argue till you're blue in the face – I'm not going to change my mind.*

FACT

sth is a fact of life something exists

and people must accept it ▶ *Stress at exam time is a fact of life for most young people.*

FACTS

the facts of life

1 the details about sex and how babies are born ▶ *Mum told me the facts of life when I was eight.*

2 the way that life really is, with all its problems and difficulties ▶ *It didn't take them long to discover the harsh financial facts of life.*

FAIR

fair and square in a fair and honest way ▶ *I want to win fair and square, without anybody's help.*

fair do's

1 that's fair! ▶ *They're keen to make extra money, and if they're willing to do the work, fair do's.*

2 be fair! ▶ *Come on, fair do's, let Ben have a piece.*

fair's fair that's fair! ▶ *If Antony is getting time off, we should have time off too. Fair's fair.*

FAIRIES

sb is away with the fairies someone is slightly crazy ▶ *I always thought Sue was away with the fairies since I saw her singing to the flowers.*

FAIT ACCOMPLI

a fait accompli something that is already decided or done, and unable to be changed ▶ *The closure of the factory is a fait accompli, and*

workers are already looking for other jobs.

FALL

fall flat to have little or no effect ▶ *His carefully prepared jokes fell completely flat.*

fall foul of

1 to suffer because of (a rule or law) ▶ *Careless drivers may fall foul of tough new laws.*

2 to have problems dealing with (an opponent or someone in authority) ▶ *He fell foul of the police in Spain and had to leave the country.*

be falling over yourself to do sth to try very hard and very eagerly to do something ▶ *Bank managers were falling over themselves to lend people money.*

fall short (of sth) to be less than something ▶ *He made an offer, but it fell well short of the $5000 we needed.*

be heading for a fall *also* **be riding for a fall** to be likely to fail ▶ *The business is heading for a fall – the management don't seem to know what they're doing.*

FAMILIARITY

familiarity breeds contempt when you know someone or something better, you have less respect for them ▶ *You never see the head talking to the students. She believes that familiarity breeds contempt.*

FANCY

a passing fancy when you like someone or something only for a short time ▶ *She's seen a house she wants to buy but I'm hoping it's just a passing fancy.*

take your fancy to be attractive, interesting, or amusing to you ▶ *I like to spend time at the market, buying whatever takes my fancy.*

FAR

as far as _____ goes considering something (used to introduce a subject) ▶ *As far as money goes, we have very little in the budget for anything.*

far and away definitely ▶ *The microchip is far and away the company's most important product.*

far from it no, it is not true ▶ *"Is your son a good student?" "Far from it, I'm afraid."*

FASHION

after a fashion not very successfully or well ▶ *She keeps the house clean, and she cooks after a fashion.*

do sth like it's going out of fashion *also* **do sth like it's going out of style** to do a lot or too much of something ▶ *He was eating chips like they were going out of fashion.*

FAT

chew the fat to talk in a relaxed and friendly way ▶ *They go to the pub to chew the fat every evening.*

the fat is in the fire there will suddenly be trouble ▶ *If your father hears of this the fat will be in the fire.*

live off the fat of the land to have a comfortable life when others are poor ▶ *The rulers live off the fat of the land while the poor struggle to survive.*

FATE

a fate worse than death the most unpleasant situation you can imagine ▶ *His parents thought he should be a lawyer, which he regarded as a fate worse than death.*

tempt fate

1 to do something that involves unnecessary risks ▶ *I wouldn't sail alone without a radio. That would be tempting fate.*

2 to attract bad luck by saying all will go well ▶ *I'm not going to tempt fate by saying that we can definitely win.*

FATHER

like father, like son *also* **like mother, like daughter** a child looks and behaves like their parent ▶ *The illness has proved she's a real fighter – like mother, like daughter, I suppose.*

FAULT

_____ to a fault so much of a good quality, such as honesty or kindness, that it can cause problems ▶ *She's honest to a fault – sometimes to the point of rudeness.*

FAVOUR

curry favour (with sb) to try to make someone like you by praising them or doing things for them ▶ *Election promises are usually designed to curry favour with voters and not to meet the needs of the country.*

FEAR

put the fear of God into sb to frighten someone ▶ *He's a fast driver but that accident put the fear of God into him.*

FEAST

a feast for the eyes/ears something that is good to look at or to hear ▶ *The little bay is a feast for the eyes – the perfect place for a lazy holiday.*

it's feast or famine there always seems to be too much or too little of something ▶ *Rainfall has been very erratic – it's been feast or famine for the farmers.*

a movable feast an event with no definite date or time ▶ *The barbecue is a movable feast – it depends entirely on the weather.*

F

A movable feast is one of several religious holidays in the Church, which happen about the same time every year, although the date changes from year to year.

FEAT

sth is no mean feat something is very difficult to achieve ▶ *I managed to beat my nephew at chess, which is no mean feat.*

FEATHER

a feather in your cap something to be proud of ▶ *A win today would be quite a feather in the team's cap.*

you could've knocked me down with a feather I was extremely surprised ▶ *When I heard that Joe had got married, you could've knocked me down with a feather!*

FEATHERS

ruffle sb's feathers to upset or annoy someone slightly ▶ *The success of his first novel ruffled the feathers of some older authors.*

smooth ruffled feathers to make angry people calmer ▶ *She was very good at smoothing ruffled feathers when the customers complained.*

FED UP

be/get fed up (with sth) to be or become annoyed or bored ▶ *I'm fed up with being told to work harder; I'm doing as much as I can.* ▶ *He got very fed up waiting for the doctor.*

FEEL

feel yourself to feel better after an illness ▶ *I'm feeling more myself this morning. I think I'll go to work.*

FEELERS

put out feelers to start asking people for their opinion or help in getting something ▶ *She's already putting out feelers for a job in Los Angeles.*

FEELING

a/the sinking feeling (that) *also that sinking feeling* the feeling that you get when you realize suddenly that something unpleasant has happened or is going to happen ▶ *I had a sinking feeling that the storm was destroying all our trees.*

FEELINGS

no hard feelings I'm not angry with you and hope that you are not angry with me ▶ *No hard feelings, Pat – I was the one who was wrong.*

FEET

be/get back on your feet to be or get better again after illness or difficulties ▶ *She was back on her feet by the end of the month.* ▶ *The idea was to get the company back on its feet before the Christmas rush.*

dead on your feet extremely tired ▶ *Why don't you get some sleep? You must be dead on your feet.*

drag your feet *also drag your heels* to take too much time doing something ▶ *He accused the government of dragging its feet over the prison reform bill.*

fall on your feet *also land on your feet* to be lucky in a situation ▶ *He really fell on his feet when he joined Mark's company.*

F

This idiom comes from the idea that when cats fall from something, they always land on their feet.

find your feet to become more confident or successful in a new situation ▶ *New students don't take long to find their feet at college.*

get cold feet to feel afraid to do something that you have planned ▶ *We got cold feet about spending so much and cancelled the holiday at the last minute.*

get under your feet also *be under your feet* to annoy you by being in the same place as you ▶ *When her husband retired she found he sat around the house and got under her feet all day.*

have feet of clay to be normal, with human faults; not to be perfect ▶ *It is a shock when we realize our parents have feet of clay.*

have/get itchy feet to (start to) want to travel or to change your job ▶ *I've always had itchy feet so I was delighted when they offered me a job in India.*

have two left feet to move in a very awkward way when you dance ▶ *"Will you dance with me?" "I'm afraid I've got two left feet."*

keep your feet (firmly) on the ground also *have both feet on the ground* to think or behave in a sensible way ▶ *She's got a very glamorous job but*

she's kept both feet firmly on the ground.

be light on your feet to move quickly and gracefully ▶ *It's unusual for a man who is that large to be so light on his feet.*

be rushed off your feet also *be run off your feet* to be extremely busy ▶ *On Friday evenings we're rushed off our feet at the bar.*

be six feet under to be dead ▶ *I hope I'll be six feet under by the time they're cloning people.*

stand on your own two feet to be independent and take care of yourself ▶ *It's time your son was standing on his own two feet.*

sweep sb off his/her feet to make someone love you very quickly ▶ *He swept me off my feet with poetry and wonderful love letters.*

think on your feet to make effective decisions quickly ▶ *A lawyer must be able to think on her feet.*

vote with your feet to show that you do not like a situation by leaving it ▶ *Many people voted with their feet and went to work abroad.*

walk sb off their feet to make someone tired by making them walk a long way ▶ *Granddad's tired. I think we've walked him off his feet today.*

FENCE

sit on the fence to refuse to give a definite answer or opinion ▶ *There are four people in favour and three against and Jan's sitting on the fence as usual.*

FENCES

mend (your) fences to improve a relationship with someone that you have had an argument with ▶ *Is it too late to mend fences with your ex-wife?*

F

FEW

have had a few too many ➤ have had **ONE** too many

few and far between not many or not often ▶ *In the world of antiques, bargains are few and far between.*

FIDDLE

fit as a fiddle also *fit as a flea* to be completely healthy ▶ *He was in hospital over Easter but he's as fit as a fiddle now.*

play second fiddle (to sb) to be less important or powerful than someone else ▶ *He turned down the job because he didn't like playing second fiddle to Philip.*

FIELD

have a field day to enjoy yourself by doing or saying what you like ▶ *If the journalists find out about that conversation, they'll have a field day.*

lead the field to be the best ▶ *The company has led the field in computer technology for the last five years.*

play the field to have many different romantic relationships ▶ *I'll never get married. It's too much fun playing the field.*

FIGHT

fight it out to continue fighting or competing until someone wins ▶ *The top two teams will go on to the next round, while the other four fight it out in the play-offs.*

be fighting fit to be very healthy ▶ *He is fighting fit and will be ready to play again next season.*

fight shy of doing sth to avoid doing something, or be unwilling to do something ▶ *The report fights shy of criticizing any particular individual.*

FILL

have had your fill (of) to have had enough (of) ▶ *At 29, Sarah had had her fill of married life and decided to go abroad to live.*

FINDERS

finders keepers (losers weepers) if you find something, you can keep it ▶ *I've found some coins under the sofa – finders keepers!*

FINGER

have a finger in every pie also **have a finger in several pies** to be involved in many different

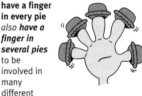

activities, often to get an advantage for yourself ▶ *Johnson has a finger in several pies and is now getting involved in local politics.*

keep a finger on the pulse to make sure you know what is new and interesting in a particular area ▶ *She makes sure she keeps a finger on the pulse of fashion and pop culture.*

> Your pulse is the regular beat that can be felt as your heart pumps blood around your body.

not lift a finger also **not raise a finger** to be too lazy or unconcerned to help ▶ *Two employees watched the man being robbed without lifting a finger to help him.*

point the finger (of blame) also **point an accusing finger** to blame ▶ *He pointed the finger at Justin, who had been seen leaving the house.* **finger-pointing** N ▶ *After months of* *name-calling and finger-pointing, leaders from both countries have promised to try and stop the violence.*

put your finger on sth to know or be able to explain (what is wrong or different) ▶ *The house looks odd – I can't quite put my finger on why.*

wrap sb around your little finger *also* **twist sb round your little finger** to make someone do what you

want by persuading them or by being nice to them ▶ *She had always known how to wrap her mother round her little finger.*

FINGERNAILS

hang (on) by your fingernails *also* **cling (on) by your fingernails** to continue to survive although you are close to failure ▶ *This is our third defeat, but we're hanging on by our fingernails.*

FINGERPRINTS

sb's fingerprints are all over sth something is typical of a particular person, so they must have been involved in it ▶ *That complicated arrangement has Ernie's fingerprints all over it.*

FINGERS

cross your fingers *also* **keep your fingers crossed (that)** to hope for good luck (the first and second fingers are often crossed over each other for luck) ▶ *I'm crossing my fingers here, but we're expecting £5000.* ▶ *"Are you going to university?" "Yes, fingers crossed!"*

get your fingers burned *also* **burn your fingers** to suffer unpleasant results from doing something so that you don't want to do it again ▶ *Investors had their fingers burnt once too often, and kept away from oil shares.*

have (got) green fingers to be able to grow plants successfully ▶ *Look at those beautiful roses! You've certainly got green fingers.*

let sth slip through your fingers to fail to take an opportunity or offer ▶ *Don't let this chance slip through your fingers – you've got to think of the children.*

work your fingers to the bone to work extremely hard ▶ *Their mother has worked her fingers to the bone for them.*

FINGERTIPS

have sth at your fingertips to have information about something immediately available ▶ *He'll have the numbers you need at his fingertips.*

to your fingertips completely; in every way ▶ *George was a professional to his fingertips.*

FIRE

breathe fire to show you are very angry or determined to get what you want ▶ *Mrs Peters came out breathing fire when she heard the noise in the corridor.*

come under fire to be severely criticized ▶ *Parents have recently come under fire for giving their children too much freedom.*

F

hang fire to be delayed ➤ *I'm afraid plans for the extension are still hanging fire.*

light a fire under sb to make someone work harder or show more interest ➤ *We've got to light a fire under the sales people.*

be playing with fire to be taking unnecessary risks ➤ *She knew she was playing with fire, given Mick's reputation with women.*

FIRING LINE

be in the firing line also **be in the line of fire** to be in a position in which you may be attacked ➤ *When customers complain, he's the first in the firing line.* ➤ *The chairman found himself in the line of fire at today's board meeting.*

be out of the firing line also **be out of the line of fire** to be away from a position in which you may be attacked ➤ *Things are bad at work – I've been trying to keep myself out of the firing line.*

FIRST

first come, first served the people who arrive earliest, or those who ask first get something ➤ *There are 30 seats, but it's first come, first served, so get there early.*

FISH

a big fish in a small pond also **a big fish in a little pool** someone who is important only in a small place ➤ *She had been a big fish in a very small pond until she came to the London office.*

drink like a fish to drink a lot of alcohol very often ➤ *My flatmate drinks like a fish at weekends but he stays sober during the week.*

feel like a fish out of water also **be like a fish out of water** to feel uncomfortable because you are in a situation that does not suit you ➤ *I felt like a fish out of water all the time I was living on the farm.*

have other fish to fry to have other, more important things to do ➤ *He isn't concerned with office procedure; he's got other, bigger fish to fry.*

there are plenty more fish in the sea also **there are other fish in the sea** you can find someone else to love ➤ *I'm not really upset about losing Oliver – there are plenty more fish in the sea.*

FIST

an iron fist in a velvet glove someone who seems to be kind at first but who is actually determined to get what they want ➤ *They soon realized that soft-spoken Lee was an iron fist in a velvet glove.*

rule sb with an iron fist to have strict, often cruel, control over someone ➤ *My father ruled us with an iron fist and hit us if we disobeyed him.* **iron-fist** ADJ ➤ *Arrests, torture, and executions are all part of the government's iron-fist policy.*

FIT

fit to drop extremely tired ➤ *After the performance, he looked fit to drop.*

have a fit also **throw a fit** to get very angry and upset ➤ *My mother'll have a fit if she finds you here – you'd better go.*

FITS

by fits and starts also **in fits and starts** happening for a time, then stopping for a time, then starting again ➤ *Stock prices have continued to rise by fits and starts all week.*

FIVE

give me five! (said when you want to hit someone's open hand with your hand) that's good, or good to see you! ► *We did it – give me five!* ► *Hey, what's happening? Give me five!*

take five to rest for a short time ► *OK, everyone, let's take five. We'll start again at 2 o'clock.*

FIX

get/have a fix on to find out or know all about a situation or person ► *Just when you think you've got a firm fix on Peter, he does something completely unpredictable.*

in a fix having problems ► *I'm in a bit of a fix – can you pick the girls up from school?*

a quick fix a fast and easy way of solving a problem ► *I'm afraid there's no quick fix for her poor English results.* **quick-fix** ADJ ► *Environmentalists have warned that quick-fix schemes to deal with global warming may be risky.*

FLAG

keep the flag flying to continue to support an idea, team etc in spite of difficulties ► *This school has kept the sports flag flying even though funds have been cut.*

show the white flag to show that you accept defeat ► *By half-time the Dragons were beginning to show the white flag.*

FLAME

an old flame a person that someone used to have a romantic relationship with ► *She didn't know what to say when she met her old flame at the party.*

FLAMES

fan the flames to do something that makes a bad or difficult situation worse ► *Her angry speech fanned the flames of the human rights debate.*

go up in flames to be completely destroyed by fire ► *I watched, horrified, while a whole year's work went up in flames.*

be shot down in flames to be told that what you are saying is completely wrong ► *Anyone who tried to argue with Dad was shot down in flames.*

FLAP

be/get in a flap to be or become worried and nervous, usually because you are having to do too much ► *I really got in a flap when our guests turned up a day early.*

FLASH

a flash in the pan popular or successful for only a short time ► *Early in his career, critics called him a flash in the pan.*

FLAVOUR

be flavour of the month *also* **be flavour of the week** a person or thing that is very popular now, but will not be for long ► *That boy band is flavour of the month for now, but they won't be in the charts for long.* **flavour-of-the-month/week** ADJ ► *He's ready to lend his support to any flavour-of-the-week political causes.*

F

FLEA

fit as a flea ➤ fit as a FIDDLE

send sb away with a flea in his/her ear to refuse to accept someone's idea or request ▶ *She came to ask for a loan but I sent her away with a flea in her ear.*

FLESH

be flesh and blood to be human ▶ *It's hard to believe the old movie stars were flesh and blood like us.* **flesh-and-blood** ADJ ▶ *Those doctors are more used to looking at numbers on screens than at flesh-and-blood patients.*

in the flesh actually there in the same place as you, not on TV or in newspapers ▶ *It was a thrill to see the President in the flesh.*

sth is more than flesh and blood can stand something makes you very angry or upset ▶ *When he started criticizing my family, that was more than flesh and blood could stand.*

make your flesh creep also **make your flesh crawl** to make you feel frightened or ill ▶ *That night she told us a long ghost story, guaranteed to make our flesh creep.*

press the flesh to shake hands with people (=greet them by holding and shaking their hands) ▶ *Politicians sometimes have to press the flesh and chat to voters.*

put flesh on (the bones of) sth to add more details to something or to make more decisions about it ▶ *The task force will put more flesh on the bones of their scheme to tackle rural poverty.*

your (own) flesh and blood your own family ▶ *I was shocked at the way she was treating her own flesh and blood.*

FLIES

be dropping like flies also **be going down like flies** to become ill or injured, or die in large numbers ▶ *Sue came in with flu, and the next day the whole office started dropping like flies.*

(there are) no flies on sb someone is intelligent and cannot easily be deceived ▶ *There are no flies on Richard, however bad his classwork may be.*

FLIGHT

a flight of fancy an idea that is full of imagination but is not sensible ▶ *My aunt named her yacht The Love Boat in a flight of fancy she was later to regret.*

FLOOD

be in full flood ➤ be in full FLOW

FLOODGATES

sth opens the floodgates also **the floodgates open**

1 lots of people want to do something that one person does ▶ *An apology would open the floodgates to compensation claims.* ▶ *The floodgates have opened and now thousands of people are selling their houses on the Internet.*

2 something makes you express all of your thoughts or feelings ▶ *Tony's unexpected kindness had opened the floodgates and she suddenly burst into tears.*

FLOOR

floor it to make a car go very fast ▶ *I had to floor it to get away from the cops.*

wipe the floor with sb to defeat someone completely ▶ *They wiped the floor with us and went on to win the whole tournament.*

FLOW

go with the flow to accept new or different situations, without worrying about them or trying too hard to control them ▶ *Just relax and go with the flow. You expect too much of yourself!*

be in full flow also **be in full flood** to continue smoothly, without stopping ▶ *I'm sorry to interrupt your speech while you're in full flow, but we simply must finish now.* ▶ *The morning rush hour was in full flood and I was late for work.*

FLY

a/the fly in the ointment something difficult or unpleasant that spoils a good situation ▶ *Henry loved his work – the only fly in the ointment was that his boss didn't like him.*

to be a fly on the wall to hear and see what people say and do in a private situation ▶ *I'd like to be a fly on the wall when she tells her boss she wants a pay rise.* **fly-on-the-wall** ADJ ▶ *We watched a fly-on-the-wall documentary about the hotel industry.*

sb wouldn't hurt a fly also **sb wouldn't harm a fly** someone is very harmless and gentle ▶ *Mike looks fierce but he wouldn't hurt a fly.*

FLYING

be flying blind to have to guess how

to do something ▶ *Often we're flying blind because we don't have any really reliable data.*

FOG

in a fog (of) very confused and unable to think clearly ▶ *She stumbles through life in a fog of drugs and music.*

FOGGIEST

not have the foggiest (idea) not to know anything at all about something ▶ *"Where does he work?" "I haven't the foggiest."*

FOOD

food for thought something that makes you think carefully ▶ *Some doctors are refusing to treat people with problems caused by smoking. That's food for thought, isn't it?*

FOOL

a fool and his money (are soon parted) also **a fool and his money (are easily parted)** someone is spending too much money too quickly ▶ *I've updated my car to this year's model – a fool and his money are soon parted!*

sb is nobody's fool someone cannot easily be deceived or tricked ▶ *She may be young and inexperienced but she's nobody's fool.*

more fool you/him etc you etc are being stupid ▶ *"She watches television all evening while I cook dinner and clear away." "More fool you for letting her."*

play the fool to behave in a silly or irresponsible way ▶ *Josh was playing the fool and tipped green paint all over the carpet.*

FOOLS

fools rush in (where angels fear to tread) you may do something

F

frightening or brave when you don't understand about the problems of the situation ▶ *We didn't know much about adopting a teenager – in fact it was a case of fools rushing in.*

not suffer fools (gladly) not to be patient or polite with stupid people ▶ *She's probably fair to the students, but she doesn't suffer fools gladly.*

FOOT

the boot is on the other foot also **the shoe is on the other foot** the situation has been turned around the other way ▶ *He used to beg me for work, but now he's successful the boot's on the other foot and it's me that's chasing him.*

catch sb on the wrong foot to cause someone to make a mistake or be socially awkward ▶ *Her sudden arrival caught me on the wrong foot, and I said something really rude.* **wrong-foot** v ▶ *The director was wrong-footed several times during questioning.*

get off on the wrong foot to begin badly ▶ *If you want to make a good impression, don't get off on the wrong foot by looking untidy.* **get off on the right foot** ▶ *I wanted to start my new job on the right foot, but I seem to have upset the production manager already.*

get your foot in the door to get your first opportunity to be involved in something ▶ *She got her foot in the door by taking a job in local radio.*

have a foot in both camps also **have a foot in each camp** to be involved with two opposite groups of people ▶ *As a vegetarian married to a butcher, you might say she has a foot in both camps.*

have one foot in the grave to be very old or ill ▶ *My grandsons treat me*

as if I had one foot in the grave already.

not put a foot wrong to do something without making mistakes ▶ *Our defenders have hardly put a foot wrong all afternoon.*

put your foot down
1 to refuse to allow something to happen ▶ *I asked if I could borrow the car again but Mum put her foot down this time.*
2 to make a car go faster ▶ *As soon as he was on the motorway, Jim put his foot down.*

put your foot in your mouth also **put your foot in it** to say something embarrassing, by mistake ▶ *He is a kind and intelligent man, but he has an amazing talent for putting his foot in his mouth.* ▶ *I really put my foot in it with your mother – I'm sorry!*

shoot yourself in the foot to make a mistake or stupid decision that spoils something that you do ▶ *I can't tell my clients about other agents – that would be shooting myself in the foot, wouldn't it?*

FOOTSTEPS

follow in sb's footsteps to do what someone else has done ▶ *Printing was one of the few trades where daughters could follow in their fathers' footsteps.*

FORCE
a force to be reckoned with a person or group that has enough power to be important ▶ *The new company is a force to be reckoned with in the global software market.*

FOREWARNED
forewarned is forearmed if you are warned that something will happen, it is easier to deal with it
▶ *Management is talking about restructuring. I shouldn't be telling you this, but forewarned is forearmed.*

FORT
hold (down) the fort to be responsible when the person who usually does this is away ▶ *I'm off to the dentist's now – can you hold the fort?*

FORTUNE
a small fortune quite a lot of money
▶ *Her engagement ring must have cost a small fortune.*

FOX
crazy like a fox seeming crazy but really intelligent ▶ *"Take no notice of him, he's crazy." "Well, crazy like a fox maybe – he always seems to get what he wants."*

FRAME
be in a ___ frame of mind to have a particular attitude at a particular time ▶ *She came back from her holiday in a much better frame of mind.*

be in the frame to be likely to be chosen or blamed ▶ *Taylors were never in the frame for this contract.*
▶ *The police would like to put him in the frame for the robbery.*

FREEFALL
go into freefall to start falling very

quickly ▶ *The housing market went into freefall just before we wanted to sell.*

FRIEND
a fair-weather friend someone who only wants to be your friend when you are successful, and leaves you when you have problems or need help
▶ *The rich tend to attract fair-weather friends.*

man's best friend a dog ▶ *The ideal present for man's best friend is a fur-lined basket for cold winter evenings.*

FRIENDS
have friends in high places to know important people who are willing to help you ▶ *He kept his job so he must have friends in high places.*

FRINGE
the/a lunatic fringe the people in a group who have the most extreme opinions ▶ *Only a lunatic fringe of the animal rights activists use violence.*

FRITZ
on the fritz not working properly ▶ *It was a long, boring trip, and the car radio was on the fritz.*

FROG
have a frog in your throat to have difficulty in speaking because your throat is blocked for a moment
▶ *In the middle of the speech he got this terrible frog in his throat.*

This idiom comes from an old belief that if you drank water containing the eggs of a frog (=small green animal that lives in or near water), the frogs would grow inside your body. The difficulty in speaking was supposed to be caused by the frog trying to escape.

FRONT

on the ___ front in a particular situation ▶ *On the traffic front, there are delays on the Newbury to Oxford road.*

FRUIT

bear fruit to produce the good results that you wanted ▶ *Our policies are bearing fruit, and the economy is getting stronger.*

forbidden fruit something or someone that seems attractive because you are not allowed to have it ▶ *She thinks we shouldn't ban kids from smoking because forbidden fruit is always more attractive.*

FRUITCAKE

nutty as a fruitcake slightly crazy ▶ *I'm not going out with her – she's nutty as a fruitcake.*

A 'fruitcake' is a cake with nuts and dried fruit in it, often eaten at Christmas. 'Nutty' is slang for 'crazy'.

FRYING PAN

out of the frying pan (and) into the fire from a bad situation to a worse one ▶ *I don't want promotion – that would be jumping out of the frying pan into the fire.*

FUEL

add fuel to the fire to do something that makes a bad situation much worse ▶ *Things are bad enough without the lawyers adding fuel to the fire.*

FULL

be full of yourself to be too proud of yourself ▶ *Julie's a good-looking woman, but she's really full of herself.*

sb is full of it someone usually says untrue or stupid things ▶ *He's so full of it – he's always talking about the wonderful jobs that he's turned down.*

FUN

poke fun at to make a joke about someone in an unkind way ▶ *Don't poke fun at him – he didn't do anything to you.*

FUNERAL

it's/that's your funeral you must deal with the results of your own actions! ▶ *I think you're heading for trouble, but if you don't want any help, that's your funeral.*

FUNNY

so ___ it's not (even) funny too much of a particular quality ▶ *I find her so boring it's not even funny.*

FURNITURE

be part of the furniture to be someone that people hardly notice ▶ *I've been doorman here for five years so I'm part of the furniture now.*

FUSE

sb has a short fuse someone becomes angry very easily and quickly ▶ *A teacher with a short fuse has more problems in the classroom than the slow, silent type.*

FUTURE

there is no future in sth something is not likely to continue or succeed ▶ *I can't see that there's any future in our relationship.*

F

Gg

GAFF

blow the gaff to tell a secret
▶ *Unfortunately, he blew the gaff
to the kids.*

GALLERY

play to the gallery to do something
for its effect on other people ▶ *Some
teachers lose respect because they
enjoy playing to the gallery.*

> The gallery is the part of a theatre
> which has the cheapest seats. If
> an actor plays to the gallery, he or
> she tries to do things that make
> people in those seats laugh or
> clap (=hit their hands together to
> show approval).

GAME

be ahead of the game also **stay ahead
of the game** to accept and use new
methods, machines etc ▶ *We've
invested in the latest equipment so
we're well ahead of the game.*

beat sb at their own game to do or try
to do something more successfully
than someone else ▶ *JetFire's aim was
to beat commercial airlines at their
own game.*

be fair game to be a fair subject for
questions or criticism ▶ *Should
politicians' private lives be fair game
for newspapers?*

the game is up something wrong or
dishonest has been discovered ▶ *He
knew the game was up when he saw
the police car outside his house.*

give the game away to let people
know a secret ▶ *It was supposed to be*
*a surprise party but Jack gave the
game away.*

sth is a mug's game something is a
stupid thing to do ▶ *The doctor
described smoking as a mug's game.*

play the game to do things in a way
that is acceptable to those in authority
▶ *He refuses to play the game, so he
will never be promoted.*

play a waiting game to wait and see
how a situation develops ▶ *Police are
playing a waiting game outside the
kidnappers' house.*

GAMES

play games (with) to talk or behave in
a way that is not direct, honest, or
serious ▶ *Just stop playing games and
tell us what you want.* ▶ *If you try
playing games with your department's
budget, you will only cause trouble.*

GAMUT

run the gamut to include every one of
a particular type of thing ▶ *The main
character ran the gamut of emotions
from happiness to despair.*

GANDER

take a gander at to look at ▶ *Take a
gander at the food on that buffet
table!*

GAP

bridge the gap to reduce the amount
of difference between two things ▶ *It's
hard bridging the gap between
traditional values and modern ideas.*

GARDEN

common or garden ordinary; not
special ▶ *It was common or garden
greed that made me take this job.*

everything in the garden's rosy also
everything in the garden's lovely
everything seems to be going well

▶ *I never said everything in the garden would be rosy if you came to live with me.*

lead sb up the garden path to deceive someone by telling them things that

are not true ▶ *Phil admitted that he'd led her up the garden path.*

GAS

be running out of gas to have less energy or desire to continue than before ▶ *I took over the firm in 2000, and now I feel I'm running out of gas.*

GASP

the last gasp the end of a long process or period of time ▶ *It was a hot day in early September – the last gasp of summer.*

GAUNTLET

run the gauntlet of to be criticized, attacked, or annoyed by ▶ *The proposals will have to run the gauntlet of the directors' questions.*

> Running the gauntlet was a form of punishment in the military in which soldiers with weapons stood in two lines facing each other and beat the person who was being punished as he ran between them.

take up the gauntlet also **pick up the gauntlet** to accept an invitation to argue or compete ▶ *If you think*

another driver is challenging you to a race, don't pick up the gauntlet.

throw down the gauntlet to invite someone to argue or compete ▶ *The coach had thrown down the gauntlet by stating that they would not lose a single game.*

> This idiom comes from an old tradition of throwing a gauntlet (=glove) onto the ground in order to show that you wanted to fight someone. If someone agreed to fight you, they would pick up the gauntlet.

GEAR

get into gear to start to happen or work in the right way ▶ *Local beauty queens are getting into gear for the forthcoming pageant.*

GENIE

the genie is out of the bottle an event has taken place that has made a big change in people's lives ▶ *The Internet has let the genie of unrestricted information out of the bottle.*

put the genie back in the bottle to try to make a situation like it was before ▶ *I've talked to reporters and now it's too late to put the genie back in the bottle.*

GET

get away from it all to go to a different place so that you can forget your problems, work etc ▶ *When we want to relax and get away from it all, we go to the mountains.*

get it together to get organized and be in control of a situation ▶ *I need a day or two to get it together and then I'll phone you.*

get off lightly ➤ be LET off lightly

G

get real! you are not being sensible or practical ▶ *You think he's the best player they've got? Get real! He's useless.*

get this! listen to this ▶ *Get this, Kim says we'll all be getting a bonus this year!*

be getting there to be working successfully towards finishing or achieving something ▶ *"Have you finished your report yet?" "No, but I'm getting there."*

get what's coming to you to get what you deserve for doing something bad ▶ *In most Hollywood movies the bad guy gets what's coming to him and the good guy wins in the end.*

got it in one what you have guessed is correct ▶ *"You think that Lee is lying?" "Got it in one."*

when you get (right) down to it ➤ when it COMEs (right) down to it

sb will get there (in the end) someone will finish or achieve something despite the problems it involves ▶ *It may take six months or a year, but we'll get there in the end.*

GHOST

give up the ghost to stop doing something, or stop working completely ▶ *I'm afraid his car's given up the ghost so he's back to cycling.*

not have a ghost of a chance (of doing sth) also **not stand a ghost of a chance (of doing sth)** to be unable to succeed or to be impossible ▶ *Our team got through to the finals, but we*

don't stand a ghost of a chance of winning.

lay the ghost of to deal with a problem from your past ▶ *He has been working hard to lay the ghost of last year's failure.*

GIFT

gift of the gab the ability to talk a lot, or with great effect ▶ *He's a big man with a ready smile and an engaging gift of the gab.*

to think you are God's gift to think you are very sexually attractive and that anyone would want to be romantically involved with you ▶ *The trouble with him is, he thinks he's God's gift to women.*

GIVE

give and take when two people or groups are each willing to let the other have or do some of the things they want ▶ *In all successful marriages there has to be give and take.*

give as good as you get to treat your opponent as effectively as he or she treats you ▶ *She certainly gives as good as she gets in an argument.*

give it to me straight tell me (something unpleasant) in a direct and honest way ▶ *Give it to me straight – are we still getting married?*

give or take ___ used to show the amount by which a calculation may be wrong ▶ *He arrived two hours ago, give or take a few minutes.*

I'll give you/him etc that I accept that ▶ *Even if he's not a great actor, he's a good dancer – I'll give you that.*

GLASS

glass ceiling an imaginary limit preventing someone (often a woman) from reaching the top of an organization ▶ *Some claim there is a glass ceiling preventing disabled workers from getting management posts.*

GLEAM

a gleam in sb's eye a plan or project that is being considered ▶ *At that time, the nightclub was still a gleam in her eye.*

GLORY

bask in sb's reflected glory also **bathe in sb's reflected glory** to enjoy the praise or fame that a friend or family member is experiencing ▶ *When he got to the final we were all happy to stand back and bask in his reflected glory.*

GLOVE

fit sb like a glove to be exactly right for someone ▶ *This job seems to fit you like a glove.*

GLOVES

the gloves are off the fight has started ▶ *The gloves are off in this aggressive advertising campaign.*

treat sb with kid gloves also **handle sb with kid gloves** to treat someone very carefully so as not to upset them ▶ *Hotel managers have to learn to treat awkward guests with kid gloves.*

GLUTTON

a glutton for punishment someone who seems to enjoy doing something unpleasant ▶ *We'll get a cab from the station – we aren't gluttons for punishment.*

A glutton is someone who eats too much.

GO

go all out to try, using a lot of energy and determination ▶ *She believes in going all out for academic success.*

go bust (of a business) to fail ▶ *What rights do consumers have if an airline company goes bust?*

go deep ➤ RUN deep

go easy on sb/sth not to punish or criticize someone or some behaviour which would usually be punished or criticized ▶ *They went easy on me as it was my first day at work.* ▶ *The school does not go easy on under-age drinking.*

go for broke to take big risks to try to achieve something ▶ *I decided to go for broke and launch my own company.*

go for it do it ▶ *That sounds interesting. I should go for it if I were you.*

go off at half cock also **go off half cocked** to do something without planning it properly ▶ *We need to restructure but we must make sure we don't go off at half cock.*

go one better (than) to do a better thing ▶ *I wanted Mum to do the graphics for me but she went one better and bought me the software.*

go spare to suddenly become very angry ▶ *Dad'll go spare if I'm not home by midnight.*

have a go at sb to speak angrily to someone ▶ *He had a go at me for losing the contract.*

let's not even go there don't ask or talk about that ▶ *"Why's he in such a*

G

bad mood, anyway?" "*Let's not even go there!"*

be on the go to be very busy ▶ *I've been on the go all day and I'm dying for a proper meal.*

GOAL

score an own goal to make a mistake or stupid decision that spoils something that you do ▶ *She was right to criticize him, but she scored an own goal by losing her temper.*

GOALPOSTS

move the goalposts to change the aims or decisions of an organization suddenly, so that people are

confused ▶ *The last time the exam system was changed, teachers weren't happy. Now the goalposts have been moved again.*

> Goalposts are the two posts that you kick a ball through in sports such as football to score points. Moving the goalposts would make this difficult.

GOAT

get sb's goat to annoy someone very much ▶ *That speaker really got my goat – I nearly walked out.*

GOING

do sth while the going's good to do something while there is an opportunity ▶ *You'd better take that job while the going's good – there aren't that many opportunities here.*

be heavy going to be difficult or

boring to deal with ▶ *I tried reading his poems but I found them heavy going.* ▶ *Linda's a nice girl, but she's rather heavy going.*

when the going gets tough when a situation becomes difficult ▶ *When the going gets tough she always runs to her parents.*

GOLD

strike gold to find something that makes you successful or rich ▶ *As I blew the dust off the ancient book, I knew I'd struck gold.*

GOLDFISH

live in a goldfish bowl to be in a situation where a lot of people know about your life ▶ *For the first few months after their success, they didn't mind living in a goldfish bowl.*

GOLDMINE

be sitting on a goldmine to own something very valuable ▶ *Her house is full of antiques – she must be sitting on a goldmine.*

GOOD

as good as so nearly that any difference is not important ▶ *I haven't written the final chapter, but the book's as good as finished.* ▶ *You as good as promised me the job and now I see it's advertised in the paper.*

GOODBYE

say goodbye to sth also **kiss sth goodbye** to accept the fact that you will lose or not have something ▶ *He's just kissed goodbye to half a million dollars in bad investments.*

GOODS

deliver the goods also **come up with the goods** to do something as well as you are expected to do it ▶ *She's a* *good player who consistently delivers the goods.*

get/have the goods on sb to find out or know things about someone ▶ *Reporters are trying to get the goods on one of Chicago's biggest crime families.*

GOOSE

kill the goose that lays the golden egg(s) also **kill the golden goose** to destroy or spoil something that brings you a lot of money ▶ *Those awful flats were built before the tourist board realized that they were killing the golden goose.*

wouldn't say boo to a goose to be very shy and quiet ▶ *She looks as if she wouldn't say boo to a goose but she can be quite stubborn.*

GOOSEBERRY

play gooseberry to be the unwanted third person with two people who want to be alone together ▶ *You two go to the cinema without me – I don't want to play gooseberry.*

GOSPEL

take sth as gospel to believe that something is completely true ▶ *Newspaper reports shouldn't always be taken as gospel.*

> The gospel is another word for the stories and ideas in the New Testament in the Bible. You may also hear people say that something "is the gospel truth" when they want to emphasize that it is true.

GRABS

up for grabs available to anyone ▶ *Five city council seats are up for grabs in the coming election.*

GRACE

fall from grace to stop being liked or trusted by someone in authority ▶ *You fell from grace after she overheard that phone conversation.*

sb's/sth's saving grace a good quality that prevents someone or something from being completely bad or disappointing ▶ *Craig's boring and lazy and his only saving grace is that he isn't talkative.*

GRACES

in sb's good graces liked by someone ▶ *Any politician has to get into the voters' good graces.*

GRADE

make the grade to succeed ▶ *He's a talented player who has a good chance of making the grade.*

GRAIN

go against the grain to be very different from your natural behaviour or beliefs ▶ *I don't trust him and it really goes against the grain to give him the money.*

GRAPES

sour grapes a bad attitude that makes someone criticize something because they want it but cannot have it ▶ *She keeps making jokes about your diamond ring, but it's just sour grapes.*

GRAPEVINE

hear sth on the grapevine to know something because the information

G

has been passed from one person to another ▸ *We've heard on the grapevine that you're looking for some bar staff.*

GRASS

the grass is (always) greener (on the other side of the fence) something else always seems better than what you have ▸ *I used to long for retirement – you know how it is, the grass is always greener.*

the grass roots the ordinary people in an organization, not the leaders ▸ *We ought to be listening to the grass roots.* **grass-roots** ADJ ▸ *He was appealing for more funding at grass-roots level.*

not let the grass grow under your feet to waste no time ▸ *We're not letting the grass grow under our feet – the new gym will be ready in May.*

be put out to grass ➤ be put out to PASTURE

GRAVE

dig your own grave to do something that will cause serious problems for you later ▸ *I knew that if I borrowed more money I'd be digging my own grave.*

sb would turn (over) in their grave someone who is dead would be very angry or upset about something that

is happening now ▸ *Mozart would turn*

in his grave if he heard that band messing up his symphony.

GRAVY

a/the gravy train something from which many people can make money and have a nice life ▸ *The building trade regard these government contracts as a gravy train.*

GREEK

it's (all) Greek to me I can't understand it ▸ *I tried to read the computer manual, but it was all Greek to me.*

GRIEF

give sb grief to criticize or complain about someone ▸ *The actors were giving him grief for cancelling the show.*

GRIN

grin and bear it to accept a difficult or unpleasant situation because there is nothing you can do about it ▸ *There's no chance of a pay rise this year – even the union says we'll just have to grin and bear it if we don't want redundancies.*

wipe the grin off sb's face to do something that makes someone less pleased or satisfied ▸ *Ask him to pay for the damage – that should wipe the grin off his face.*

GRIP

get a grip (on yourself) to take control of yourself ▸ *If you don't get a* grip and start doing some work, you're going to fail the exam.

get a grip on sth to deal with a situation or come to understand something ▶ *We need to get a grip on the changes in the exam system.*

be in the grip of to be in a bad situation that you cannot control ▶ *The Northeast is in the grip of the worst snowstorm for 50 years.*

lose your grip to become less confident and less able to deal with a situation ▶ *He's making a lot of mistakes these days – do you think he's losing his grip?*

GRIPS

get to grips with sth also **come to grips with sth** to start to deal with a problem ▶ *It took her years to get to grips with the fact that Alex was dead.*

GRIST

be (all) grist to the mill to be available for use, usually to someone's advantage ▶ *Arguments between famous people are all grist to the journalists' mill.*

> 'Grist' is a quantity of grain that is to be ground (=crushed into small pieces) at one time.

GROOVE

in the groove doing an activity easily and well ▶ *It takes a while to get back in the groove after a holiday.*

GROUND

break new ground to do or discover something completely new ▶ *Young designers long to break new ground in the world of fashion.*

common ground ideas or aims that two or more people share ▶ *We talked about a number of things, trying to find some common ground, but failed.*

cover a lot of ground to deal with a lot of things or parts of a subject ▶ *This book attempts to cover a lot of ground, from the Middle Ages to the present day.*

cut the ground from under sb's feet also **cut the ground from under sb** to do something that destroys someone's argument or fails to support them ▶ *The chief witness didn't turn up, cutting the ground from under the defence's feet.*

fall on stony ground to be unsuccessful ▶ *All her pleas for help fell on stony ground.*

gain ground to make progress ▶ *The concept of Internet shopping has gained ground rapidly.*

get off the ground to start to run successfully ▶ *We need some good marketing ideas to get the scheme off the ground.* ▶ *The course got off the ground with an excellent seminar.*

go over the same ground also **cover the same ground** to say or deal with something again ▶ *Their arguments always seem to go over the same ground.*

go to ground to hide ▶ *The latest lottery winner went to ground after a day of interviews and phone calls.*

hit the ground running to start something with a lot of energy and with some advantages ▶ *A generous investor*  *helped us hit the ground running.*

G

lose ground to do worse or become less effective ▶ *I've lost some ground since I've been ill, but I'll catch up next week.* **regain/recover lost ground** ▶ *Shares that fell earlier in the week regained all lost ground today.*

sb's old stamping ground the place where someone often used to be ▶ *We visited my old stamping ground, the pubs around the King's Road.*

be on dangerous ground to be behaving in a way that involves risk ▶ *If you start criticizing his cooking, you'll be on dangerous ground.*

be on safe ground also **be on firm ground** to be doing something that you are certain about ▶ *When the conversation turned to education, I was on safe ground again.*

prepare the ground to do things which will make it easier for something to happen ▶ *They did a really good job of preparing the ground for the drama festival.*

run sb into the ground to make someone work very hard ▶ *Mill owners often used to run their workers into the ground.*

run sb/sth to ground ➤ run sb/sth to EARTH

shift your ground also **change your ground** to change your aims or opinions ▶ *Each time she argues about it she shifts her ground.*

stand your ground also **hold your ground** to refuse to change your opinion ▶ *When someone shouts at you like that, it's not easy to stand your ground.*

suit sb (right) down to the ground to be exactly what someone wants ▶ *That little cottage would suit Mum down to the ground.*

take the moral high ground also **take**
the high moral ground to think your decision or opinion is morally better than other people's ▶ *In voting against the bill, he is taking the moral high ground.* ▶ *She attempts to take the high moral ground but I'm not convinced.*

thin on the ground not much, not many ▶ *When we were in need of funds, potential backers were thin on the ground.*

worship the ground sb walks on also **worship the ground under sb's feet** to admire or love someone very much so that you think everything they do is right ▶ *She worships the ground you walk on, though it may not be obvious.*

GROUND FLOOR

be/get in on the ground floor to be or become involved from the beginning ▶ *Luckily, we got in on the ground floor when the project was first proposed.*

GUARD

catch sb off guard to cause someone to do something badly because they are not prepared for it ▶ *We were caught off guard by the huge numbers of orders.*

lower your guard also **let your guard down** to stop being careful about what you do or say ▶ *He finally lowered his guard and agreed to give us an interview.*

be on your guard to pay careful attention to what is happening ▶ *The police have warned us to be on our guard against forged banknotes.*

GUESS

be anybody's guess not to be certain or known ▶ *I put my passport down* *here, but where it is now is anybody's guess.*

your guess is as good as mine I do not know the answer ▶ *"Who do you think will win?" "Your guess is as good as mine."*

GUESSES

(I'll give you) three guesses the answer is very easy to guess ▶ *Someone has been talking about you and I'll give you three guesses who!*

GUEST

be my guest please do (what you have asked to do) ▶ *"Could I borrow your pen?" "Be my guest."*

GUINEA PIG

a guinea pig someone on whom new ideas are tested ▶ *Two overweight people have agreed to be guinea pigs for our new exercise programme.*

GUN

hold a gun to sb's head to force someone to do something ▶ *Nobody's holding a gun to your head – if you don't want to buy the house, don't do it.*

jump the gun to do something too early ▶ *The college has jumped the gun and announced new courses before it has people to teach them.*

GUNNING

be gunning for sb to look for opportunities to criticize or harm someone ▶ *Several members of the Senate are gunning for the president.*

GUNS

the big guns the most important and powerful people in an organization ▶ *Let's try to sort this out before the big guns get involved.*

do sth with (all) guns blazing to use all your energy, skill, and knowledge against an opponent ▶ *Our team came out with all guns blazing, scaring the Dragons into making some silly mistakes.*

be going great guns to be very successful ▶ *The club's going great guns, and we hope to expand next year.*

spike sb's guns to stop someone from being successful ▶ *We brought down all our prices to spike the competition's guns.*

stick to your guns to refuse to change your opinion about something ▶ *He stuck to his guns and told the same story to the police.*

GUT

at gut level through your emotions, as opposed to your intelligence ▶ *We know that we must die, but at gut level we feel it might not happen to us.* **gut-level** ADJ ▶ *What goes on in the country's prisons has set off gut-level reactions.*

bust a gut to work very hard ▶ *I'd like it next week but you don't have to bust a gut to get it done.*

sb's gut reaction someone's first and immediate feelings ▶ *My gut reaction is that kids would really like these toys.*

GUTS

hate sb's guts to hate someone very much ▶ *Barry thinks I like him, but I hate his guts.*

G

sb will have your guts for garters
someone will be angry with you
▶ *Have you spilt coffee on it? Dad'll have your guts for garters!*

spill your guts to tell someone a lot of personal or secret facts ▶ *Have you seen those talk shows where the guests spill their guts about their relationships?*

GUTTER

the gutter press popular newspapers that print shocking stories ▶ *The gutter press has done its best to give the college a bad reputation.*

GUY

fall guy someone who is blamed for something bad that someone else did ▶ *The colonel was made the fall guy for the assassination.*

A fall guy is another name for a stunt man. Stunt men are used instead of actors to do the dangerous things in films so that the actors are not hurt.

no more Mr Nice Guy! I'm going to stop behaving kindly and fairly ▶ *The new policy is no more Mr Nice Guy, so look out!*

G

Hh

HACK

sb can hack it to have the ability needed to succeed ▶ *They promoted him, but he just couldn't hack it.*

HAIR

a bad hair day a day when you feel annoyed and ugly, and things go wrong ▶ *Today is definitely a bad hair day – I'll be glad when it's bedtime.*

get sb out of your hair to stop someone annoying you because they are always near you or interfering with what you are doing ▶ *I don't care what you tell him, just get him out of my hair.*

a/the hair of the dog (that bit you) an alcoholic drink that is supposed to make you feel better when you have drunk too much alcohol the night before ▶ *The bar opened at 10 a.m. for those who just wanted a little hair of the dog.*

a hair shirt a sign that someone is feeling guilty ▶ *The company put on its hair shirt for a few weeks after the accident.*

> A hair shirt was a rough, uncomfortable shirt worn by some very religious Christian people to punish themselves for something or to show that they did not care about comfort.

let your hair down to enjoy yourself and relax, especially after working hard ▶ *New Year in Scotland is a time for letting your hair down.*

sth makes your hair curl something is surprising or shocking ▶ *I could tell you a few things about him that would make your hair curl.*

tear your hair out to be very angry, frustrated, or worried ▶ *Mum has been tearing her hair out over the wedding arrangements.*

not turn a hair not to be affected or upset ▶ *Both boys were covered in blood, but my grandmother didn't turn a hair.*

HAIRS

split hairs to talk about small, unimportant differences between things as if they were important ▶ *Saying that you don't hate him, you just hate his behaviour, may be splitting hairs.* **hair-splitting** N ▶ *The lawyers wasted days on minor details and hair-splitting.*

HALE

hale and hearty very healthy and active ▶ *Dad was hale and hearty until he was 95.*

HALF

sb doesn't (even) know the half of it a situation is much worse than it appears to someone ▶ *"These have certainly been difficult negotiations." "You don't know the half of it."*

how the other half lives what life is like for other people, especially if they are richer or poorer than you ▶ *What a fantastic hotel – so this is how the other half lives!*

H

sb's other half also **sb's better half** someone's husband, wife, or partner ▶ *I've met her a couple of times, but I don't know her other half.*

too ___ by half having too much of a particular quality ▶ *His presentation was considered to be too clever by half.*

HALFWAY

meet sb halfway to accept some of someone's opinions in order to reach an agreement ▶ *We're prepared to meet her halfway – we'll give her a part-time assistant.*

HALT

grind to a halt to stop working gradually ▶ *Ferry and rail services ground to a halt as the storm increased.*

HALVES

not do things by halves to do something properly and put a lot of effort into it ▶ *You've got enough food for 50 people – you don't do things by halves, do you?*

HAMMER

come under the hammer also **go under the hammer** to be offered for sale at an auction (=public meeting where things are sold) ▶ *Her favourite silver teapot came under the hammer for only £100.*

hammer sth home to repeat something until people understand it or agree with it ▶ *Doctors are still trying to hammer home the message about the connection between smoking and heart disease.*

HAMMERING

take a hammering ➤ take a BEATING

HAND

a big hand approval of someone shown by clapping loudly (=making a noise by hitting your hands together)

▶ *And now, let's have a big hand for the jazz band!*

bite the hand that feeds you to behave in an ungrateful way towards someone who has helped or supported you ▶ *The staff aren't*

likely to bite the hand that feeds them by criticizing company policy.

sb can do sth with one hand tied behind his/her back someone can do something very easily ▶ *I could beat him with one hand tied behind my back.*

be caught with your hand in the cookie jar to be caught taking something that you should not ▶ *He had been caught with his hand in the cookie jar once too often.*

be a dab hand at/with sth to be good at doing or using something ▶ *I'm quite a dab hand with a drill – I put these shelves up all by myself.*

the dead hand of used about an idea or system that prevents progress and development ▶ *Many teachers claim* *that the dead hand of bureaucracy is hindering their work.*

a firm hand strict control ▶ *Those kids just run wild – what they need is a firm hand.*

(at) first hand by direct personal experience ▶ *Students can experience the world of engineering at first hand.* **first-hand** ADJ ▶ *Her book is based on first-hand accounts of the war.*

force sb's hand to make someone do something sooner than they wanted to do it ▶ *I don't want to force your hand, but we do need a decision by Monday.*

get out of hand to become very difficult to control ▶ *I was taught how to spot a drinking problem before it gets out of hand.*

get the upper hand to get or have more power than someone or something else ▶ *Firefighters battled to get the upper hand against the forest fire.*

give sb a free hand to allow someone to do something in the way that they choose ▶ *The board gave me a free hand with recruitment.* **sb has a free hand** ▶ *I had a free hand when I was choosing the designs.*

give (sb) a hand also **lend (sb) a hand** to help (someone) ▶ *Can you give me a hand with these desks?* **sb needs a hand** ▶ *We'll need a hand with the accounts this year.*

go hand in hand (with) two things are closely related and often appear together ▶ *Sunshine and a relaxed lifestyle don't always go hand in hand.*

hand in glove closely involved with each other ▶ *Drug dealers were working hand in glove with gun-running organizations.*

have sb eating out of (the palm of) your hand someone is willing to do

whatever you want ▶ *She's another young star who has the director eating out of her hand.*

have a hand in to be involved in ▶ *We've had a hand in all aspects of the catering industry.*

the heavy hand (of) also **a heavy hand** power used in a strict or cruel way ▶ *Political opposition struggled to survive under the heavy hand of the secret police.* ▶ *He was known to run the department with a heavy hand.*

hold sb's hand to help someone in an unfamiliar or frightening situation ▶ *This cookbook holds your hand throughout the preparation of complicated dishes.*

keep your hand in to practise a skill so that you do not lose it ▶ *I always take painting materials on holiday with me, just to keep my hand in.*

live (from) hand to mouth to have very little money to live on ▶ *I hope I won't still be living from hand to mouth when I'm 30.* **hand-to-mouth** ADJ ▶ *My wife was willing to share the hand-to-mouth existence of a young writer.*

an old hand (at sth) someone who has a lot of experience (of something) ▶ *The bar was full of old hands making fun of the new recruits.*

be on hand to be available ▶ *The health advisor will be on hand to answer your questions.*

on the other hand by comparison ▶ *The pub is cheap – on the other hand, the restaurant will have much nicer food.*

reject sth out of hand also **dismiss sth out of hand** to decide immediately not to accept something ▶ *The idea for a new road was rejected out of hand because it would cost far too much.*

the right hand doesn't know what the

H

left hand is doing also **the left hand doesn't know what the right hand is doing** there is not enough communication in an organization ▶ *Because the right hand didn't know what the left hand was doing, I was given two completely different instructions.*

show your hand to let other people know your plans where this might give them an advantage ▶ *He told us not to show our hand too soon.*

> If you show your hand in a game of cards, you let other people see which cards you are holding. This gives them the advantage of knowing what you are likely to do next in the game.

take sb/sth in hand to take responsibility for dealing with someone or something ▶ *She took her grandchildren in hand and put a stop to their wild behaviour.* ▶ *We've asked the head teacher to take the matter in hand.*

to hand near and easy to find or reach ▶ *I smashed the window with the nearest thing that came to hand.*

try your hand at sth to try doing something new ▶ *More and more actors are trying their hand at directing films.*

turn your hand to sth to do something that is not what you usually do ▶ *If you work in a small company you have to be able to turn your hand to anything that needs doing.*

wait on sb hand and foot to do everything for another person ▶ *She isn't one of those mothers who wait on their sons hand and foot.*

work hand in hand (with) to work closely together ▶ *Conservationists*

have been working hand in hand with the government to save the whales.

you/I have to hand it to sb also **you've/I've got to hand it to sb** someone deserves praise for what they have done, although you may not be willing to give it ▶ *You have to hand it to him – he does play well under pressure.*

HANDCUFFS

golden handcuffs a lot of money paid to an important person in a company so that they do not leave ▶ *Their golden handcuffs scheme was designed to lock all their best managers into their jobs.*

HANDLE

fly off the handle to get very angry suddenly ▶ *I was trying to explain that it was an accident, but he flew off the handle.*

get a handle on to understand a situation so that you can deal with it more successfully ▶ *After a few days she'd got a handle on what the job required.*

HANDS

at the hands of sb because of the actions of ▶ *Elephants and lions had suffered at the hands of big-game hunters.*

change hands to be given or sold to another person ▶ *Over a hundred million shares changed hands on the New York stock exchange today.* ▶ *A lot of money has changed hands during this deal.*

dirty your hands also **soil your hands** to get involved in an activity that is dishonest or unpleasant ▶ *Some scientists do not want to dirty their hands with weapons research.*

fall into the wrong hands to be found by people who may use it in a way that harms others ▶ *The agreement should prevent test weapons falling into the wrong hands.*

get your hands dirty to be involved in the practical parts of an activity ▶ *We need factory managers who aren't afraid to get their hands dirty.*

sb's hands are tied someone cannot help someone achieve something, even though they may want to  ▶ *They need extra staff, but their hands are tied because of budget cuts.*

have sth on your hands to have to deal with something ▶ *If we don't do something now, we'll have a disaster on our hands.*

have your hands full to have a lot to do ▶ *Don't ask me to help, I've got my hands full already.*

in safe hands safe, protected ▶ *Don't worry, you're in safe hands – she's a brilliant doctor.*

it's all hands on deck everyone has to be available to work hard ▶ *When the wedding party arrives, it'll be all hands on deck.*

lay your hands on to be able to find or get something ▶ *We're trying to lay our hands on the original report.*

play (right) into sb's hands to do something that helps somebody else gain an advantage over you ▶ *If we respond with violence, we'll be playing into their hands – they'd love a fight.*

sit on your hands to do nothing useful in a situation ▶ *The board was accused of sitting on its hands and waiting for the problem to go away.*

take sb/sth off sb's hands to take responsibility for someone or something ▶ *Our son is going to take the business off our hands.*

sb/sth is off sb's hands ▶ *Your kids will be off your hands in a few years' time.*

wash your hands of sb/sth to refuse to accept responsibility for something any longer ▶ *It's no longer possible for us to wash our hands of students who don't perform well.*

This idiom comes from a story in the Bible. Pilate, the Roman ruler, washed his hands at Jesus' trial (=a process during which it is decided if someone is guilty of a crime) and said he was not responsible for what happened to Jesus.

win hands down also **beat sb/sth hands down** to win or beat completely and easily ▶ *Their team won hands down, 5-1.*

HANDSHAKE

a golden handshake a large amount of money given to someone important when they leave their job ▶ *Our boss got a golden handshake of a million pounds.*

HANG

get the hang of sth to gradually find the right way of doing something ▶ *Using the Internet is easy, once you get the hang of it.*

hang in there! continue doing what you are trying to do ▶ *Hang in there – you've nearly finished!*

hang loose stay calm and relaxed

▶ *Just hang loose until we find out what's going on.*

hang sb out to dry to do nothing to help someone who is in trouble ▶ *He was hung out to dry after the muddle with the computers.*

hang up your ___ to stop doing a job where you wear or use (a particular thing) ▶ *I'll be hanging up my boxing gloves in a couple of years' time.*

HARD

hard done by unfairly treated ▶ *She feels hard done by, as she hasn't had the same opportunities as her sister.*

be hard put to do sth also **be hard pressed to do sth** to find it difficult to do something ▶ *He'll be hard put to find a publisher for his poetry.* ▶ *I'd be hard pressed to name the best film at the festival.*

be hard to come by to be difficult to get or find ▶ *Jobs were hard to come by in the countryside.*

HARDBALL

play hardball (with sb) to do things in a determined way so that you get what you want ▶ *We don't want to anger a company that's famous for playing hardball.*

HARNESS

in harness
1 working together ▶ *Local and central government should work in harness to create more jobs.*
2 working at your job ▶ *He is now back in harness after his illness.*

HARVEST

reap the harvest to get the results you deserve ▶ *She is reaping the harvest of putting her social life before her studies.*

HASH

make a hash of sth to do something very badly, so that it fails or is destroyed ▶ *He tried to repair the CD player and made a complete hash of it.*

HASTE

more haste less speed if you do something too quickly you will have to spend more time fixing the problems ▶ *Don't try and paint this wall before the plaster's dry – more haste less speed.*

HAT

go hat in hand to ask for money or help in a very respectful way ▶ *I'm not going to them hat in hand to ask for my job back.*

have your ___ hat on also **wear your ___ hat** influenced by the job you are doing or the situation you are in at that time ▶ *I think night clubs are fun but when I have my parental hat on, I am not so enthusiastic.*

keep sth under your hat to keep something a secret ▶ *I'm leaving in January, but please keep it under your hat.*

old hat not new or interesting ▶ *The Internet is already old hat to academic researchers.*

pass around the hat to collect money from a group of people ▶ *We passed round the hat and got her a nice leaving present.*

pull sth out of a/the hat also **pull a rabbit out of a/the hat** to suddenly produce a solution to a problem

▶ *Let's contact Pete and see if he can pull something out of the hat.*

I take my hat off to sb I admire someone for what they have done ▶ *Congratulations, I take my hat off to you!*

sb is talking through his/her hat someone is talking as if they know something when they do not ▶ *He was talking through his hat when he said this computer would be just right for me.*

throw your hat into the ring also **toss your hat into the ring** to announce officially that you are going to compete for a job or in an election ▶ *Palmer has now thrown his hat into the ring as a candidate for school governor.*

wear more than one hat to have more than one job ▶ *She wears more than one hat – she's directing the play and is also in charge of the costumes and lighting.*

HATCHET

bury the hatchet to agree to stop arguing ▶ *I've more or less buried the hatchet with my father.*

HATTER

as mad as a hatter completely crazy ▶ *We don't have much to do with my wife's family. Mad as hatters, the lot of them.*

HAVE

sb has been had someone has been deceived ▶ *You've been had, I'm afraid. You should have tried the car before you bought it.*

sb has it coming (to him/her) something bad is going to happen to someone and they deserve it because they have done something bad too

▶ *George has it coming to him, after the way he's treated my sister.*

sb has (got) it in for sb someone wants to harm someone else ▶ *They've been burgled four times – I think someone's got it in for them.*

have had it up to here (with) also **have had it (with)** to be very annoyed (with someone or something) and not to want to deal with them or think about them any more ▶ *I've had it up to here with the phone company – you talk to them!*

have (got) it made to have everything you need in order to have a good life ▶ *You've got exactly the job you wanted, where you wanted it – I'd say you've got it made.*

have it out with sb to talk to someone who you are angry with and try to come to a conclusion ▶ *I had it out with the saleswoman, and I finally got my money back.*

have sb (right) where you want them to have an advantage over someone you are dealing with ▶ *You have the committee right where you want them, so ask for the money now.*

have what it takes to have the qualities that are needed in order to be successful ▶ *He has what it takes to get on in professional football.* ▶ *This mobile phone has what it takes – we've sold twice as many of this model than of any other brand.*

sb is having sb on someone is tricking someone else ▶ *Of course they didn't tell him what you said – they're just having you on.*

HAVOC

play havoc with also **wreak havoc** to cause a lot of trouble or confusion ▶ *Mobile phones play havoc with*

H

aircraft landing systems. ➤ *The storms have wreaked environmental havoc in Florida.*

HAWK

watch sb like a hawk to watch someone very carefully, in case they try to do something wrong ➤ *That saleswoman always watches young customers like a hawk.*

HAY

hit the hay ➤ hit the SACK
make hay (while the sun shines) to take the opportunity to do something now ➤ *When the big cruise ships come into the harbour, the shopkeepers can make hay.*

HAYWIRE

go haywire to do strange and unexpected things ➤ *Sorry this report is late; the computers went haywire this morning.* ➤ *She went a bit haywire after her husband died.*

HEAD

bite sb's head off to speak to someone suddenly in a very angry way ➤ *I only asked if he could move his car, but he bit my head off.*

bring sth to a head to make a situation suddenly get much worse so that it has to be dealt with ➤ *Her threat to resign was a deliberate move to bring matters to a head.* **come to a head** ➤ *The arguments came to a head at last week's meeting.*

bury your head in the sand also **stick your head in the sand** to ignore a problem or danger because you do not want to deal with it ➤ *If you find your debts building up, don't bury your head in the sand – talk to your bank.*
head-in-the-sand ADJ ➤ *Many hospitals need to abandon their head-in-the-sand mentality and face up to reality.*

> Some people believe that ostriches (=very large birds that cannot fly) put their heads in the sand when there is trouble or danger.

sb can do sth standing on his/her head someone can do something very easily ➤ *I could do the biology test standing on my head.*
sb can't make head or tail of sth somebody cannot understand something ➤ *See if you can understand this letter – I can't make head or tail of it.*

fall head over heels (in love) to feel a strong romantic love for someone ➤ *I fell head over heels for Mike the first time I met him.*

from head to toe also **from head to foot** all of someone's body ➤ *Tom came home soaked from head to toe.* ➤ *She was dressed in red from head to foot.*
get/have a head start to get or have an advantage when you start doing something ➤ *She got a head start because she's bilingual in English and*

Spanish. **give sb a head start** ▶ *Give your child a head start by sending her to nursery school.*

get/be in over your head to get or be involved in a situation that is too difficult or complicated ▶ *He got in over his head and had to close the restaurant after three months.*

get it into your head that to have an idea that is not true ▶ *He'd got it into his head that Kim was coming, but I'm sure she never intended to.*

give sb his/her head to give someone the freedom to behave how they want ▶ *We thought we'd give the art director his head, and see what happened.*

go head to head (with sb) to compete in a direct and determined way (with someone) ▶ *We knew we couldn't go head to head with the new supermarket.*

go over sb's head to avoid getting permission for something from the usual person, by asking someone more important ▶ *If Ken won't arrange training for us, we'll just have to go over his head.*

go over your head to be too difficult or complicated to understand ▶ *Half the instructions he gave us went straight over my head.*

sth goes to your head

1 something makes you behave as though you are very important ▶ *Don't tell Leo you think he's gorgeous – it would only go to his head.*

2 (of alcohol) to make you feel drunk very quickly ▶ *Whisky just goes straight to my head – I'll stick to beer.*

sb has a good head on his/her shoulders someone is intelligent and sensible ▶ *Adam will do well, he's got a good head on his shoulders.*

sb has his/her head screwed on (right) someone is sensible ▶ *Anyone with their head screwed on will see that his offer is absurd.*

have your head in the clouds to think a lot about things that you would like to happen so that you do not see what is really happening around you ▶ *As a child I always had my head in the clouds, travelling the world in my imagination.*

be a head case to be crazy ▶ *I went to a school where half the teachers were head cases.*

be head and shoulders above to be much better than ▶ *He's head and shoulders above his rivals in the business.*

keep a cool head to stay calm and reasonable ▶ *Throughout the exam I tried to keep a cool head.*

keep your head above water to manage to deal with all your problems or work ▶ *I'm advertising for an assistant as I'm struggling to keep my head above water.*

keep your head down to make sure that people do not notice you ▶ *During his boss's frequent panics, John just keeps his head down.*

laugh/scream etc your head off to laugh, scream, etc a lot for a long time ▶ *Dave saw a huge spider and started screaming his head off.*

lose your head to behave in a crazy or strange way ▶ *One of the soldiers lost*

his head and started shooting. **keep your head** ➤ *Luckily, the driver kept his head and steered the bus to the side of the road.*

sb needs his/her head examined sb has said or done sth wrong or stupid ➤ *Anyone who takes a boat out in storms like this needs his head examined.*

off the top of your head quickly, without thinking too much ➤ *"How many students take German?" "Off the top of my head – about 40 or 50."*

be off your head to be crazy ➤ *"Are you off your head? It's too cold to go camping in February."*

on your (own) head be it you must be responsible for what you have decided to do ➤ *I don't think you should have said that – on your own head be it if he gets angry.*

be out of your head ➤ be out of your MIND

sth rears its (ugly) head also **sth raises its (ugly) head** something (unpleasant) appears or becomes active ➤ *It seems that drug-related crime is raising its ugly head in our small town.*

turn heads to impress people and make them notice you, especially by looking very attractive ➤ *Our new advertisement is designed to turn heads.*

turn sth on its head also **stand sth on its head**

1 to show that an idea is the opposite of what it seems ➤ *The professor's theories turn logic on its head.*

2 to change the way people think about something ➤ *The Beatles' Sergeant Pepper album stood the music industry on its head.*

sth turns your head to think that you are more important than you were before ➤ *When she first went to Paris to model it really turned her head.*

HEADLINES

grab the headlines to be so shocking or unusual as to be in the newspapers ➤ *A series of violent robberies have been grabbing the headlines this week.*

HEADS

heads will/must roll some people will or must lose their jobs because they are responsible for things going wrong ➤ *Heads must roll after this latest financial scandal.*

knock sb's heads together also **knock heads** to force two people to reach an agreement ➤ *Those two are always arguing – it's time someone knocked their heads together.*

put your heads together to work together in order to solve a problem

➤ *We need to put our heads together and work out some kind of compromise.*

HEAR

can't hear yourself think there is so much noise that it is stopping you from thinking clearly ➤ *Will you be quiet! I can't hear myself think.*

HEART

be ___ at heart to be basically a particular sort of person ➤ *I guess I'm*

just a country girl at heart – I'd do anything to get out of the city.

a bleeding heart someone who feels too much sympathy for people with few advantages ▶ *You don't have to be a bleeding heart to feel saddened by the imprisonment of young people.*

bleeding-heart ADJ ▶ *We are letting bleeding-heart liberals dominate our courts.*

break sb's heart to make someone very sad ▶ *It breaks my heart to see our lakes and rivers destroyed by pollution.* ▶ *Sue broke his heart when she left him.*

close to sb's heart very important to someone ▶ *Ireland and its people will always be close to my heart.*

cross my heart (and hope to die) I promise ▶ *I won't tell anyone what you've just told me – cross my heart.*

sb doesn't have the heart to do sth someone is unwilling to upset someone else by doing something ▶ *I didn't have the heart to tell her I'd lost her picture.*

eat your heart out you will wish you had or could do this! ▶ *I shook the winner's hand, and he gave me his autograph – so eat your heart out!*

(straight) from the heart honest and showing strong feeling ▶ *She welcomed us with a warmth that came straight from the heart.*

get to the heart of sth to understand or deal with the most important part of something ▶ *Reorganization alone will not get to the heart of the problem.*

have a change of heart to begin to feel differently about something ▶ *After starting a law course, she had a change of heart and swapped to politics.*

have a heart! don't be strict or unkind! ▶ *I can't climb any faster, have a heart!*

have a heart of gold to be very kind even though you may not appear to be ▶ *Your uncle always seemed rather rude, but he had a heart of gold.*

have a heart of stone to be unkind or unsympathetic ▶ *I asked for time off to look after my little boy, but my boss has got a heart of stone.*

sb's heart is in the right place even though someone does not seem very kind, they do care about other people ▶ *She's a very strict teacher, but her heart's in the right place.*

in your heart of hearts in your most private thoughts ▶ *I encouraged Lucy to apply for a new job, but in my heart of hearts I hoped she'd stay with us.*

lose heart to stop wanting to continue because you think you will not succeed ▶ *I started out on the marathon, but lost heart when I fell and bruised my knee.*

a man/woman after your own heart a person you like because they do the same kind of thing you do ▶ *"He sits around talking instead of getting on with his work." "Ah, a man after my own heart."*

pour out your heart (to sb) also **open your heart (to sb)** to tell someone everything that you are feeling ▶ *He poured out his heart to me that night, saying that he had never loved his wife.*

set your heart on (doing) sth to want (to do) something very much ▶ *He's set his heart on a career in law.* ▶ *I've set my heart on passing my driving test before the summer.*

sick at heart very sad or upset ▶ *I was sick at heart when I told Mum the news.*

H

take heart to be encouraged and feel you will do well ▶ *People with bad backs can take heart from a new medical procedure.*

take sth to heart to be strongly affected by something, often a criticism ▶ *I took the teacher's comments to heart and worked a lot harder.* ▶ *Don't take those spiteful remarks to heart – she didn't mean them.*

the way to sb's heart the way to please someone ▶ *The best way to my father's heart is to give him a good bottle of wine.*

wear your heart on your sleeve to show your true feelings openly ▶ *Nick tends to wear his heart on his sleeve and some girls find this puts them off.*

This idiom comes from the very old custom of a man wearing something on his sleeve that was given to him by the woman he loved.

with all your heart with very strong feelings ▶ *It was obvious that she loved him with all her heart.*

young at heart (of an older person) having the feelings and attitudes of a young person ▶ *They put on a pensioners' dance night for the young at heart.*

your heart goes out to sb you feel great sympathy for another person ▶ *He looked so lonely and afraid that her heart went out to him.*

your heart isn't in it you do not really want to do what you are doing ▶ *She's getting bored with that job and it's obvious that her heart's not in it.*

your heart skipped a beat also **your heart missed a beat** you were very excited, surprised, or frightened ▶ *My heart skipped a beat when he smiled at me.*

your heart was in your mouth you felt very nervous or frightened ▶ *My heart was in my mouth – I was sure the car was going to hit him.*

HEARTSTRINGS

tug at sb's heartstrings to make someone feel very sad ▶ *She knew her children would be safe, but parting with them tugged at her heartstrings.*

HEAT

the heat is on a situation is not relaxed, especially because people are expecting you to do something ▶ *When the heat is on at work, make sure you get enough sleep.*

This idiom was first used by criminals talking about the police, whom they called 'the heat'. If the police were looking for you, then the heat was on. When the police were not looking for you, the heat was off.

in the heat of the moment without stopping to think because you are excited or angry ▶ *My decision to leave was made in the heat of the moment.*

turn up the heat (on sb) to criticize or threaten someone so that they do what you want ▶ *The lecturers have turned up the heat on lazy students this week.*

HEAVEN

be in seventh heaven to be in a very happy situation ▶ *He's in seventh heaven whenever he's climbing mountains.*

move heaven and earth to do sth to work very hard to do something ▶ *I'd move heaven and earth to get to their wedding.*

HEEL

down at heel also **down-at-heel** looking old, poor, or in a bad condition ▶ *A few of the houses were shabby and down at heel, but most had just had a fresh coat of paint.*

HEELS

dig your heels in also **dig in your heels** to be determined not to change your mind ▶ *I wanted to go on holiday in May, but Mike dug his heels in, so we went in August as usual.* ▶ *Mother dug in her heels and refused to move house.*

drag your heels ➤ drag your FEET

hot on the heels of sth also **hard on the heels of sth** happening very soon after something else ▶ *The arrest came hot on the heels of accusations in the Sunday papers.*

take to your heels to run away ▶ *The thieves took to their heels with a bag of watches and jewellery.*

HELL

all hell breaks loose a situation suddenly becomes bad, disorganized, or violent ▶ *When one of the singers jumped off the stage, all hell broke loose.*

come hell or high water whatever happens, in spite of any problems ▶ *I'm going to make him listen to me, come hell or high water.*

for the hell of it without having any good reason; for fun ▶ *We used to climb the tree and steal pears, just for the hell of it.*

give sb hell to be angry with someone and shout at them ▶ *Dad was giving him hell for breaking the CD player.*

go through hell to experience a very difficult or bad situation ▶ *We went through hell, not knowing if our son would live or die.*

not have a (snowball's) chance in hell (of) also **not have a hope in hell (of)** it is impossible for someone (to) ▶ *Frankly, you didn't have a snowball's chance in hell of winning.*

sb is hell-bent on (doing) sth ➤ sb is BENT on (doing) sth

hell for leather very fast or with a lot of energy ▶ *We were driving hell for leather across Texas.*

a living hell an extremely unpleasant place or situation ▶ *A jealous husband can make your life a living hell.*

raise hell to complain angrily ▶ *If we dismiss Lawrence, he'll raise hell with the directors.*

be shot to hell also **be blown to hell** to be completely ruined ▶ *After he'd been using the car for a few weeks, the brakes were shot to hell.*

there'll be (all) hell to pay there will be a lot of trouble ▶ *You'd better have the report ready on Tuesday, or there'll be all hell to pay.*

to hell with sb/sth I don't care about

H

somebody or something ▶ *I'll say what I want, and to hell with the job.*

when/until hell freezes over never ▶ *"When are you going to apologize*

to Carl?" "When hell freezes over."

HERE

here goes! I'll start now! (said just before you start something that you are nervous about) ▶ *I've never spoken in public before, but here goes!*

HERO

the/an unsung hero someone who is not famous for something that they have done, although they deserve to be ▶ *People who care for the elderly are the unsung heroes of our society.*

HERRING

a red herring information mentioned deliberately to turn people's attention from the real problem ▶ *Discussing the exact wording of the law is a red herring to prevent us looking at the facts.*

HET UP

be/get het up to be or become anxious or upset ▶ *You get het up over the silliest things.*

HIDE

have a hide like a rhinoceros not to be affected by people's criticism or suggestions ▶ *A politician has to have a hide like a rhinoceros or stop reading the newspapers.* ▶ *She doesn't seem to realize we don't want her with us – she's got a hide like a rhinoceros!*

HILL

be over the hill to be too old ▶ *Peter's been dropped from the team now he's over the hill.*

HILT

(up) to the hilt as much as possible ▶ *He borrowed up to the hilt to buy that house – and now interest rates have gone up.*

HIP

shoot from the hip to say what you think in a direct way ▶ *Now I'm going to shoot from the hip, so don't take offence.*

HISTORY

sb/sth is history someone or something is finished and no longer active or important ▶ *If you do anything wrong in this job, you'll be history.*

...(and) the rest is history everyone knows the rest of a story that you have been telling ▶ *She met Antonio on holiday in Spain, and the rest is history.*

HIT

hit and miss also **hit or miss** not carefully planned or organized ▶ *His driving lessons have been rather hit or miss so he may not pass his test.*

hit it off (with sb) to like someone as soon as you meet them ▶ *I hit it off with Fred right from the start, and we've been friends ever since.* ▶ *Didn't you two hit it off?*

hit sb when he/she is down to harm someone when they are already in a bad situation ▶ *I'm not telling him now – I can't hit a man when he's down.*

hit sb where it hurts (most) to do the thing that you know will hurt someone (most) ▶ *The law will hit drug dealers where it hurts – in their pockets.*

HOG

go the whole hog to do something in a complete and thorough way ▶ *We decided to go the whole hog and hire a limousine.*

live high on the hog to have a rich style of living ▶ *These people travel the world living high on the hog.*

HOLD

hold sb/sth dear to love someone or something ▶ *Worst of all, I've lost the respect of the person I hold most dear.*

put sth on hold to delay doing or starting something ▶ *My dreams for the future have been put on hold since I lost my job.*

HOLDS

no holds barred with no controls or conditions ▶ *The two of them argued it out, no holds barred – it certainly cleared up any misunderstandings.*

no-holds-barred ADJ ▶ *The programme will have a no-holds-barred approach to religious discussion.*

HOLE

burn a hole in your pocket (of money) to be ready for spending immediately ▶ *I've got my £100 winnings burning a hole in my pocket.*

need sth like a hole in the head not to need something at all ▶ *I need visitors tonight like I need a hole in the head.*

HOLES

be full of holes to have many faults ▶ *He said that many of the theories about air pollution are full of holes.*

pick holes in sth to criticize something ▶ *It's better not to pick holes in other people's performances.*

HOME

bring it home (to you) to make you realize how serious or dangerous a situation is ▶ *His news brought it home to me how selfish people can be.*

hit home also **strike home** to have a strong effect ▶ *Her colleagues' criticism of her report hit home.*

home (away) from home a place where you feel as comfortable as in your own home ▶ *Our family provides a home from home for foreign students.* ▶ *The hotel was built as a home away from home for American servicemen.*

a home truth a fact about someone that is true but unpleasant ▶ *I told him a few home truths before I left.*

HOMEWORK

do your homework to find out about a

H

subject before you have to deal with it ▶ *TV presenters have to do their homework on the people they interview.*

HONEYMOON

the honeymoon is over someone or something that was popular at first has begun to have problems ▶ *Usually, the honeymoon is over for a president after the first year.* **a/the honeymoon period** ▶ *When you first meet a client, there is usually a honeymoon period when everyone seems to like each other.*

HOOK

by hook or by crook using whatever methods you can ▶ *She's going to find a man to support her, by hook or by crook.*

let/get sb off the hook to allow or help someone to get out of a difficult situation ▶ *This is the law, and no one will be let off the hook.* ▶ *Just saying sorry won't get you off the hook.*

HOOKS

get your hooks into sb to get control over someone ▶ *Once the money lenders have got their hooks into you you're stuck.*

HOOPS

make sb go through (the) hoops also **put sb through (the) hoops** to make someone do a lot of difficult things or answer a lot of difficult questions

▶ *We put all the candidates through the hoops and only take 10%.*

> A hoop is a large ring that some animals can be trained to jump through to perform.

HOOT

don't care a hoot also **don't give two hoots** not to care ▶ *Tim doesn't care a hoot about money.* ▶ *My mother doesn't care two hoots whether I'm married or not.*

HOPE

be hoping against hope to keep hoping that something will happen although it is unlikely ▶ *I'm hoping against hope that I'll be well enough to travel.*

HOPES

pin your hopes on to depend only on ▶ *He pinned all his hopes on winning the gold medal.*

HORIZON

be on the horizon to be expected to happen soon ▶ *There don't seem to be any jobs on the horizon so I'm moving to London.*

HORIZONS

broaden your horizons to experience new situations and new ideas ▶ *Working with disabled people really broadened my horizons.*

HORNS

lock horns (with sb) to disagree strongly ▶ *The companies locked horns over patent laws.* ▶ *He locked horns with his father on several occasions.*

be on the horns of a dilemma not to know which of two unpleasant choices to make ▶ *This job offer has put me on the horns of a dilemma.*

This idiom comes from the idea that an angry bull will throw you, whichever horn you try to hold on to.

HORSE

back the wrong horse also **pick the wrong horse** to support someone who is not successful ▶ *I backed the wrong horse when I went to work for her.*

a dark horse someone in a competition who is not well known ▶ *Alan was a bit of a dark horse until he won the tournament last year.*

don't look a gift horse in the mouth do not criticize a present, or something that is free ▶ *Don't look a gift horse in the mouth – any holiday is better than none!*

This idiom comes from the fact that you can tell how healthy a horse is by looking at its teeth. If someone gave you a horse as a gift, it would be foolish to worry about its health.

sb gets on his/her high horse someone is behaving as if they are better than everyone else ▶ *She tends to get on her high horse and give the men a hard time.*

you can lead a horse to water (but you can't make it drink) you can give someone an opportunity, but you cannot force them to do anything they do not want to ▶ *Parents must provide an education, but they should remember that you can lead a horse to water – they can't force their children to learn.*

HORSES

change horses (in midstream) to change your support from one person or plan to another ▶ *Our candidate was ill so we had to change horses in midstream.*

hold your horses wait, be patient ▶ *Now, hold your horses a moment, that isn't what I said.*

wild horses wouldn't drag me also **wild horses wouldn't make me** I will

not do that ▶ *He's invited me, but wild horses wouldn't drag me to that wedding.*

HOT

(all) hot and bothered annoyed, worried, or upset ▶ *She was all hot and bothered because she couldn't find her key.*

be hot to trot to be eager to start or get involved ▶ *Our company is hot to trot and can provide all your computer needs.*

be too hot to handle to be too shocking to be played or shown to the public ▶ *Broadcasters have decided the song is too hot to handle.*

HOT CAKES

sell like hot cakes to be bought by lots of people in a short time ▶ *The CD is selling like hot cakes and will probably reach number one next week.*

H

HOUR

the eleventh hour the latest possible time you can do something ▶ *New evidence was uncovered at the eleventh hour.*

sb's finest hour the most important, most successful, and best time in someone's life ▶ *His finest hour came when he won the Championship.*

sb's hour of need the time when someone or something needs help ▶ *Tom was the only person who came to see me in my hour of need.*

HOURS

the small hours the early morning, between about 1 o'clock and 4 o'clock ▶ *The party went on into the small hours of Sunday morning.*

HOUSE

bring the house down also **bring down the house** (of someone who is performing) to get a lot of applause (=people hitting their hands together to show how much they like something) ▶ *He brought the house down with his drum solo.*

eat sb out of house and home to eat too much of someone's food ▶ *Since Mike's been here he's been eating me out of house and home.*

get on like a house on fire to like each other very much ▶ *She understands me – we've always got on like a house on fire.*

a house of cards a weak plan or organization ▶ *The peace agreement is a house of cards that could collapse at the first sign of trouble.*

on the house paid for by the bar or restaurant ▶ *After-dinner coffee is on the house tonight.*

put your (own) house in order also **set your (own) house in order** to put right everything in your business or personal affairs ▶ *You should look for ways of putting your own house in order before you criticize me.*

HOUSEHOLD

a household name used about someone or something that is very well known ▶ *Television made him a household name.*

HOUSES

people who live in glass houses (shouldn't throw stones) you should not criticize other people when you have equally bad faults ▶ *I don't think you have any right to complain – people who live in glass houses, after all.*

shout sth from the housetops ➤ shout sth from the ROOFTOPS

HOW

how does sth grab you? do you like this suggestion? ▶ *How does a fortnight in Zanzibar grab you?*

HUE

hue and cry angry protests ▶ *He'll be safer with us until the hue and cry is over.*

HUMAN

sb is only human someone may be expected to make mistakes or show weaknesses ▶ *I'm so sorry about the mix-up, but our staff are only human you know.*

HUMP

get/be over the hump to deal with or have dealt with the most difficult part of a situation ▶ *Once I'd finished the essay question I was over the hump.*

HUNG UP

hung up on sth thinking or worrying too much about something ▶ *Don't get hung up on small details; just concentrate on the general impression you're making.*

HURDLE

clear a hurdle to deal successfully with a problem ▶ *If you've passed the accounting exam, you've cleared the first hurdle. None of the others are as hard.*

HUSH

hush money money that you pay so that someone keeps something secret ▶ *He was paying the lawyer plenty of hush money to keep quiet about the contract.*

H

Ii

ICE

break the ice to do something that makes people relax when they have just met each other ▶ *It's hard to break the ice at these formal dinners.*

not cut much ice (with) also **cut no/little ice (with)** not to impress or influence ▶ *His environmental policies do not cut much ice with big business.*

keep sth on ice also **put sth on ice** to decide to stop moving something forward ▶ *The project will be kept on ice until the new manager comes.*

be (skating) on thin ice to be taking a risk ▶ *You'll be on thin ice if you take any more time off.*

ICING

icing on the cake something that makes a good situation even better ▶ *The film's doing really well, and this award is the icing on the cake.*

> Icing is a sweet substance made from sugar and water or lemon juice or egg whites etc and put on cakes.

IDEAS

bounce ideas off sb to discuss ideas before you make a decision ▶ *Some writers work in groups and bounce ideas off each other.*

ILL

ill at ease nervous and embarrassed ▶ *The new students were standing around in the hallway, looking ill at ease.*

IMAGE

be the spitting image of sb to look exactly like someone else ▶ *Paul's the spitting image of his father.*

IN

be in for it about to be in trouble ▶ *You're in for it now; Mum was keeping that cake for tonight.*

INCH

give sb an inch (and he/she will take a mile) if you let someone do one small thing, they will try to do a lot more ▶ *Give a kid like Joey an inch, and he'll certainly take a mile.*

beat sb (to) within an inch of their life also **thrash sb (to) within an inch of their life** to hit someone very hard many times ▶ *Granddad stole an apple when he was little and got beaten to within an inch of his life.*

INFLUENCE

under the influence having drunk a lot of alcohol ▶ *The police caught him driving under the influence.*

INS

the ins and outs of all the details and facts of ▶ *Our students are taught the ins and outs of contract law.*

INSULT

(to) add insult to injury someone who has harmed you is making things worse ▶ *The bus company is providing fewer night services and, to add insult to injury, they are charging higher fares.*

IRON

strike while the iron is hot to take an opportunity at a time when you are likely to succeed ▶ *Your father's in a good mood, so strike while the iron's hot.*

IRONS

irons in the fire opportunities or activities ▶ *I'm not worried, I've got other irons in the fire.* ▶ *Eric had so many irons in the fire that he was hardly ever home.*

ISSUE

force the issue to force someone to make a decision or take action ▶ *We're hoping she'll take the job,* *but we don't want to force the issue.*

take issue with sb/sth to disagree with someone and start a discussion about a subject ▶ *I have to take issue with you on the subject of teaching standards.*

ITEM

be an item to be having a romantic relationship ▶ *You and Rose seem to be an item.*

IVORY

in an ivory tower completely involved in reading and ideas, and unable to face ordinary problems ▶ *It's easy for people in their academic ivory tower to be critical.*

Jj

JACK

(be) a jack of all trades (and master of none) to be able to do a lot of different jobs but none of them very well ▶ *What we really need around the office is a jack of all trades.*

JACKPOT

hit the jackpot to be very successful or lucky, or exactly right ▶ *Our local TV station hit the jackpot with its new game show.* ▶ *"I think Roy is going out with Anna." "You may have hit the jackpot there."*

This idiom comes from gambling (=the practice of risking money on card games, horse races etc). If someone hits the jackpot when they are gambling, they win lots of money.

JAW

sb's jaw dropped someone was very surprised ▶ *John's jaw dropped when he saw his son's bruised face.*

JEKYLL AND HYDE

Jekyll and Hyde a person who has two very different parts to their character, one good and one bad ▶ *She's Jekyll and Hyde: one moment sweet and generous and the next*

spreading malicious gossip about her friends. **Jekyll-and-Hyde** ADJ ▶ *Wilkinson is rather a Jekyll-and-Hyde character.*

This idiom comes from R.L. Stevenson's book *The Strange Case of Dr Jekyll and Mr Hyde* in which Dr Jekyll finds a drug that changes him into a person called Mr Hyde, who has all of Dr Jekyll's most evil qualities.

JELLY

turn to jelly also **feel like jelly** to feel very weak ▶ *Before the interview my legs turned to jelly and my palms started to sweat.*

JOB

fall down on the job to fail to do the work you are supposed to do ▶ *The council has fallen down on the job of keeping the streets clean.*

a snow job lies and tricks that someone uses in order to hide the truth ▶ *The whole story is a major snow job, if you ask me.*

JONESES

keep up with the Joneses to spend money getting all the things that people around you have ▶ *They got into debt because they insisted on keeping up with the Joneses.*

Jones is a common family name in English. 'The Joneses' is often used to mean the ordinary family.

JUDGMENT

sit in judgment (on/over) to criticize someone's behaviour ▶ *I don't think you should sit in judgment on other people's relationships.*

JUGULAR

go for the jugular to attack someone in a way that will damage them ▶ *Some journalists go for the jugular when they interview celebrities.*

> The jugular is a large vein (=tube that blood flows through) in your neck that goes directly to your heart.

JUICE

let sb stew in his/her own juice to let someone suffer as a result of their own actions ▶ *No, I'm not going to ring her; let her stew in her own juice for a while.*

JUMP

stay one jump ahead of sb to have an advantage over someone ▶ *Intelligence services were trying to stay one jump ahead of the enemy.*

JUNGLE

concrete jungle an area of unpleasant and ugly concrete buildings in a city ▶ *The front of the building has a harbour view, but the back overlooks a concrete jungle.*

JURY

the jury is still out (on sth) people do not yet know enough to decide whether something is good or bad ▶ *The jury is still out on genetic engineering.*

> A jury is the group of people who decide if someone is guilty of a crime in a court of law. 'The jury is out' means the jury has left the court room to make their decision.

JUST

it's just as well (that) it is lucky, or all for the best (that) ▶ *It's just as well for everyone that Paul retired when he did.*

JUSTICE

do justice to sb/sth *also* **do sb/sth justice** to deal with someone or something in a reasonable and fair way ▶ *Do you think the film does justice to the book?* ▶ *He's really done justice to your cooking – look, he's eaten the whole pie!*

poetic justice when bad or good luck happens to someone who deserves it ▶ *That's poetic justice – nearly all the stolen money came from dishonest deals.*

rough justice when people are punished or rewarded in an illegal or unsympathetic way ▶ *Villagers used to deal out rough justice to those suspected of a crime.*

J

Kk

KEEL

(back) on an even keel steady and without problems ► *It took a long time to get her life on an even keel after the accident.*

KEEP

earn your keep

1 to earn the money that you need to live ► *I started earning my keep at 14.*

2 to bring in money or business for a company ► *Olly was a good salesman and soon began to earn his keep.*

keep sb guessing to keep your actions secret until the last minute ► *A good thriller writer keeps the reader guessing all the way through.*

keep sb posted to give someone news as it happens ► *Keep me posted; I'll be interested to hear what happens.*

you can keep ___ I do not want or like ► *You can keep your wild parties – I prefer the quiet life.*

KEN

sth is beyond sb's ken somebody does not know or understand anything about a subject ► *How he keeps that job is beyond my ken.*

KETTLE

another kettle of fish also *a different kettle of fish* a completely different situation from the one you are talking about ► *Her last job was very dull but the new one is another kettle of fish.*

KEYED UP

be/get keyed up to be or become worried, nervous, or excited ► *The students were all keyed up for their oral test.*

KICK

better than a kick in the teeth better than nothing ► *Winning $10 is better than a kick in the teeth, I suppose.*

get a kick out of (doing) sth to think something is exciting and fun to do ► *I get a real kick out of performing on stage.*

kick sb upstairs to give someone a job at a higher level but with less power than before ► *Our tired executives often get kicked upstairs for a few years before retirement.*

KICKS

get your kicks from sth also *do sth for kicks* to do something for excitement ► *The local kids get their kicks from racing stolen cars.*

KIDDING

who is sb kidding? also *who does sb think he's/she's kidding?* someone's reasons or excuses are completely unbelievable and would not deceive anyone ► *You two are just good friends, are you? Who are you kidding here?*

KILL

move in for the kill also *close in for the kill* to try in a determined way to defeat your opponent ► *When he admits his mistake, move in for the kill.*

KILLING

make a killing to make a lot of money in a short time ► *We were lucky* *enough to make a killing on the Hong Kong stock market.*

KILTER
out of kilter out of balance ▶ *Our budget was thrown out of kilter by the recession.*

KISS
be the kiss of death (for sb/sth) *also* **give sb/sth the kiss of death** to make someone or something fail ▶ *Baggy trousers were the kiss of death for the fashion-conscious woman that year.*
be the kiss of life (for sb/sth) *also* **give sb/sth the kiss of life** to help to make someone or something continue or succeed ▶ *Lottery money has been the kiss of life for many small theatre groups.*

KNEES
be the bee's knees to be very nice, attractive, good, etc
▶ *He thought he was the bee's knees because he'd been to college.*

bring sth to its knees *also* **bring sb to his/her knees** to damage someone or something badly ▶ *Bad management has brought the hospital to its knees.*
go down on your knees *also* **go down on bended knee** to ask for something in an eager and emotional way ▶ *I refuse to go down on my knees to get a job.*

KNELL
to sound the death knell of to cause

something to fail or stop existing ▶ *E-mail has sounded the death knell of the fax machine.*

> A death knell is the sound made by a bell that is rung when someone has died.

KNIFE
go under the knife to have a medical operation ▶ *They've set a date for me to go under the knife.*
twist the knife (in the wound) *also* **stick the knife in** to do something that hurts or embarrasses someone even more ▶ *Twisting the knife in the wound, he asked her to repeat her apology in front of everyone.*
you could (have) cut the air with a knife *also* **you could (have) cut the atmosphere with a knife** you could feel that the people you were with were very angry or upset, although no one was saying anything ▶ *The moment I walked into the room, I knew my parents were having another argument. You could have cut the air with a knife.*

KNIFE-EDGE
be on a knife-edge to be in a situation where either of two opposite things could happen ▶ *After the cutbacks, my job was on a knife-edge.* ▶ *The play is on the knife-edge between humour and tragedy* **knife-edge** ADJ ▶ *The governor will be facing a knife-edge vote in next week's elections.*

KNIGHT
a knight in shining armour a brave, romantic, and protective man ▶ *She won't marry until she finds a knight in shining armour.*

KNOCK

don't knock it don't criticize or complain about something ▶ *I've taken up judo – don't knock it, you can meet some nice people!*

knock it off! stop doing that ▶ *Knock it off, you two – I'm sick of your arguing.*

KNOCKS

hard knocks difficult or unpleasant experiences that you learn from ▶ *He told us about the hard knocks he'd had in the business world.*

KNOT

cut the Gordian knot to deal with a very difficult and complicated situation, especially in a quick, simple way ▶ *The Gordian knot had been cut, and the peace talks could begin.*

tie the knot to get married ▶ *Over 150*

couples tied the knot on Valentine's Day.

KNOTS

tie yourself in knots to become confused when dealing with something complicated ▶ *The more she tried to justify her behaviour, the more she tied herself in knots.*

KNOW

sb didn't know what hit him/her someone was very surprised or shocked ▶ *My first day teaching I didn't know what had hit me.*

be in the know to understand or have the necessary information ▶ *People in the know are saying 50 jobs will go.*

know sth backwards to know something very well ▶ *Ben knows the motor industry backwards.*

know sb/sth inside out to know someone or something very well ▶ *I know these people inside out – they'll love your idea.*

not know whether you're coming or going to feel very confused and busy ▶ *I've got so much to do, I don't know whether I'm coming or going.*

there's no knowing ➤ there's no TELLING

KNUCKLES

have your knuckles rapped ➤ be given a RAP across the knuckles

K

IDIOM ACTIVATOR

This special section contains 10 basic 'concept words', for example **PROBLEM**. Each concept word is divided into groups of idioms that have similar meanings. So, for example, under **PROBLEM** you have a general group called **'having problems'**, a group called **'cause problems for yourself'**, and so on. Looking at these groups of idioms and checking their definitions in the main part of the dictionary can help you to understand how each idiom is different from or similar to the others. The capital letters in each idiom show you where to find an entry in the A–Z list. For example, you will find **a THORN in sb's side** under 'thorn'.

I
D
I
O
M

PROBLEM

cause problems for yourself
- the CHICKENS (have) come home to roost
- dig your own GRAVE

having problems
- in/into deep WATER
- in a FIX
- in/into hot WATER
- not be out of the WOODS (yet)
- be up the CREEK (without a paddle)

sth makes life difficult/unhappy
- be the BANE of sb's existence
- a THORN in sb's side

cause problems for sb
- DROP sb in it
- put the CAT among the pigeons
- stir up a hornet's NEST

A
C
T
I
V
A
T
O
R

sth prevents progress/achievement
- be a DRAG on sth
- a sticking POINT
- a stumbling BLOCK

in a situation with difficult choices
- between the DEVIL and the deep blue sea
- a CATCH 22 (situation)
- (caught) between a ROCK and a hard place
- Hobson's CHOICE

137

I D I O M

A C T I V A T O R

feeling angry
▶ be/get hot under the COLLAR
▶ be/get STEAMed up
▶ in high DUDGEON

angry/frustrated
▶ tear your HAIR out

sth makes you angry/annoyed
▶ get sb's GOAT
▶ sth makes your BLOOD boil
▶ raise sb's HACKLES
▶ get sb's BLOOD up
▶ sth is (like) a red RAG to a bull

angrily complain about sth
▶ be up in ARMS (about sth)
▶ raise HELL

say/do a lot because you are angry
▶ let off STEAM
▶ vent your SPLEEN

angrily criticize/insult sb
▶ bite sb's HEAD off
▶ cut sb down to SIZE
▶ give sb HELL
▶ give sb a PIECE of your mind
▶ have a GO at sb
▶ jump down sb's THROAT

two people/groups angry with each other
▶ be at DAGGERS drawn

deliberately annoy sb
▶ push (sb's) BUTTONS
▶ rattle sb's CAGE
▶ ruffle sb's FEATHERS

ANGRY

suddenly become very angry
▶ blow your TOP
▶ fly off the HANDLE
▶ go APE
▶ go BALLISTIC
▶ go BANANAS
▶ go off the deep END
▶ GO spare
▶ go through the ROOF
▶ have a FIT
▶ lose your COOL
▶ SEE red

I
D
I
O
M

A
C
T
I
V
A
T
O
R

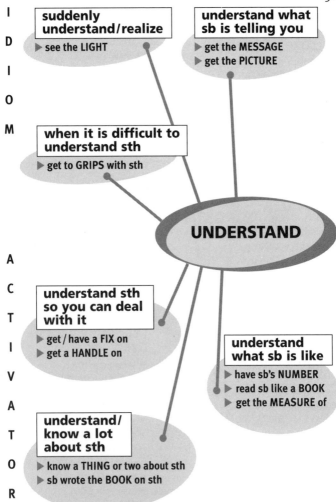

suddenly understand/realize
▶ see the LIGHT

understand what sb is telling you
▶ get the MESSAGE
▶ get the PICTURE

when it is difficult to understand sth
▶ get to GRIPS with sth

UNDERSTAND

understand sth so you can deal with it
▶ get / have a FIX on
▶ get a HANDLE on

understand what sb is like
▶ have sb's NUMBER
▶ read sb like a BOOK
▶ get the MEASURE of

understand/ know a lot about sth
▶ know a THING or two about sth
▶ sb wrote the BOOK on sth

I D I O M

not understand/ know anything

▶ not have a CLUE
▶ it's (all) GREEK to me
▶ not know the first THING about
▶ be out of TOUCH (with)

not understand/know, although sb explains

▶ sb can't make HEAD or tail of sth
▶ go over sb's HEAD
▶ be none the WISEr
▶ be out of your DEPTH

NOT UNDERSTAND/KNOW

A C T I V A T O R

nobody understands/knows

▶ be anybody's GUESS
▶ the BLIND (are) leading the blind
▶ be an unknown QUANTITY

not understand sth correctly

▶ don't get me WRONG
▶ get the wrong END of the stick
▶ miss the POINT

said when you do not understand/know sth

▶ (it) BEATs me
▶ not have the FOGGIEST (idea)
▶ SEARCH me!
▶ you've got me THERE

I
D
I
O
M

A
C
T
I
V
A
T
O
R

start doing sth

▶ be off the (starting) BLOCKS
▶ get down to BUSINESS
▶ get CRACKING
▶ get / keep the SHOW on the road
▶ get your TEETH into sth
▶ hit the ROAD
▶ start the BALL rolling
▶ set up SHOP

start happening or being used

▶ get into GEAR
▶ get off the GROUND
▶ get / be under WAY

START

start sth new or try again

▶ a clean SLATE
▶ from SCRATCH
▶ try your HAND at sth
▶ turn your HAND to sth

eager to start or try sth

▶ be champing at the BIT
▶ be RARING to go / to do sth
▶ be straining at the LEASH
▶ hit the GROUND running

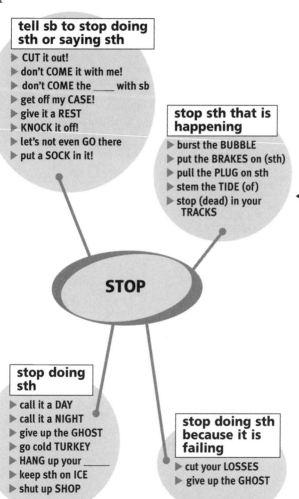

tell sb to stop doing sth or saying sth

- ▶ CUT it out!
- ▶ don't COME it with me!
- ▶ don't COME the _____ with sb
- ▶ get off my CASE!
- ▶ give it a REST
- ▶ KNOCK it off!
- ▶ let's not even GO there
- ▶ put a SOCK in it!

stop sth that is happening

- ▶ burst the BUBBLE
- ▶ put the BRAKES on (sth)
- ▶ pull the PLUG on sth
- ▶ stem the TIDE (of)
- ▶ stop (dead) in your TRACKS

STOP

stop doing sth

- ▶ call it a DAY
- ▶ call it a NIGHT
- ▶ give up the GHOST
- ▶ go cold TURKEY
- ▶ HANG up your _____
- ▶ keep sth on ICE
- ▶ shut up SHOP

stop doing sth because it is failing

- ▶ cut your LOSSES
- ▶ give up the GHOST

I
D
I
O
M

A
C
T
I
V
A
T
O
R

I D I O M

A C T I V A T O R

sb does sth easily

▶ sb can do sth in his/her SLEEP
▶ sb can do sth standing on his/her HEAD
▶ sb can do sth with one HAND tied behind his/her back
▶ no SWEAT
▶ take to sth like a DUCK to water

sth is easy

▶ as easy as falling off a LOG
▶ be a BREEZE
▶ be a PIECE of cake

EASY

sth will be easy because the difficult part is done

▶ be DOWNHILL (all the way) from here
▶ break the BACK of sth
▶ get/be over the HUMP

DIFFICULT

sth is difficult to do

- sth is a tall ORDER
- sth is hard to SWALLOW
- no BED of roses
- sth is no mean FEAT
- sth is no PICNIC
- sth TAKES some doing
- that's / it's EASIER said than done

sb has difficulty doing sth

- be HARD put to do sth
- have your WORK cut out (for you)
- be thrown in at the deep END

be in a difficult situation

- go through HELL
- (with) your BACK to the wall
- the HEAT is on

I
D
I
O
M

A
C
T
I
V
A
T
O
R

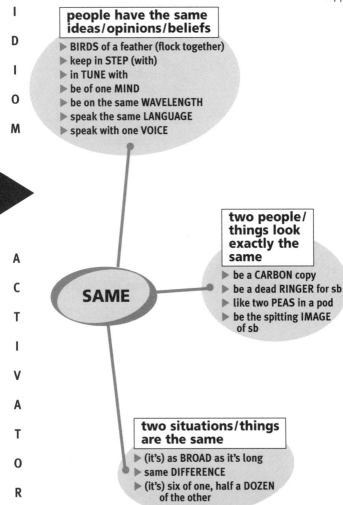

people have the same ideas/opinions/beliefs
- ▶ BIRDS of a feather (flock together)
- ▶ keep in STEP (with)
- ▶ in TUNE with
- ▶ be of one MIND
- ▶ be on the same WAVELENGTH
- ▶ speak the same LANGUAGE
- ▶ speak with one VOICE

SAME

two people/things look exactly the same
- ▶ be a CARBON copy
- ▶ be a dead RINGER for sb
- ▶ like two PEAS in a pod
- ▶ be the spitting IMAGE of sb

two situations/things are the same
- ▶ (it's) as BROAD as it's long
- ▶ same DIFFERENCE
- ▶ (it's) six of one, half a DOZEN of the other

two situations are different
- another KETTLE of fish
- be a far CRY from
- it's a (whole) new BALL GAME

two people/things are different
- be at LOGGERHEADS (with sb)
- be at ODDS (with)
- be (like) CHALK and cheese
- a different ANIMAL
- be on a (totally) different WAVELENGTH
- be POLES apart
- not see EYE to eye
- THEM and us
- be WORLDS apart

DIFFERENT

a group of different kinds of things/people
- from all WALKS of life
- be a mixed BAG
- THIS, that, and the other (thing)

different from other people
- go against the CURRENT
- stick out like a sore THUMB
- they broke the MOULD when they made sb

LI

LABOUR
a labour of love something that you do because you like doing it, not for money ▶ *This garden is a labour of love, created by Mrs Townsend over 20 years.*

LADDER
climb (up) the ladder also **move up the ladder** to become more important and successful in your work ▶ *Climbing swiftly up the ladder of corporate responsibility, Sam became managing director in five years.*

LADIES' MAN
a ladies' man a man who likes to spend time with women and is successful with them ▶ *Simon's a real ladies' man; he has so many women friends.*

LADY
it ain't over till the fat lady sings the final result cannot be known until something is completely finished ▶ *We're losing 4-0, but it ain't over till the fat lady sings.*

LAM
on the lam trying to escape and hide from someone, especially the police ▶ *Sykes was arrested after three weeks on the lam.*

LAMB
go like a lamb to the slaughter to accept a bad situation because you have no choice or do not realize how bad it will be ▶ *She's a tyrant! When she employed me to clean her house I went like a lamb to the slaughter.*

LAND
be in the land of the living to be alive or awake ▶ *I'm amazed your grandfather is still in the land of the living.*

sb is (living) in cloud-cuckoo land someone has ideas about the world that are not true or sensible, and thinks that things are much better than they really are ▶ *Anyone who wants to ban the use of animals in medical research is living in cloud-cuckoo land.*

a land of milk and honey a perfect place or situation, where there are no problems ▶ *Some new arrivals in the capital expect a land of milk and honey, but most are more realistic.*

This idiom comes from a story in the Bible in which the people of Israel were promised a land full of plenty of food where life would be good. This land is described as 'flowing with milk and honey'.

land sb in it ▶ DROP sb in it
the lie of the land also **how the land lies** the basic facts about a situation ▶ *Before accepting the job, you should get to know the lie of the land.*

LANGUAGE
speak the same/sb's language to have the same interests and opinions as someone else ▶ *Jake and I got on from the start; we spoke the same language.*

LAP

fall into your lap also **drop into your lap** to come by chance and good luck ▶ *My life changed when the opportunity to travel to America fell into my lap.*

the last lap the final part of something that has taken a long time ▶ *We climbed into the little train for the last lap of our journey.*

live in the lap of luxury to have a very pleasant and comfortable life with plenty of money ▶ *She's married to a film star and they live in the lap of luxury.*

LARGE

at large

1 as a group; in general ▶ *We have to find out what the public at large want from their health service.*

2 free; not in prison ▶ *Fiona's killer remains at large 15 months after her death.*

LARK

be up with the lark to get up out of bed very early in the morning ▶ *John's always up with the lark. He likes to get to work before anyone else.*

LAST

last but not least the last person or thing mentioned is no less important than the others ▶ *I want to thank my editor, my researcher, and last but not least my husband who supported me when times were hard.*

LAUGH

have the last laugh (on sb) to be successful, or receive proof that you are right, after being defeated or criticized ▶ *My book was published last year, so I finally had the last laugh on the editors who had rejected it.*

sb will be laughing someone will be in a good situation and feel very pleased ▶ *We bought the house for £60,000, so if we can sell it for £75,000 we'll be laughing.*

LAURELS

look to your laurels to watch out for someone as good as you are who will compete with you ▶ *There are some brilliant young players coming up – the champion must look to his laurels.*

rest on your laurels to stop trying to achieve anything new because you are satisfied ▶ *It's great that you got to university, but you can't afford to rest on your laurels.*

> In ancient times, leaves from a laurel tree were given to people such as poets and athletes as an honour.

LAW

sb is a law unto himself/herself someone does what they want to, instead of what they are told to do ▶ *Ever since she was a teenager, she's been a law unto herself.*

the law of the jungle a situation in which people look after themselves and the strongest people have all the advantages ▶ *There were no rules in that business – the law of the jungle was the guiding principle.*

lay down the law to tell people what to do very firmly ▶ *Ian is never happier than when he's laying down the law.*

L

Murphy's law if something can go wrong, it will ▶ *"Why is the traffic always worst when you're already late?" "Murphy's law."*

> Murphy's law is a humorous rule that says: Whatever can go wrong, will go wrong. There are other rules like this that are often called Murphy's Laws, such as: Nothing is as easy as it looks and Everything takes longer than you think it will. Although many people have ideas about who Murphy might be, no one is sure.

take the law into your own hands *also* **take matters into your own hands** to deal with a problem yourself, often in a violent or illegal way ▶ *Local people took the law into their own hands and removed the statue from the park.*

LAY

lay it on thick *also* **lay it on with a trowel** to say something with a lot of false emotion ▶ *I wondered if I was laying it on too thick, but the lawyer seemed impressed.*

lay sb low to make someone ill ▶ *An outbreak of flu laid the whole family low for a week.*

lay sb to rest to bury a dead person ▶ *The President was laid to rest in Arlington National Cemetery.*

lay sth to rest *also* **put sth to rest** to stop something spreading or happening ▶ *The leaders' friendly smiles were designed to put to rest any rumours about disagreements between them.*

lay yourself (wide) open (to sth) ➤ LEAVE yourself (wide) open (to sth)

LEAF

turn over a new leaf to start behaving better ▶ *Andy says he's turned over a new leaf, and that he's going to be an ideal husband from now on.*

LEAGUE

be in league with sb to be helping someone in a harmful or illegal plan ▶ *They discovered that the train drivers were in league with the robbers.*

be (way) out of your league
1 to be trying to do something that is too difficult for you ▶ *I'm good at chess, but I was out of my league playing our regional champion.*
2 to be too attractive, expensive etc for you ▶ *"Jane's lovely." "Yes, but she's way out of your league!"*

LEAN

lean over backwards ➤ BEND over backwards

LEAP

a leap in the dark an important decision you make, not knowing what the result will be ▶ *Rusty took a leap in the dark and accepted the job in New York.*

LEAPS

by leaps and bounds very quickly ▶ *Our company is expanding by leaps and bounds.*

LEASE

a new lease of life *also* **a new lease on life** a new basis for being active and happy again ▶ *I was hoping that a new job would give me a new lease of* *life.* ▶ *Since I stopped drinking I have a new lease on life.*

LEASH

be straining at the leash to be eager to start doing something ▶ *The training went well, and they're all straining at the leash.*

LEAST

to say the least something is even more extreme than you are saying it is ▶ *Their complaints about our service are unkind, to say the least.*

LEAVE

leave sb high and dry to leave someone in a difficult situation without any help ▶ *I'll stay until Monday – I don't want to leave you high and dry.*

leave a lot to be desired also **leave much to be desired** to be worse than it should be ▶ *I'm afraid my cooking often leaves a lot to be desired.*

leave well (enough) alone to not do anything to change a situation because you do not want to make it worse than it was ▶ *She's tired of your interfering – why can't you leave well alone?*

sth leaves you cold something does not interest or excite you at all ▶ *The idea of working in a big organization leaves me cold.*

leave yourself (wide) open (to sth) also **lay yourself (wide) open (to sth)** to do things that make it likely that something bad will happen to you ▶ *We've left ourselves open to investigation by the tax inspectors.* ▶ *Matt's laid himself wide open to criticism in the press.*

LEG

break a leg! good luck! (especially

before a stage performance) ▶ *"I've never been on stage before." "You'll be fine – break a leg!"*

sb can talk the hind leg off a donkey someone talks too much ▶ *Donald is a bit boring, and he can talk the hind leg off a donkey.*

not have (got) a leg to stand on to have nothing to support your opinion, legal position etc ▶ *If they take John to court, he won't have a leg to stand on.*

leg it to run very quickly ▶ *Just grab the money and leg it before she changes her mind.*

a leg up help given to a person or group ▶ *The Arts Centre is getting a financial leg up from the council this year.*

be pulling sb's leg to tell someone something that is not true, as a joke ▶ *Has Susan forgotten, or is she pulling my leg?*

LEGS

have legs (of an idea or plan) to be a good one that is likely to succeed ▶ *I like the idea of running summer courses; I think it has legs.*

be on her/its etc last legs to be old and weak ▶ *You don't have to do everything for me – I'm not on my last legs yet.* ▶ *This computer's certainly on its last legs.*

LENGTH

keep sb/sth at arm's length also **remain at arm's length from sb** to

L

avoid being closely involved with someone or something ▶ *The family found it impossible to keep reporters at arm's length.*

LENGTHS

go to great lengths to do sth also **go to considerable lengths to do sth** to do a lot in order to achieve something ▶ *He will go to great lengths just to find a free parking space.*

LEOPARD

a leopard can't/doesn't change its spots someone cannot or does not easily change their bad qualities ▶ *"He's had a huge fight with his latest girlfriend too." "I guess a leopard doesn't change its spots."*

LET

let fly
1 to try and get a goal, point etc ▶ *He headed towards the goal and let fly a superb shot.*
2 to criticize angrily ▶ *In her autobiography, she lets fly against Hollywood and the film industry.*

let sb have it to shout at someone because you are angry with them ▶ *I saw her hitting that little boy and I just let her have it.*

let it all hang out to relax and do what you feel like without worrying what everyone else thinks ▶ *This is Carnival – a time when normally sober and hard-working citizens let it all hang out.*

be let off lightly also **get off lightly** to

be punished less severely than expected or deserved ▶ *Martin's been let off lightly – he got a fine instead of a prison sentence.* ▶ *Don't think you're going to get off lightly this time.*

let rip
1 to criticize strongly ▶ *TV audiences love a fight, especially when well-known people let rip at each other.*
2 to do something with energy and enthusiasm ▶ *The orchestra let rip with a jazzed up version of the William Tell overture.*

let sth slide also **let sth ride** to ignore something or let it become worse ▶ *She was rude to me again today, but I just let it slide.* ▶ *After his divorce he let things slide and got into debt.*

let (it) slip (that) to say something that is supposed to be a secret ▶ *The secretary let slip plans for an emergency meeting.* ▶ *Linda let it slip that she had a few famous clients who were in serious legal trouble.*

LETTER

the letter of the law the exact words of a law or agreement, rather than the general meaning ▶ *Sticking to the letter of the law, the border guard would not accept a passport with a torn cover.*

to the letter exactly (according to rules or instructions) ▶ *Security staff had to obey these rules to the letter.*

LEVEL

be on the level to be honest, legal, or true ▶ *She seemed to be on the level, but maybe she was just a good actress.*

LICENCE

a licence to print money an unfair chance to make a lot of money very

L

easily ▶ *People see music publishing as a licence to print money, but it can be a risky business.*

LICKED
have (got) sth licked to have succeeded in dealing with something ▶ *We've got the problem licked and we should get the orders out by tomorrow.*

LID
keep a lid on to control something or keep it secret ▶ *He keeps a tight lid on his private life, and rarely speaks to the press.*

take the lid off sth also **blow the lid off sth** to let people know the truth about a situation ▶ *He was the person who took the lid off the financial scandal.* ▶ *It took a year for the press to blow the lid off the relationship.*

LIE
give the lie to to prove that something is not true ▶ *His exam results give the lie to his teachers' gloomy predictions.*

lie in wait (for)
1 to hide in a place and wait for someone so that you can attack them ▶ *The four men were lying in wait for Collins behind the shed.*
2 to be about to happen to someone ▶ *When you're testing a new product, you have no idea what challenges are lying in wait for you.*

live a lie to live in a way that makes you feel dishonest and unhappy with yourself ▶ *Before you start that secret affair, think whether you'll be able to live a lie every day.*

a white lie a small lie that you tell because you do not want to upset someone ▶ *She asked if I liked her*

new boyfriend – well, I just told her a little white lie and said yes.

LIFE
you can't do sth to save your life you have never been able to do something ▶ *No, I'm not joining the choir – I can't read music to save my life.*

I can't for the life of me I can't in any way ▶ *I can't for the life of me understand what he sees in her.*

a charmed life a life in which someone has a lot of good luck ▶ *He's led a charmed life, having survived a train crash and a car accident without a scratch.*

for dear life with all your strength and attention ▶ *The cat was hanging onto a branch of the tree for dear life.*

get a life! you are boring or lazy! ▶ *"Have you tried these computer games?" "Oh, get a life!"*

(as) large as life really there ▶ *I went to the door, and there was John, as large as life.*

larger than life more exciting or interesting than ordinary people ▶ *Singers and stage performers are always a little larger than life.* **larger-than-life** ADJ ▶ *The chef is a larger-than-life character who is genuinely passionate about his job.*

the life (and soul) of the party someone who is the centre of attention in social situations ▶ *He really enjoys being the life and soul of the party.*

L

life in the fast lane an exciting way of living that involves dangerous and expensive activities ▸ *Tired of living life in the fast lane, several older celebrities have retired to quiet houses in the country.*

life's too short I don't want to waste time on boring or unimportant things ▸ *Life's too short to worry about the colour of your shoes and handbag!*

live the life of Riley also **lead the life of Riley** to have a very comfortable, easy life without having to work hard or worry about money ▸ *I was living the life of Riley until my business partner died.*

not on your life! definitely not ▸ *I'm not going to that doctor – not on your life!*

put your life in sb's hands to cause someone to be responsible for what happens to you ▸ *It's scary putting your life in the hands of a young surgeon.* **sb's life is in your hands** ▸ *There was a moment during the fire when the child's life was in my hands.*

take your life in your (own) hands to do something very dangerous ▸ *If you drive fast on these icy roads, you're taking your life in your hands.*

LIGHT

bring sth to light to make something known ▸ *Her research brings to light many new facts about dinosaurs.*

come to light ▸ *Details of the theft came to light after a second girl came forward to give evidence.*

give sb/sth the green light to give someone permission to do something ▸ *A revolutionary approach to cancer research was given the green light this week.* **get the green light** ▸ *More funding for education*

has finally got the green light.

sb hides his/her light under a bushel someone does not show their abilities and skills to other people ▸ *Harry was never tempted to hide his light under a bushel.*

in the cold light of day when you are calm and sensible ▸ *In the cold light of day, their argument seemed ridiculous.*

a leading light an important person ▸ *Morris is one of the leading lights of our drama group.*

the light at the end of the tunnel hope for the future, after a long and difficult period ▸ *The war may have ended, but we won't see the light at the end of the tunnel for many months to come.*

the light of sb's life the person someone loves most ▸ *Iris was his only child and the light of his life.*

make light of sth to treat something important and serious as unimportant or funny ▸ *I don't want to make light of your problems, but I do have a train to catch.*

be out like a light to fall into a deep sleep very quickly ▸ *I was out like a light at 9.30.*

see sb/sth in a ____ light also **view sb/sth in a ____ light** to understand someone or something in a particular way ▸ *I hope the interviewers will see my two years' travelling in a positive light.*

see the light to understand or realize something suddenly ▸ *Small business owners are hoping the government will see the light and give them some concessions.*

see the light of day to become known or seen ▸ *These documents haven't seen the light of day for 30 years.*

shed (new) light on sth also **throw (new) light on sth** to provide new information about something ▶ *Max has shed new light on the events leading up to the fire.*

show sb/sth in a _____ light to make someone or something seem to have more of a particular quality ▶ *The book shows Beethoven in a new and interesting light.*

LIGHTNING

lightning never strikes twice someone is not likely to have the same kind of luck twice ▶ *On the theory that lightning never strikes twice, I parked my new car in the street where the old one had been stolen.*

LIGHTS

the bright lights the excitement and activity in a big city ▶ *At 18, Ned left the village for the bright lights of Liverpool.*

LIKE

if sb doesn't like it he/she can lump it also **like it or lump it** it doesn't matter whether someone likes a situation or not ▶ *There's pizza for dinner, and if you don't like it you can lump it.* ▶ *Like it or lump it, we're stuck with organizing a big family Christmas.*

LIKES

the likes of me/him etc people like me, him etc ▶ *She'd never be attracted to the likes of Matthew.*

LILY

gild the lily to spoil something by adding too much decoration or making it too complicated ▶ *Far from gilding the lily, the candles provided a welcoming atmosphere.*

LIMB

go out on a limb to be the only person who takes a risk ▶ *Any airline that goes out on a limb by raising fares will risk losing business.*

tear sb limb from limb to attack someone in a violent way ▶ *I thought the dogs were going to tear me limb from limb.*

LIMITS

overstep the limits ➤ see overstep the MARK

LINE

all along the line also **right down the line** at all times ▶ *We owe our success to the people who've supported us all along the line.*

the bottom line the basic, most important part of a situation ▶ *The bottom line is that we have to act now to prevent the situation from getting any worse.*

> This idiom comes from business accounts in which the bottom line is the final line that shows how much profit a company has made or how much money was lost.

bring sth into line (with) to make something fit with another system or set of rules ▶ *These changes will bring*

L

the safety standards into line with the rest of Europe.

cross the line also **step over the line** to become offensive or extreme ▶ *When does artistic expression cross the line into obscenity?* ▶ *If their behaviour steps over the line between peaceful protest and riots, the police will take action.*

down the line also **down the road** in the future ▶ *I'd like to teach abroad a few years down the line.* ▶ *She's going to be sorry a couple of months down the road.*

draw a line under sth to try to forget about a bad situation, so that you can start again ▶ *Vicky and I agreed to draw a line under our disagreements and make a fresh start.*

draw the line at to refuse to do something because you think it is wrong or unpleasant ▶ *She's been in lots of romantic movies, but she draws the line at anything really sexy.*

drop sb a line to write a short letter to someone ▶ *I thought I'd drop you a line to see how you are.*

fall into line to change or behave so as to obey the rules or laws of a company, organization etc ▶ *An official said that aid would be cut off if the country did not fall into line with others that were receiving funds.*

feed sb a line also **spin sb a line** to tell someone something that is not true in order to get an advantage ▶ *Brian feeds all the girls the same line – he says he's terribly shy.* ▶ *The salespeople tend to spin you a line about product reliability.*

a fine line between a slight difference between two things, one of which is bad ▶ *There's a fine line between aiding suicide and making drugs*

available to relieve the pain. ▶ *As a manager, he trod a fine line between firmness and force.*

in the front line
1 involved in or responsible for the latest developments in something ▶ *The laboratory is in the front line of medical research.*
2 doing a dangerous job, dealing with big problems ▶ *As a cop, you are in the front line every day – you have to be prepared for that.* **front-line** ADJ ▶ *The crisis centre is a front-line service providing vital support to the community.*

be in the line of fire ▶ be in the FIRING LINE

lay it on the line to tell someone the truth about what they have to do in a very direct way ▶ *Let me lay it on the line for you. If we don't get this product on the market now, someone else will.*

the line of least resistance a course of action that will cause fewest problems for you and will result in the least opposition from other people ▶ *Mum always took the line of least resistance, which resulted in Dad becoming a bit of a tyrant.*

be (way) out of line to be behaving badly, or in a way that is not acceptable ▶ *He was way out of line for yelling at you like that.*

be out of line with sth not to match or work in the same way as something else ▶ *Our estimate of the funds needed was out of line with the official one.*

be out of the line of fire ▶ be out of the FIRING LINE

put sth on the line also **lay sth on the line** to risk losing something very important to you ▶ *Racing drivers are* putting their lives on the line every time they compete. ▶ *You shouldn't have to lay your neck on the line for your rights.*

sign on the dotted line  to make a legal promise that you have to keep ▶ *Make sure you consult a lawyer before signing on the dotted line.*

step out of line to do something that is not allowed ▶ *Dad gives us a hard time if we step out of line.*

take a hard line to be determined to make people behave in the way that you want ▶ *He has taken a hard line with teachers' contracts.* **hard-line** ADJ ▶ *Hard-line elements in the government have criticized the proposal.* **hard-liner** N ▶ *There are few hard-liners left in the present government.* **take a soft line** ▶ *So far police have been taking a soft line on peaceful demonstrations.*

toe the line to say or do what someone in authority expects you to ▶ *Formerly, newspaper editors had to toe the line or risk being beaten up by the secret police.*

LINES

along the same lines also **on the same lines** or **along these lines** similar to, or done in a similar way to, what you are talking about ▶ *Our group is organized on the same lines as many consumers' associations in America.* ▶ *Here's a kitchen we designed last year – I could do you something along these lines.*

on the right lines working towards the right result ▶ *If we're on the right lines and Dora did take the money, we must tell the police.* **on the wrong lines** ▶ *No, she's never been here – you're on the wrong lines there.*

read between the lines to understand something that is only suggested (in something spoken or written) ▶ *Chrissie assured me that she was happy, but reading between the lines I could see that something was bothering her.* ▶ *Most company literature requires skill at reading between the lines.*

LINK

the weak link (in the chain) the one person or thing in a group that does not work or perform as well as the others ▶ *Our sales figures are down, and I'm afraid it's Trevor who is the weak link.*

A link is one of the rings in a chain.

LION

brave the lion in his den also **beard the lion in his den** to go and see someone who has power over you ▶ *I'm seeing Bob about my pay rise now – time to brave the lion in his den.*

LIP

button your lip also **zip your lip** to stop yourself from saying something unpleasant, or telling a secret ▶ *It's not worth arguing with her, just button your lip.*

pay lip service to to say that you like an idea without doing anything to support it ▶ *The store pays lip service to caring for the environment and then insists on wrapping everything in layers of plastic.*

L

stiff upper lip strict control over showing your feelings although you are very upset ▶ *Dad kept a stiff upper lip at the funeral but burst into tears when he got home.*

LIPS

sb is licking his/her lips also *sb is licking his/her chops* someone is very excited about something that is going to happen ▶ *The journalist was licking her lips at the thought of the exclusive interview.*

sth is on everyone's lips something is being talked about a lot ▶ *I think the same question is on everyone's lips.*

sb's lips are sealed someone won't tell (a secret) ▶ *I asked her who she was seeing, but her lips are sealed.*

read my lips believe me! ▶ *Read my lips, Nico. I do not want to go out with you.*

LITMUS TEST

a litmus test something that clearly shows what someone or something is like ▶ *This survey of local people is an interesting litmus test of how the parties are doing a year after the election.*

LIVE

sb can live with sth someone can accept an unpleasant situation ▶ *If you publish this you'll ruin a man's life – can you live with that?*

sb lives and breathes sth someone loves being involved in a particular

activity very much ▶ *My daughter lives and breathes horses.*

(you) live and learn I have just learnt something new ▶ *I didn't realize there was a second phone line in the office – well, you live and learn.*

live it up to do exciting or expensive things that you enjoy ▶ *The landlord's living it up somewhere in the Mediterranean.*

LOCK

lock, stock, and barrel all or every part of something ▶ *When his wife left, he moved back to his Mum lock, stock, and barrel.*

LOG

as easy as falling off a log very easy ▶ *He says using the Internet is as easy as falling off a log.*

sleep like a log also *sleep like a baby* to sleep very well ▶ *I slept like a log despite the noise outside.*

LOGGERHEADS

be at loggerheads (with sb) to disagree or quarrel ▶ *The sisters have been at loggerheads for years.* ▶ *Jake's at loggerheads with him about some family money.*

LOINS

gird (up) your loins to get ready to do something difficult ▶ *The players were girding their loins for the most important match of the season.*

LONG

be long on ___ but short on ___ also *be short on ___ but long on ___* to have too much of one quality and not enough of another one ▶ *His arguments were dismissed as long on emotion and short on facts.*

the long and the short of it is *also* ***that's the long and short of it*** the basic facts about a situation are ▶ *The long and short of it is, you failed the test.* ▶ *She's going into hospital, they'll do tests today and we'll have the results by Friday – that's really the long and short of it.*

LOOK

give sb a dirty look to look at someone in an angry or disapproving way ▶ *I said that Simon would be happy to cook dinner, and he gave me a dirty look for not asking him first.*

look before you leap to think about the results of your actions before doing something ▶ *It sounds like the opportunity of a lifetime, but remember to look before you leap.*

take a long, hard look to think very hard about what is wrong with something ▶ *After last year's appalling figures, the company is taking a long, hard look at itself.*

LOOSE

on the loose free; not prevented from doing what you want ▶ *Zookeepers say there's a lion on the loose.* ▶ *I could hardly wait for my parents to leave – I was on the loose in London at last!*

LORD

lord it over sb to act in a way that shows how important or powerful you think you are ▶ *Now she's been promoted, she likes to lord it over everyone.*

LOSE

lose it

1 to lose control of your behaviour or temper ▶ *I went into the interview and lost it completely – they must think I'm an idiot.* ▶ *He tends to lose it when he's had a few drinks.*

2 to stop being good at a job or activity ▶ *She used to be a good manager, but she's lost it in the last few months.*

LOSS

be at a loss (to do sth) *also* ***be at a loss for words*** not to know what to do or say in a difficult situation ▶ *I'm at a loss to understand why she left in such a hurry.* ▶ *For once my mother seemed at a loss for words.*

be a dead loss to be completely useless ▶ *I gave their boy a job, but he was a dead loss.*

LOSSES

cut your losses to stop doing something that is costing you money or emotional energy ▶ *House prices were going down, so we cut our losses and sold our home for £5000 less than we paid for it.* ▶ *Nicky's had enough heartbreak with him; she should cut her losses and look for someone new.*

LOST

get lost go away ▶ *One of those salesmen came to the door and I told him to get lost.*

LOT

a fat lot of good *also* ***a fat lot of help*** not helpful or useful in any way ▶ *"I'm going to stop paying my rent as a protest." "A fat lot of good that'll do you – he'll throw you out."* ▶ *There's a post office in the town, but that's a fat lot of help if you don't drive.*

L

sb/sth has a lot to answer for someone or something is partly responsible for the way that a person or group of people thinks or behaves ▶ *Early movies have a lot to answer for because they disguised the true nature of marriage.*

throw in your lot with sb to join or support someone ▶ *Atkins was an independent firm but in 2000 they threw in their lot with CB Chemicals.*

LOVE

all's fair in love and war people do not always keep to the rules in some situations involving competition ▶ *"I'm going out with Kitty's boyfriend tonight!" "Well, all's fair in love and war, I suppose."* ▶ *All's fair in love and war, and in the music business you do whatever you have to to promote a record.*

not... for love nor money also **not for love or money** not at all ▶ *I can't get that spare part for love nor money.*

there is no love lost (between) (of two people or groups) they dislike each other ▶ *There's no love lost between the students and the local residents, who complain about noisy parties and drunken behaviour.*

LOWDOWN

the lowdown (on sb/sth) the most important and useful facts about someone or something ▶ *We're meeting someone who has the lowdown on the reorganization plans.*

LUCK

bad luck also **hard luck** I'm sorry you're having problems ▶ *"I've got to work until seven tonight." "Oh, bad luck."*

beginner's luck unusually good luck you have when you do something for t

he first time ▶ *"I won £100 on the first race!" "Beginner's luck – it won't happen again!"*

chance your luck ➤ chance your ARM

be down on your luck to be having bad luck or problems, usually for a long time ▶ *I heard you were down on your luck, and I wondered if this job might suit you.*

the luck of the devil also **the luck of the Irish** good luck ▶ *He's got the luck of the devil, walking away from the crash without a scratch.* ▶ *Another win for O'Neill – he calls it the luck of the Irish.*

it's the luck of the draw the result of something depends on chance ▶ *You'll probably pass your test, but it's the luck of the draw – some of the examiners are stricter than others.*

no such luck no, not at all ▶ *I thought that he might offer me something to drink, but no such luck.*

push your luck also **be pushing it** to risk doing or asking for something too much or too often ▶ *"I'm going to ask for a day off as well as a bonus." "Don't push your luck."* ▶ *We've got room for 15 students – 20 would be pushing it.*

tough luck I do not care about that problem ▶ *If he doesn't like what's for dinner, it's tough luck.*

worse luck I do not like the situation I am in ▶ *"Are you coming tonight?" "No, I can't. I've got to work, worse luck."*

LUMP

a lump in your throat the feeling that you cannot speak because you want to cry ▶ *Every time I watch that film I get a lump in my throat.*

LUNCH

be out to lunch to be slightly crazy ▶ *I tried having a conversation with him, but he's really out to lunch, isn't he?*

there is no (such thing as a) free lunch you cannot get anything without working for it or paying for it ▶ *We must face the fact that there is no free lunch – there is a tax bill for every improvement in public transport.*

LURCH

leave sb in the lurch to leave someone without any help or support ▶ *She left her students in the lurch just before the exams began.*

L

Mm

MAJORITY

the silent majority the large number of people in society who do not make their political opinions known publicly ▶ *It's well known that the silent majority are in favour of peace.*

MAKE

sth can make or break sb/sth also ***sth is make or break (for sb)*** something is important enough to make a person or thing succeed or fail ▶ *A review by our theatre critic can make or break a show.* ▶ *These negotiations are extremely important; it's make or break for everyone involved.* **make-or-break** ADJ ▶ *This is a make-or-break game for the Lions.*

be made (for life) to be so rich that you will never have to work again ▶ *The business is going well – we're not made for life, but we're getting there.*

make good to become rich and successful after being poor and unknown in your early life ▶ *He was a poor farm boy who made good.*

make it big to become very successful and famous ▶ *She's always had dreams of making it big as a singer.*

be on the make to be always trying to get money or advantages for yourself ▶ *The financial world has always attracted young men on the make.*

MAKINGS

have the makings of sth to have the ability or qualities needed to become a particular kind of person or thing ▶ *The story has all the makings of a major political scandal.*

MAN

be as ___ as the next man/woman also ***do sth as ___ as the next man/woman*** to have as much of a quality as anyone else, or to be able to do something as well as anyone else ▶ *I'm as adventurous as the next man, but I'm not attracted to white-water rafting.* ▶ *Don't worry about me, I can take rejection as well as the next woman.*

every man for himself a situation in which people look after themselves and do not help each other ▶ *We just jumped into the water, and it was every man for himself.*

the grand old man of sth a man who has been involved in a particular activity or profession and is greatly respected by people ▶ *He is fondly regarded as the grand old man of science fiction.*

if you want…, sb is your man/woman also ***if you want…, sb is the man/woman*** a particular man or woman is the best person to help someone or to do a particular job for them ▶ *If you want a great hairstyle at a reasonable price, Jill's your woman!*

sb is a marked man someone is in danger because someone else wants to harm or defeat him ▶ *After the scandal, he was a marked man, and left within a year.*

a man's gotta do what a man's gotta do also ***you gotta do what you gotta do*** I have to do something although I do not want to ▶ *I hate organizing office parties, but sometimes a man's gotta do what a man's gotta do.*

M

sb's right-hand man/woman the person who works most closely with someone to help and support them ▶ *The mayor's former right-hand woman is now campaigning against him.*

to a man including every one of the group you are talking about ▶ *The islanders, patriotic to a man, are prepared to fight for their independence.*

you can't keep a good man/woman down if someone is determined and good at what they do, they will succeed in spite of difficulties ▶ *You shouldn't be surprised at how well she's doing; you can't keep a good woman down, you know.*

be your own man/woman someone does what they want, without being influenced or controlled by other people ▶ *In spite of pressure on him to conform, he was very much his own man.*

MANNER

do sth as (if) to the manner born to do something easily and naturally, although it is an unusual and unfamiliar thing for a person to do ▶ *It was the first time she'd hosted a big party, yet she accomplished it as if to the manner born.*

MAP

put sb/sth on the map to make a place, person, or thing well-known ▶ *The excellence of the university is helping to put this town on the map.*

wipe sth off the map to destroy a place or a community completely ▶ *The earthquake wiped entire villages off the map.*

MARBLES

lose your marbles to start behaving in a crazy way ▶ *I have no idea why he started to tell these fantastic lies – he must have lost his marbles.*

'Marbles' is a game that children play, using small, coloured glass balls.

MARCH

steal a march on sb to get an advantage over someone by doing something before they do it, or before they expect you to do it ▶ *We stole a march on the rest of the industry by modernizing at the right time.*

MARK

a black mark (against sb) something that makes people dislike or disapprove of someone ▶ *I'm sure his fierce temper is a black mark against him.*

be close to the mark also **be near the mark** to be mostly true, or almost exact ▶ *My job title is administrator, but office psychologist would be closer to the mark.*

hit the mark
1 (of a statement) to be true and exact ▶ *He described her as a poor little rich girl, which hits the mark precisely.*

M

2 to be successful in getting the effect that you want ▶ *Her stage performance as a fussy mother really hits the mark.* **miss the mark** ▶ *His songs still miss the mark for most people because of his gloomy voice.*

A mark is what you aim at when you practise shooting a gun.

leave your mark (on sb/sth) to have an important effect (on something or someone) for a long time ▶ *Years of poverty have left their mark on the family.*

make your mark (in/on) also **make a mark (in/on)** to do something new, special, or successful that makes people notice you ▶ *Every journalist wants to make their mark and be remembered.*

be (way) off the mark not to be correct or true ▶ *Her answers to most of the questions were way off the mark.*

overstep the mark also **overstep the limits** to offend people by doing or saying things that you should not do or say ▶ *He's overstepped the mark again, speaking to the press about our private lives.*

be quick off the mark to be good at understanding a situation quickly and taking action ▶ *You have to be quick off the mark to find a genuine bargain.* **be slow off the mark** ▶ *I answered the question correctly, but I was too slow off the mark.*

The mark is the place where runners begin a race.

be wide of the mark to be not very exact or true ▶ *The election result showed that all the opinion polls had been wide of the mark.*

MARKET

corner the market (in sth) to gain control of the whole supply (of something) ▶ *There isn't another bike shop in this town, so we've managed to corner the market.*

be in the market (for sth) to be interested in buying (something) ▶ *The armchair's beautiful, but I'm not really in the market for an antique.*

MASK

sb's mask slips someone who is hiding their real feelings shows them for a moment ▶ *"Really, is it worth that much?" she said, her mask of polite interest slipping for a moment.*

MASTER

be a past master (at sth) to be very good (at something) ▶ *He's a past master at getting everyone else to do the work.*

MATCH

meet your match to have difficulty in a competition, sport etc because your new opponent is as strong, clever, or skilful as you are ▶ *After dazzling performances in the early stages of the tournament, she met her match in the final.*

the whole shooting match everything ▶ *I was thinking of buying the farmhouse without the land, but they want to sell the whole shooting match.*

MATTER

as a matter of course as part of what is usually done ▶ *A large company should supply their customers with this information as a matter of course.*

be no laughing matter also **not be a laughing matter** (of a situation) to be serious ▶ *News of the cancellation is*

M

no laughing matter for the hundreds of fans who bought tickets for the concert.

MCCOY

the real McCoy real, and not a copy ▶ *This watch isn't a fake, it's the real McCoy.*

MEAL

make a meal (out) of sth to spend too much time, effort, or emotion doing something ▶ *OK, he's crashed into my new car, but it can be fixed – no need to make a meal out of it.*

a meal ticket a person or thing that someone uses to get money ▶ *Rich girls are often worried that they are being used as a meal ticket by their boyfriends.*

a square meal a good meal that fills your stomach ▶ *You'll feel better once you've got a good square meal inside you.*

MEANING

sb doesn't know the meaning of (the word) ___ someone has never experienced a particular emotion or situation, or has deliberately ignored it ▶ *He appears not to know the meaning of the word work.*

MEANS

by all means yes; of course ▶ *If you think he'd be interested in the talk, by all means bring him along.*

by no means also **not... by any means** not in any way ▶ *He isn't a bad cook by any means, but some of his dishes are too spicy for me.*

sth is a means to an end something is only done or used in order to obtain something else ▶ *For me, money is just a means to an end – all I want is a reasonably comfortable life.*

MEASURE

for good measure to add to what has already been done or used ▶ *The new CD will feature his band with a few guest artists thrown in for good measure.*

get the measure of also **take the measure of** to discover what someone or something is like ▶ *It's only taken a day for the students to get the measure of the new teacher, and start behaving badly.*

MEAT

sb is dead meat someone is going to be in trouble ▶ *Touch that TV and you're dead meat!*

one man's meat is another man's poison something that one person likes very much may be greatly disliked by another person ▶ *When it comes to jobs, one man's meat is very often another man's poison.*

MEDICINE

a dose of your own medicine also **a taste of your own medicine** bad treatment that is like the treatment you give someone else ▶ *Unhealthy doctors got a dose of their own medicine when they were told to eat less and exercise more.* ▶ *Give him a taste of his own medicine – refuse to negotiate with him.*

MEDIUM

a/the happy medium a way of doing something that is somewhere between two possible choices ▶ *Can you find a happy medium between being strict*

M

with your children and letting them do anything they like?

MEET

meet sb halfway (of one of two people or groups) to agree to do something the other wants ▶ *I don't like the terms he's proposing, but I'm prepared to meet him halfway to get the job.*

MEMORY

have a memory like a sieve to keep forgetting things ▶ *I forgot you were coming this morning – I've got a memory like a sieve these days.*

take a trip down memory lane *also* **take a stroll down memory lane** to spend some time remembering your past ▶ *Take a trip down memory lane at the college reunion on August 14th.*

MEN

separate the men from the boys *also* **sort out the men from the boys** to show clearly which people have the

ability to do something and which do not ▶ *We all have the same training – it's how you play on the day that separates the men from the boys.*

MEND

be on the mend to be getting better ▶ *He's had flu, but he's on the mend now.*

MESSAGE

get the message to understand and accept what someone is telling or asking you ▶ *I've told her over and over again that she has to change her attitude, but she doesn't get the message.*

METHOD

there's method in sb's madness even though someone is behaving strangely, there is a sensible reason for what they are doing ▶ *She's trying to make me jealous, that's all. There's method in her madness.*

METTLE

put/keep you on your mettle to make or keep you determined to do your best ▶ *The first candidate was smiling as she came out of the interview, which put me on my mettle.*

be on your mettle ▶ *We were on our mettle, determined not to lose a point.*

MIDAS

the Midas touch the ability to earn money very easily ▶ *He seems to have had the Midas touch since he first started investing.*

> This idiom comes from the old story of King Midas who had the ability to turn anything he touched into gold.

MIDDLE

(out) in the middle of nowhere far away from any towns, houses, people etc ▶ *My car broke down in the middle of nowhere, and it took hours to get help.*

MIDNIGHT

burn the midnight oil to work or study until very late at night ▶ *I was burning the midnight oil last night, doing some last-minute revision.*

M

MILE

go that extra mile also **go the extra mile** to make a special effort or do more than you have been asked to do, in order to achieve something ▶ *Our company goes that extra mile and provides a free helpline for our customers.*

sb would run a mile someone is very unwilling to do something or be involved in a situation ▶ *He'd run a mile if I suggested bringing Mum to live with us.*

MILK

it's no use crying over spilt milk you should not worry about something bad that has already happened ▶ *You've wrecked the computer, but it's no use crying over spilt milk. At least it was insured.*

MILL

go through the mill to have a long, unpleasant, and difficult experience ▶ *You are in the right, but is it worth going through the mill of a long court case?* **put sb through the mill** ▶ *They didn't want to put their children through the mill of competitive exams.*

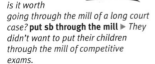

MILLSTONE

a millstone around your neck a problem that is stopping you from succeeding or progressing ▶ *That big old house has been a millstone around his neck for years.*

MINCEMEAT

make mincemeat (out) of sb to defeat someone easily in an argument, competition etc ▶ *She's no good as a witness – a lawyer would make mincemeat of her.*

MIND

all in the mind not real; existing only in your imagination ▶ *She was tired of the doctor telling her that her pain was all in the mind.*

blow your mind (of an experience) to be very impressive, unusual, or shocking ▶ *The new sound and light show would blow your mind.* **mind-blowing** ADJ ▶ *I saw some mind-blowing photographs of the moon.*

bored out of your mind also **bored out of your skull** extremely bored ▶ *After two hours of speeches I was bored out of my mind.*

sth crosses your mind you think about (doing) something suddenly, or for a short time ▶ *It crossed my mind that you should have a copy of this report.* ▶ *Cleaning the bath? It never crosses his mind!*

give sb a piece of your mind to tell someone how angry you are with them and why ▶ *If I see that rude woman again, I'm going to give her a piece of my mind.*

go out of your mind to become so confused, worried, frightened etc that you feel you are going crazy ▶ *He's ill in hospital, and his parents are going out of their minds with worry.*

sb has a mind of his/her own someone is capable of doing what they want to do, not what they are told to ▶ *I don't need your advice, thanks, I've got a mind of my own.*

M

have a good mind to do sth to be considering doing something because you are angry, especially when you probably will not do it ▶ *I've got a good mind to phone your mother and tell her just what you've been doing.*

have half a mind to do sth to want to do something which might be silly or wrong ▶ *He had half a mind to leave work early, but he knew his boss would find out.*

have a one-track mind to think or talk about only one subject most of the time ▶ *She's got a one-track mind – all I ever hear about is her different boyfriends.*

have an open mind (about) *also* **keep an open mind (about)** to be willing to listen to other people's opinions and change your ideas if you agree ▶ *I'm keeping an open mind until I've heard all the evidence.* **open-minded** ADJ ▶ *They have always been open-minded about politics.*

have sth on your mind to keep thinking about something or worrying about it ▶ *I'm sorry I forgot to call, I've had a lot on my mind lately.* **be on your mind** ▶ *He's been on my mind all week – do you think I'm in love?*

if/when you put your mind to it if or when you decide to make an effort ▶ *He could do really well in maths if he put his mind to it.*

know your own mind to be sure of what your opinions are, and what you want to do ▶ *When I was younger I didn't really know my own mind, so I just did what other people did.*

the mind boggles an idea, action, or event is so surprising that it is difficult to imagine ▶ *"Rachel's mum is writing a romantic novel." "The mind boggles."* **mind-boggling** ADJ ▶ *The*

magazine has made a mind-boggling £150 million this year.

mind over matter you can do something that seems very difficult, or even impossible, if you really want to ▶ *He's convinced it's just mind over matter, and you can stop yourself getting ill.*

nobody in his/her right mind would do sth *also* **no___in his/her right mind** it would be very stupid or unreasonable to do something ▶ *Nobody in their right mind would choose to live in that old cottage.* ▶ *No woman in her right mind would marry him.*

be of one mind *also* **be of the same mind** to have the same opinion about a particular situation or want the same things from it ▶ *I think we're all of one mind that protecting our old buildings is our top priority.* ▶ *I'm of the same mind as you.*

be out of your mind *also* **be out of your head etc** to be crazy, or affected by drugs or alcohol ▶ *Are you out of your mind? We can't ask a complete stranger to give us beds for the night.* ▶ *He slipped and fell when he was totally out of his head.*

read sb's mind to know what someone is thinking ▶ *He poured her a drink. "Thanks! You must have read my mind," she said.* **mind-reader** N ▶ *I'm not a mind-reader – you need to tell me how you feel.*

it/sth slipped your mind you temporarily forgot something you were supposed to do ▶ *I'm so sorry I forgot to phone you – it just slipped my mind.*

speak your mind to say exactly what you think, without feeling embarrassed or shy ▶ *She's not* afraid to speak her mind on any subject.

be a weight off your mind *also* **be a load off your mind** to no longer be a reason to worry ▶ *It's a great weight off our minds to know that she's going to recover completely.*

MINDS

be in two minds (about) to be unable to decide what to do, or what you think about something ▶ *I was in two minds about whether to come to this party, but I'm glad I did.*

MINE

be a mine of information to be able to provide a lot of information ▶ *This is your tour guide, Sheila, who's a mine of information on the history of the town.* ▶ *The text is a mine of information for anyone researching the art of this region.*

MINUTE

there's one born every minute someone is so stupid that they believe something or someone ▶ *"He's offering a fantastic deal on that car." "You believe that? Well, there's one born every minute!"*

MISERY

put sb out of their misery
1 to tell someone something after you have refused to for some time ▶ *Come on, put us out of our misery – did you pass the test?*
2 to kill an animal or person because they are suffering ▶ *I turned away as she put the mouse out of its misery.*

MISS

a miss is as good as a mile if you have failed, it does not matter whether you failed by a lot or by a little ▶ *The letter said I did very well in the* interview, but a miss is as good as a mile, if you ask me.

MOMENT

the moment of truth a time when you find out whether something will work properly, be successful etc ▶ *This is the moment of truth for the team, their first serious contest after the six regional games.*

MOMENTS

sth has its moments *also* **sb has his/her moments** some parts of an experience or someone's behaviour are surprisingly good or enjoyable, although most of it is not ▶ *Most of my duties were boring, although the job had its moments.* ▶ *"Did she sing well?" "Let's say she had her moments."*

MONEY

easy money money that you do not have to work hard to get ▶ *Modelling seems like easy money to an ambitious teenager.*

for my money in my opinion ▶ *For my money, this hotel is the best in the country.*

have money to burn to have so much money that you do not mind what you spend it on ▶ *Look how much he* *spends on that old car – he must have money to burn.*

be in the money to get a lot of money or make a profit ▶ *Two farmers suddenly found themselves in the money when they sold their old tractor at a vintage car auction.*

M

make/spend money hand over fist to earn or spend a lot of money in a short time ▶ *The theme park is making money hand over fist.*

money talks you can get what you want if you have enough money ▶ *He got ten tickets for the World Cup final which just proves that money talks.*

my money's on sb you think someone will win a competition, be chosen for a job etc ▶ *The standard of the competitors is very high, but my money's on Jane.*

put your money where your mouth is you should take action or spend money in order to make something happen, instead of just saying that you want it to happen ▶ *If the government wants to improve educational standards, it should put its money where its mouth is.*

the smart money

1 people who know a lot about making money ▶ *The smart money in the music business is backing these new bands.*

2 people who are well informed about what will happen in a particular situation ▶ *We don't yet know who is player of the match, but the smart money is on Alex.*

take the money and run to accept what is offered to you before a situation becomes

worse ▶ *Her lawyer advised her to take the money and run before her husband changed his mind.*

throw good money after bad to spend more money trying to improve a situation that has already cost a lot ▶ *Putting yet more money into these factories now would be throwing good money after bad – the whole industry is collapsing.*

throw money at sth to try to solve a problem by spending a lot of money, instead of thinking about what is really needed ▶ *He thinks that you can solve any problem if you throw enough money at it.*

MONTH

month in, month out ➤ DAY in, day out

MONTY

the full monty everything, the whole lot ▶ *For breakfast we had the full monty: eggs, bacon, sausages, tomatoes and mushrooms.*

MOON

ask for the moon to ask for something that is difficult or impossible to get ▶ *Pensioners aren't asking for the moon – they just want enough to live on.*

once in a blue moon very rarely ▶ *My daughter comes round to see me once in a blue moon.*

over the moon very happy about something that has happened ▶ *She was over the moon about the new house.*

promise sb the moon ➤ promise sb the EARTH

MOONS

many moons ago a very long time ago ▶ *When I got my first laser printer, many moons ago, it cost over £3000.*

MORE

the more the merrier I will be happy if other people join me ▶ *"Do you mind*

M

if three more come?" "No – the more the merrier."

MORNING

(the) morning after the night before a morning when someone feels ill because they have stayed up late the night before drinking alcohol ▶ *"You look rough." "Yeah, well, morning after the night before, you know how it is."*

morning, noon, and night all the time ▶ *I can't stand their music playing morning, noon, and night.*

MOTHBALLS

in mothballs not used for a time, although it may be used again later ▶ *After 16 years in mothballs, the observatory has reopened.*

MOTHER

the mother of all ____ the best, worst, biggest, most severe etc thing of its kind ▶ *Last year we experienced the mother of all storms.*

who's 'she', the cat's mother? it is rude to use 'she' about someone who is there, you should use her name ▶ *"Is she staying to lunch?" "Who's 'she', the cat's mother?" "Sorry – Sharon."*

MOTIONS

go through the motions to do something without trying very hard to succeed, or do it well because you have to do it ▶ *She said the police were just going through the motions – they weren't really interested in car thefts.*

MOULD

break the mould to do something in a way that is new, different, and better than usual ▶ *In the nineties, the newspaper broke the mould with a*

refreshing new style and lots of good articles.

> A 'mould' is a container that a liquid such as melted metal is poured into, so that it will form a particular shape when it becomes solid.

in the same mould (as) as good as or very similar to someone or something else of the same type ▶ *He's a great player, in the same mould as his grandfather.*

they broke the mould when they made sb there is no one else as good, fair, nice etc as someone ▶ *She was a great friend to us all – they broke the mould when they made her.*

MOUNTAIN

make a mountain out of a molehill to treat something as if it is very difficult or worse than it actually is

▶ *He's hopeless with computers – he makes a mountain out of a molehill just checking his e-mails.*

the mountain must go to Mohammed also **Mohammed must go to the mountain** if someone will not or cannot come to you, you have to make an effort to see them, even if this is very difficult ▶ *I realized that the mountain must go to Mohammed, so I moved to England to be near my girlfriend.*

M

This idiom is from a story in the Islamic religion. The Prophet Mohammed was trying to prove his power, and asked that Mount Safa come to him. When the mountain did not move, he said this showed that God was good because the mountain would have fallen on many people and killed them. He then went to the mountain to thank God for not sending the mountain to him.

MOUNTAINS

move mountains to do things that seem very difficult, or impossible ▶ *She is prepared to move mountains to find her daughter.*

MOUTH

down in the mouth very unhappy ▶ *When I told her what had happened, she was really down in the mouth, and I felt bad for spoiling her day.*

(straight) from the horse's mouth (of information) coming directly from the person who knows the most about it ▶ *"Are you sure he's leaving?" "I heard it straight from the horse's mouth."*

shoot your mouth off to say something offensive without thinking about it ▶ *You can't go shooting your mouth off at work; you have to control your temper.*

watch your mouth ➤ watch your TONGUE

MOVE

can't move for ___ there are so many (people or things) or there is so much (of something) that you can hardly move ▶ *On a hot summer's day, you can't move for tourists.* ▶ *You should see my office today; I can't move for paperwork.*

get a move on hurry up ▶ *Get a move on, we're going to be late.*

make the first move to be the person who tries to start a romantic relationship or to approach someone after a quarrel ▶ *Despite feminism, many women are still embarrassed to make the first move.* ▶ *I think I've got to make the first move if we're ever to be friends again.*

MOVERS

the movers and shakers the people who are responsible for very important decisions in large organizations etc, or for new ideas and activities in society ▶ *The event has attracted various movers and shakers from the world of business.*

MUCH

be much of a muchness to be about the same, and not very good ▶ *The new songs are all much of a muchness.*

MUD

(as) clear as mud not at all easy to understand ▶ *The handbook was as clear as mud, so I rang the helpline, which wasn't much better.*

drag sb through the mud also *drag sb's reputation through the mud* to harm someone by saying that they did something wrong ▶ *The newspapers dragged his reputation as a lawyer through the mud.*

sling also *throw mud* to publicly

M

criticize someone or say that they have done wrong ▶ *They are accusing us of throwing mud at their candidate.*
mud-slinging ADJ ▶ *The public will soon get tired of their mud-slinging exercises against the company.*

MULTITUDE

cover a multitude of sins also **hide a multitude of sins** to be used to hide the faults in a thing or person ▶ *The word 'development' covers a multitude of sins – could you tell us what exactly you plan to build?* ▶ *This warm winter jacket hides a multitude of sins.*

MUNCHIES

have (got) the munchies to be hungry, especially when you want something small and easy to eat ▶ *I've bought some crisps and sweets in case the kids get the munchies in the car.*

'Munchies' comes from the verb munch, meaning to chew food noisily.

MURDER

I could murder a ___ I really want to eat or drink (a particular type of food or drink) ▶ *I haven't eaten all day – I could murder a bacon sandwich.*

get away with murder to behave badly without being criticized or punished ▶ *Teachers have a hard time with children who get away with murder at home.*

MUSCLE

flex your muscle(s) to do something that shows that you have power, and intend to use it ▶ *Women in this region are starting to flex their political muscle and insist on equal rights.*

MUSIC

face the music to take responsibility for your actions, and accept criticism ▶ *I decided I'd better face the music and tell my parents that I was pregnant.*

sth is music to your ears you are very pleased to hear something ▶ *The decision to double spending on education was music to the ears of teachers and parents.*

MUSTARD

not cut the mustard to be not quite good enough ▶ *Other magazines have tried to copy us, but they've never quite cut the mustard.*

M

N

Nn

NAIL

another nail in sb's/sth's coffin also **the final nail in the coffin** something that helps to destroy someone's success,
plans, or hopes ► *The loss of so many jobs is another nail in the coffin for this region.*

hit the nail on the head to give exactly the right answer, or to describe something in exactly the right way ► *I've heard some intelligent guesses, but no one's hit the nail on the head yet.*

NAME

blacken sb's name to say unpleasant things about someone, so that other people have a bad opinion of them ► *The papers have used one bad incident to blacken his name completely.*

give sth a bad name to make people have a bad opinion of a person or thing ► *It's a pity the murder's given this pretty village a bad name.*

be ___ in all but name something or someone has all the qualities or features of a particular thing or person ► *The three colleges have been universities in all but name for many years.*

___ is sb's middle name a particular quality is typical of a person ► *He won't give you a pay rise – meanness is his middle name.*

___ is the name of the game also **the name of the game is ___** something is the most basic and important quality needed in a particular activity ► *It's the same whether you're in politics or business – marketing is the name of the game.*

make a name for yourself (as/in sth) to do something very well, so that it makes you famous ► *Sam made a name for himself as an honest politician.* ► *She's tried for years to make a name for herself in the business world.*

sb's name is mud someone is disliked for something they have done ► *As far as his employers are concerned, his name's mud.*

you name it (sb has it) there is a large variety of things that could be included in the list of things you are talking about ► *They sell everything you need for setting up an office – computers, phone systems, chairs, you name it.* ► *"What sort of drinks do you have?" "You name it, we have it."*

NAMES

call sb names to say rude or insulting things to someone ► *She told the court that her neighbours had called her names and kicked her dog.*

name names to tell people the name of the person or people involved in a particular activity ► *She told me that certain people were not happy with my work, but she didn't name names.*

NATURE

appeal to sb's better nature to try to persuade someone to do what you want by telling them it is a good, kind etc thing to do ► *"You'll be doing us* *all a great favour," she said, appealing to her sister's better nature.*

let nature take its course also **let time take its course** to wait for something to develop or pass in a natural way ▶ *I don't take any medicine for a cold, I just let nature take its course.*

NECK

break your neck (doing sth) to try very hard to do something ▶ *Don't break your neck getting this done today.*

dead from the neck up very stupid ▶ *It's nice to meet someone in this place who isn't dead from the neck up.*

in this/that neck of the woods also **in your/his etc neck of the woods** in a particular area or place ▶ *The only shop in this neck of the woods is the village post office.*

neck and neck having an equal chance of winning ▶ *The boys were neck and neck as they started the final round of the competition.*

risk your neck to do something very dangerous in which you could be hurt or killed ▶ *Afraid of risking his neck, he refused to take the boat out in the storm.*

stick your neck out to give your opinion or do something that other people are afraid to do, even though it may cause trouble for you ▶ *Nobody's prepared to stick their neck out and criticize the management.*

NEEDLE

a needle in a haystack something that is very difficult to find ▶ *Searching for the book in his office was like looking for a needle in a haystack.*

NEITHER

that's neither here nor there that is not important because it is not related to what we are talking about ▶ *My mobile phone isn't working, but that's neither here nor there. I was trying to contact him from my office phone.*

NERVE

touch a (raw) nerve also **hit a (raw) nerve** to upset someone by mentioning a particular subject ▶ *I know that in talking about adoption, I may have touched a raw nerve with some of my listeners.*

NERVES

get on sb's nerves to annoy someone ▶ *Nick's beginning to get on my nerves with his negative attitude.*

a war of nerves also **a battle of nerves** a fight or argument using threats and strength of will, but no violence ▶ *Mother and daughter stared at each other and Kate realized it was now a battle of nerves between them.*

NEST

feather your nest to get a lot of money so that you can have an easy life ▶ *She may have decided to feather her own nest by using blackmail.*

fly the nest also **leave the nest** (of a young adult) to leave their parents' home to become independent ▶ *Our children have flown the nest, so we're free to travel.*

stir up a hornet's nest to cause a lot of trouble ▶ *They are stirring up a hornet's nest, questioning the honesty of local councillors.*

N

NET

slip through the net also **fall through the net** to fail to get help or attention

who are supposed to give it ▶ *In a class of 30 children, some may slip through the net and learn very little.*

NEVER

sb (has) never looked back someone has been happy and successful since they took an opportunity or something changed in their life or job ▶ *Since he opened his own salon five years ago, he's never looked back.*

NEWS

no news is good news it is usually good that you have not received any news from someone because it probably means that nothing bad has happened ▶ *I assume they arrived safely – no news is good news.*

that's/it's news to me! I'm surprised or annoyed because someone has not told me something sooner ▶ *"I told everyone about the meeting months ago!" "Well, it's news to me."*

NICK

(just) in the nick of time just before it is too late, or just before something bad happens ▶ *The money arrived in the nick of time, so we could pay everyone before Christmas.*

NIGHT

call it a night to decide to stop doing something late at night ▶ *We've been working non-stop and I think it's time to call it a night.*

NIMBY

➤ not in my BACKYARD

NITTY GRITTY

get down to the (real) nitty gritty to discuss the most basic, important, and practical facts of something ▶ *Nobody wants to get down to the nitty gritty and sort out the problems, but we have to try.*

NOD

get the nod to get official permission or approval ▶ *They got the nod over their competitors because they had the investment capital.*

NOISES

make noises about sth to talk about something in an unclear or general way ▶ *He's been making noises about not renewing his contract.* ▶ *The retail trade is making optimistic noises about shoppers coming back to the High Street.*

make (all) the right noises to say the things that people expect or want you to say ▶ *Employees have asked for change and the new chairman is already making the right noises.*

NOSE

sb can't see beyond (the end of) his/her nose someone is too concerned with themselves and their own lives ▶ *Sometimes the management don't seem to see beyond the end of their nose.*

do sth with your nose in the air to behave as if you are better than someone else ▶ *The girls walked off with their noses in the air, leaving him wondering what he'd said to upset them.*

follow your nose

1 to keep going straight ahead ▶ *Just follow your nose to the end of the street and turn left.*
2 to follow your natural feelings, often in a situation in which there are no rules ▶ *I don't have a career plan – I just follow my nose.*

have a nose for sth to be naturally good at noticing or finding a particular type of thing ▶ *She's always had a nose for a good restaurant.*

keep your nose to the grindstone to work very hard for a long time ▶ *During the term the students kept their noses to the grindstone, but they made up for it in the holidays.*

look down your nose (at) to behave as if someone or something is not good enough for you ▶ *The fashion houses in Paris and New York tend to look down their noses at those from other places.*

pay through the nose to pay a lot or too much ▶ *I had to pay through the nose for car insurance when the boys started to drive.*

put sb's nose out of joint to annoy someone by not giving them as much respect as they think they deserve ▶ *We're looking for a simple solution that doesn't put anybody's nose out of joint.*

rub sb's nose in it/sth to keep reminding someone about something bad or embarrassing ▶ *The failure of the product was very embarrassing, and she rubbed our noses in it for months.*

stick your nose in *also* **poke your nose into sth** to become too involved in someone else's affairs ▶ *Maybe I was sticking my nose in, but I had to stop the fight.* ▶ *I don't want anyone poking their nose into my personal life.* **keep your nose out of sth** ▶ *I agreed to help him as long as he kept his nose out of my love life.*

thumb your nose (at sb/sth) to show that you do not respect someone or something ▶ *As an artist he enjoyed thumbing his nose at the authorities.*

be (right) under sb's nose to be very easy to find because it is near you ▶ *"Where are my keys?" "There, right under your nose."*

NOTHING

nothing to write home about something that is not special or interesting ▶ *That new arts magazine is nothing to write home about.*

nothing ventured, nothing gained you may achieve something if you are willing to take a risk or make an effort ▶ *Go on, apply for the job – nothing ventured, nothing gained, I say.*

think nothing of (doing) sth to think that something is not strange, special, or difficult to do ▶ *Forty years ago, children would have thought nothing of walking two or three miles to school and back.*

NOTICE

sit up and take notice to start paying attention to something because it surprises or affects you ▶ *Their eyecatching advertising campaign should make people sit up and take notice.*

NOW

now you're talking! I think your suggestion is very good ▶ *"Why don't* *we go out for a meal?" "Now you're talking!"*

NUMBER

have sb's number to understand what someone is like, so that you are able to deal with them ▶ *She had his number, and always knew when he wasn't telling her the truth.*

sb's number is up *also* **sb's number has come up** someone is about to stop being lucky or successful ▶ *Election year is when many politicians discover their number's up.*

NUMBER ONE

look out for number one *also* **look after number one** to take care of yourself and not worry about other people ▶ *My dad said that you can't trust anybody; you just have to look out for number one.*

NUT

a tough nut (to crack) *also* **a hard nut (to crack)**

1 someone who is difficult to defeat in an argument, fight, or competition, especially because they are strong and determined ▶ *He's a very tough nut to crack, having fought in international competitions for ten years.*

2 a problem or situation that is difficult to deal with ▶ *Working with inexperienced people was a hard nut, but we cracked it in the end.*

NUTS

go nuts to behave in a crazy or excited way ▶ *Some people go nuts when they have to stay at home all day, but I love it.*

be nuts about sb/sth to like someone or something very much ▶ *I'm nuts about Ireland and everything to do with it.*

the nuts and bolts of sth the practical details of something ▶ *The book deals with the nuts and bolts of travel in Spain.* **nuts-and-bolts** ADJ ▶ *I need some nuts-and-bolts advice on word processing.*

NUTSHELL

(to put it) in a nutshell *also* **that's it in a nutshell** to state the main points of an argument, discussion etc in a short, clear way ▶ *To put it in a nutshell, they were absolutely horrified.* ▶ *The city's too crowded – that's the problem in a nutshell.*

Oo

OAR

stick your oar in *also* **put your oar in** to try to be involved in other people's affairs, when they do not want you to be ▶ *I don't want him sticking his oar in. It's nothing to do with him.*

OATS

sow your wild oats to have fun while you are young, especially by having many sexual relationships that are not serious ▶ *He's sown all his wild oats and is finally ready to settle down.*

ODD

the odd one out *also* **the odd man/ woman out** someone or something that is different from the rest of the group ▶ *She was always the odd one out at school.* ▶ *In a family that lives for football, Jack and his son are the odd men out.*

ODDS

be at odds (with)
1 to disagree (with someone) ▶ *He's at odds with his family, who think music is an uncertain career.* ▶ *We seemed to be at odds on every single question.*
2 to be very different (from each other) ▶ *Transport programmes are currently at odds with environmental concerns.* ▶ *Unfortunately, theory and practice are at odds in the world of public administration.*

the odds are stacked against sb *also* **the cards are stacked against sb** it is very unlikely that someone will achieve something ▶ *She seems confident she can make the climb, though at this time of year the odds are stacked against her.*

OFF

be off with sb to behave in an unfriendly way towards someone ▶ *What's wrong with him this morning? He was really off with me at the coffee machine.*

OFF-CHANCE

on the off-chance (that) in the hope that something quite unlikely will happen ▶ *She's ringing on the off-chance that you're free to come out this evening.* ▶ *I called at her place on the off-chance – of course there was nobody there.*

OFFICES

sb's good offices help that you get from someone who has authority or who can influence people ▶ *Through his father's good offices, he obtained employment in the old family firm.*

OIL

pour oil on troubled waters to try to make people less angry ▶ *My role in the family was pouring oil on troubled waters, and they're lost without me.*

OLIVE

olive branch a sign that you want to make peace with someone during or after an argument or fight ▶ *If I had seen even the suggestion of an olive branch, I would have been prepared to forgive him.* ▶ *By admitting their mistake and arranging this meeting, they are offering you the olive branch.*

In ancient times the olive branch was used to represent peace.

ON

be on for sth to want to do something

O

or be involved in it ▶ *We're going to the club tonight. Are you on for it?*

ONCE

once and for all finally and for ever ▶ *Smokers should take this opportunity to give up their habit once and for all.*

ONCE-OVER

give sb/sth the once-over to look at someone or something carefully but quickly ▶ *Before going on holiday, give your car the once-over to make sure it doesn't need any repairs.*

ONE

have had one too many also **have had a few too many** to be very drunk ▶ *Can someone take her home? I think she's had one too many.* ▶ *We'd all had a few too many, but Tom decided he was going to climb the clock tower.*

it takes one to know one someone can understand someone else's character because they have the same faults themselves ▶ *You think she's not been honest with me? Well, it takes one to know one.*

one and the same (of two things or people) exactly alike ▶ *You can't separate sports and business these days – they're one and the same.*

be/get one up on sb to have or get an advantage over someone ▶ *She's passed her driving test so she's one up on you.* ▶ *They are hoping to get one up on their competitors when they bring out the new software.*

one for the road a last alcoholic drink before leaving a place ▶ *If you're thinking of having one for the road, make it an orange juice.*

the one that got away the thing that someone most wanted but did not get ▶ *He's had another wonderful year on the courts, but the one that got away – the regional championship – escaped him once again.*

pull a fast one (on sb) to trick or deceive someone ▶ *I know when a salesman is trying to pull a fast one, and this lad wasn't.*

OPTION

a/the soft option also **a/the easy option** a/the course of action that needs the least effort ▶ *Going into therapy is never a soft option, but it may have very positive results.* ▶ *He's always inclined to take the easy option.*

ORDER

sth is a tall order something is very difficult to do ▶ *To make a profit, we'll have to add 2000 new customers to our list, which is a tall order.*

be the order of the day to be the normal activity on a particular occasion ▶ *On our holiday relaxation was the order of the day.*

be out of order not to be working properly ▶ *The lift's out of order – we'll have to climb all those stairs!*

the pecking order the social system among a group of people or animals,

in which each one knows who is more

important and less important than themselves ► *Patients are at the bottom of the pecking order, and have very little say in the running of the hospital.*

ORDERS

get your marching orders *also* **be given your marching orders** to be ordered to leave a job, a relationship, or a place such as a sports field during a game ► *He was swindling the company for at least a year before he got his marching orders.*

OTT
➤ over the TOP

OUT

out cold unconscious, especially because of being hit ► *The man lay on the floor, out cold.*

be out of it not to know or understand what is happening because you are tired, confused, or affected by drugs or alcohol ► *After the injection I was completely out of it, so I didn't hear what the doctor said.*

OVER

over and done with completely finished ► *I'd like to get this interview over and done with so I can go home.*

OVERDRIVE

go into overdrive to start to be very

active, or to work unusually hard or well ► *She went into overdrive to get the products out on time, and made herself ill as a result.*

OWE

I owe you one said when you are thanking someone who has helped you, to tell them you will help them in future ► *Thanks for lending me your car, Fran. I owe you one for this.*

you owe me (one) said when you want to remind someone that you expect them to help you, or be nice to you, because of something you did for them, or something bad they did to you ► *"Thanks for supporting me." "That's OK, but you owe me one now!"*

OWN

get your own back (on sb) to do something bad to someone who has harmed you, as a way of punishing them ► *He thought he'd been insulted, and was waiting for a chance to get his own back.*

hold your own to defend yourself or to succeed in a difficult situation ► *The captain had radioed that he was holding his own against the storm.* ► *Knowing that he could hold his own with the great actors gave him new confidence.*

O

Pp

PACE

do sth at a snail's pace to do something extremely slowly ► *Despite all our efforts, the business is still growing at a snail's pace.*

PACES

put sb through his/her paces also **put sth through its paces** to make a person or machine show how well they can do something so that you can judge it ► *Candidates are put through their paces before a panel of local people.* ► *The designers have been busy putting the boat through its paces.* **go through his/her/its paces** ► *More than 400 people turned out at the airport to watch the helicopter go through its paces.*

PACK

ahead of the pack having more success than people you are competing with ► *Once again, this phone company is ahead of the pack.*

PAIN

no pain, no gain you should do something unpleasant because it will have a good result ► *I was aching in every muscle, but no pain, no gain, as the aerobics instructor said.*

be a pain (in the neck) to be very annoying or boring ► *I find that filling in forms is always a pain in the neck.* ► *David, stop being a pain and give Linda her doll back.*

PAINS

for your pains as a reward for your kind actions (usually said when you did not get what you hoped for) ► *I told her that she was looking attractive, and got a suspicious glare for my pains.*

growing pains problems and difficulties that are experienced in a new organization or at the start of a new activity ► *Arguments and misunderstandings are part of the growing pains of a new relationship.*

take pains to do sth also **be at pains to do sth** to make a special effort to do something ► *Most teachers take great pains to ensure that starting school is as easy as possible for young children.* ► *He was at pains to point out that he did not represent any political party.*

PAINT

be like watching paint dry also **be as exciting etc as watching paint dry** to be extremely boring ► *My father loves watching golf, but to me, it's like watching paint dry.*

PALE

beyond the pale too bad or extreme to be acceptable ► *His sexist jokes are beyond the pale.*

PALL

cast a pall over to spoil an event or occasion by making people feel sad or less confident ► *The death of five students in a road accident has cast a pall over the graduation festivities.*

PALM

grease sb's palm to give someone money in a secret or dishonest way in order to persuade them to do something ▶ *I think we'll have to grease a few palms if we want to get our shipment delivered on time.*

hold sb in the palm of your hand to influence or control someone so that they pay attention to you ▶ *She manages to hold the entire audience in the palm of her hand.*

PANTS

beat the pants off sb also **act etc the pants off sb** to defeat someone completely and easily in a game or competition, or to be much better than someone in an activity ▶ *I'm not playing with you again – you beat the pants off me last time.* ▶ *She can act the pants off any of us.*

bore/scare the pants off sb also **charm etc the pants off sb** to bore, scare, charm etc someone very much ▶ *Be aware of your audience – ask yourself, are they with me or am I boring the pants off them?*

catch sb with his/her pants down to embarrass someone by finding a weakness in them ▶ *It's the price of fame – someone will eventually catch you with your pants down and the story will be in every paper.* ▶ *We try to keep a bit of stock in reserve, so that we're not caught with our pants down.*

PAPER

sb couldn't ___ his/her way out of a (wet) paper bag someone is very bad at doing something ▶ *He'll never get the project together – he couldn't organize his way out of a paper bag.*

on paper when considering written accounts, numbers etc (in contrast with the practical facts of something) ▶ *The team look very strong on paper, but they tend not to play well under these conditions.* ▶ *On paper he is extremely wealthy, but there are rumours that his company is running into difficulties.*

be a paper tiger to appear to be a lot more powerful than you really are ▶ *The rebel army is just a paper tiger, consisting of a few officers and a rabble of badly trained men.*

not be worth the paper it's written/printed on (of a document) to have little or no value ▶ *A degree from a country like that isn't worth the paper it's printed on.*

PAR

be under par also **be below par** or **not be up to par** to fail to reach the usual or expected standard of quality, health etc ▶ *You may feel under par for three weeks or more after a viral infection.* ▶ *The team's performance has been below par for too long, and drastic action needs to be taken.* ▶ *It seemed obvious that the local schools were not up to par.*

sth is par for the course something that happens is exactly what you would expect to happen ▶ *Before lunch we'd dealt with 50 telephone calls, which is about par for the course.*

on a par (with) equal to someone or

something else ▶ *Her new salary puts her on a par with senior bankers.* ▶ *His enthusiasm is on a par with his ability.*

PARADE

rain on sb's parade to spoil someone's important or exciting plans ▶ *I'm sorry to rain on your parade, but you've just had an urgent call.*

PARADISE

be living in a fool's paradise to be happy about your situation when the state of affairs is not in fact very good ▶ *When Linda said she was leaving me, I realized that I had been living in a fool's paradise.*

PARKER

a nosy parker used about someone who wants to know something that does not concern them, especially what other people are doing ▶ *"What are you drawing?" "Nosy parker!"* ▶ *Always put personal letters away, in case some nosy parker comes snooping around your desk.*

PART

look the part to seem to be a typical person of a particular sort ▶ *When you meet clients as a financial adviser make sure you look the part – dark suit, clean fingernails, and spotless shoes.*

be part and parcel of sth to be part of something ▶ *Dialogue in television drama sounds natural, but it lacks the hesitations that are part and parcel of ordinary speech.*

take sth in good part to accept jokes or critical remarks about you cheerfully, instead of being upset ▶ *He's got a really wicked sense of humour, but his mates take it all in good part.*

the best part of also **the better part of** nearly all of ▶ *They have been living together for the best part of 30 years.*

PARTNER

sb's partner in crime someone you spend a lot of time with, especially if

you behave badly together and annoy people ▶ *Here's my son and his partner in crime, Tommy, from next door.*

PARTY

bring sth to the party to add something good to a situation or activity ▶ *The team lack the pace in attack that our players could bring to the party.*

a party pooper someone who spoils other people's fun, especially by refusing to do something that everyone else wants to do ▶ *"Let's go out." "Sorry to be a party pooper, but I need to get an early night."*

PAST

be past it to be old or in bad condition ▶ *I'm not suggesting that you're past it, but are you sure you can cope with a camping holiday?* ▶ *We're going to replace this carpet – it's getting past it.*

PASTURE

be put out to pasture also **be put out to grass** to be made to leave your job because you are too old ▶ *In jazz and*

folk music they don't put you out to
pasture for getting older – they know
that you're getting better. ▶ *Some of
the top managers have been put out
to grass this year.*

PASTURES

new pastures also **fresh pastures** a
new and different situation, especially
a better job ▶ *Most of the people who
joined the firm with me have left for
fresh pastures.*

PAT

have sth down pat also **have sth off
pat** to know something so well that
you can say it or do it without thinking
▶ *That's a difficult question. I'm afraid
I haven't got the answer off pat.*

PATCH

go through a sticky patch also **hit a
sticky patch** to experience a difficult
and unpleasant time ▶ *Their marriage
is going through a bit of a sticky patch
at the moment.* ▶ *Your bank manager
may be able to help you if you hit a
sticky patch.*

not a patch on someone or something
is not nearly as good as someone or
something else ▶ *Public transport in
London is not a patch on the system in
Paris.*

PAUSE

give you pause (for thought) to make
you stop and think ▶ *Some of the
violence in films gives parents pause
for thought.* ▶ *The results of the survey
have given us pause and we're likely to
reassess our marketing strategy.*

PEACE

hold your peace to keep quiet and say
nothing ▶ *He had some doubts about
the book's suitability, but he held his
peace.*

PEAS

like two peas in a pod also **as alike as
two peas** (of two people or things)
exactly like each other ▶ *She and her*

*sister are like two peas in a pod – I
can never tell which of them is
which.* ▶ *These bracelets are as alike
as two peas – I wonder why mine cost
more!*

PEDESTAL

place sb on a pedestal to behave to
someone and talk about them as if
they were perfect ▶ *In olden times, a
woman was either placed on a
pedestal or despised.*

PEG

take sb down a peg (or two) also
bring sb down a peg (or two) to make
someone realize they are not as
important or clever as they think they
are ▶ *He's not a bad guy, but he needs
to be taken down a peg or two.*

> This idiom comes from the time
> when the British Navy used
> sailing ships. A ship would have
> to bring its flag down to a lower
> position if a more important ship
> was in the area, and the different
> positions for the flag were shown
> by pegs (=sticks) in the ship's
> mast (=tall pole that held the
> sails).

P

PEGGED

have sb/sth pegged to understand someone or something completely so you know what they are going to do ▶ *I think I've got all my colleagues pegged now – I know who to rely on for support.*

PEN

the pen is mightier than the sword you can achieve more through communication than you can with violence ▶ *If the pen is mightier than the sword, the press should be subject to the same restraints as gun-owners!*

PENNIES

not have two pennies to rub together to have very little money ▶ *In those days, my family didn't have two pennies to rub together.*

pinch pennies to be careful to spend as little money as possible ▶ *I'll be glad when I don't have to pinch pennies any more, and I can buy a car.*

penny-pincher N ▶ *Here's a penny-pincher's guide to the best videos.*

PETARD

be hoist with your own petard also **be hoist by your own petard** to have problems because of something you have done that was intended to give you an advantage ▶ *She's been moaning about sharing an office so long that they gave her that nasty little cold one – she was really hoist with her own petard.*

This idiom comes from a line in Shakespeare's play *Hamlet*. A petard was an early kind of bomb that might explode and kill the soldier who was putting it in position.

PETER

be robbing Peter to pay Paul to take money from one part of a system or organization that needs it and use it in another part of the system or organization ▶ *They're just shifting money from one part of the social services budget to another – robbing Peter to pay Paul, in fact.*

PHRASE

to coin a phrase to invent a new phrase (when you have said something silly or changed an ordinary saying so that it sounds funny) ▶ *Dennis is the type of guy who'll have fun if it kills him, to coin a phrase.*

PICK

take your pick to choose what you want out of several things ▶ *The styles for this season are flattering, and you can take your pick from bold colours or neutral shades.*

PICNIC

sth is no picnic something is difficult and involves a lot of work ▶ *She knew that working for them would be no picnic.*

PICTURE

get the picture to understand a situation that someone is describing or explaining ▶ *I eat a lot, I gain weight, my clothes don't fit, I'm unhappy, so I eat a lot. Get the picture?*

look at the big picture to understand the whole of a situation ▶ *The ideal candidate for the job should be able to look at the big picture and prioritize work.*

out of the picture no longer involved in a situation ▶ *Of course, his son's dropped out of the picture now he's* *studying abroad.* **in the picture** ► *Life's been more exciting since she's been in the picture.*

paint a rosy picture (of sth) to describe (a situation) as better than it really is ► *Her book paints a rosy picture of social life in the last century.*

put sb in the picture to give someone information about a situation, so that they can understand it ► *Let me just put you in the picture about what's been happening in the past month.*

PIE

eat humble pie to admit that you were wrong about something, especially publicly ► *She'll have to eat humble pie and ask the company to take her back.*

pie in the sky an idea or plan that you think will never happen ► *It seems to me that the new sports stadium is just pie in the sky.*

PIECE

give sb a piece of your mind to tell someone how angry you are with them and why ► *I'm going straight to the manager and I'm going to give her a piece of my mind.*

how long is a piece of string? that's an impossible question to answer ► *"How much does a single person in London need to live on?" "How long is a piece of string?"*

sb is a nasty piece of work someone is very unpleasant and should not be trusted ► *I don't think you should talk to her about your personal life – she's a nasty piece of work.*

be a piece of cake to be very easy ► *After running a hotel, looking after a family is a piece of cake.*

a piece of the pie ➤ a SLICE of the cake

of a piece (with) in agreement (with), similar (to) ► *His letter is of a piece with the articles he's published.*

say your piece to give your opinion in a very direct way ► *The police chief said his piece and was surprised at the emotional response of the audience.*

PIECES

go to pieces to become so confused and upset that you cannot act normally ► *After the business failed, my father went to pieces.*

love sb to pieces ➤ love sb to BITS

pick up the pieces (of sth) to get a relationship or situation back to a good state, after something bad has happened and spoilt it ► *His daughter died last year and he and his wife are still picking up the pieces.*

tear sb to pieces ➤ tear sb to SHREDS

thrilled to pieces ➤ thrilled to BITS

PIG

buy a pig in a poke to buy something without looking at it carefully first ► *I'll have to test-drive the car – I don't want to buy a pig in a poke.*

PILL

a bitter pill (to swallow) something very unpleasant that you have to accept ► *Workers knew that some jobs would have to be cut to save the newspaper, but it was still a bitter pill.*

PILLAR

from pillar to post from one place or difficult situation to another ▶ *The boy's being pushed from pillar to post – he should be at home with his mother.*

PILOT

on automatic pilot not thinking about the things you are doing because you have done them many times before ▶ *After their argument, she finished her work on automatic pilot and had a good cry when she got home.*

PIN

you could hear a pin drop people are being very quiet, especially because they are listening to someone ▶ *You could have heard a pin drop in that hall while he was telling his story.*

PINCH

feel the pinch to have to live more cheaply because you have less money ▶ *Pensioners are beginning to feel the pinch as the cost of living rises.*

PIPE

be a pipe dream (of a plan) to be a nice idea but very unlikely to happen ▶ *I would like to travel for a year, but at this rate, it will always be a pipe dream.*

put that in your pipe and smoke it you must accept that, although you may not like it ▶ *A big company is paying me a lot for what you call playing about on a computer, so put that in your pipe and smoke it!*

PIPELINE

be in the pipeline to be in the process of preparation and likely to be ready soon ▶ *Also in the pipeline is a new TV series based on folk tales.*

PIPER

he who pays the piper calls the tune the person who is paying for something decides what that thing will be like ▶ *I'm not wasting money on a new family car when a second-hand one will do – in the end, he who pays the piper calls the tune.*

PITS

sth/sb is the pits I don't like or value a particular thing or person ▶ *Her boyfriends have all been horrible, but Jim's the pits!* ▶ *Parts of the city are really nice, but the bit where she lives is the pits.*

PIT STOP

make a pit stop to stop when driving on a long trip, for food, the toilet etc ▶ *We've been on the road for two hours now; let's make a pit stop soon.*

This idiom comes from the sport of car racing. Drivers make a pit stop to put more fuel in their car, check the engine etc.

PITY

more's the pity that's something to be sorry about ▶ *This Christmas we've got to go and visit her boring relatives, more's the pity.*

PLACE

all over the place
1 everywhere ▶ *The valley's beautiful – little lakes and wild flowers all over the place.*

2 not tidy or organized ▶ *His handwriting's all over the place.* ▶ *He's been all over the place since the move.*

fall into place

1 (of a series of events) to be seen in its proper position so that the whole thing can be understood ▶ *When I realized she was his sister, everything fell into place.*

2 to go well ▶ *It's wonderful, things keep falling into place – we've just been offered a cheap office building.*

be in the right place at the right time to get an interesting or useful opportunity by chance ▶ *Getting into TV journalism is hard, but if you're in the right place at the right time, you'll get your chance.*

know your place to behave in a way that shows you know which people are more important than you are ▶ *In those days, employees knew their place and didn't criticize their bosses.*

a place in the sun a situation in which you will be happy and have everything you need ▶ *After their years of study, bright corporate lawyers can usually find a place in the sun.*

put sb in his/her place to show someone that they are not as important as they think they are ▶ *If a caller to the show gets too personal, he puts them in their place.*

take second place (to) to be considered less important than someone or something else ▶ *Concern about overpopulation has begun to take second place to worries about pollution.*

PLACES

be going places to be likely to be very successful ▶ *I heard them for the first time on Friday, and I can tell you, this band's going places.*

PLATE

hand sth to sb on a (silver) plate to make it very easy for someone to get something or succeed at something ▶ *The team began the match badly and handed their opponents their first three goals on a plate.* ▶ *I don't expect a decent job to be handed to me on a silver plate.*

have a lot on your plate also **have enough on your plate** to have a lot of work to do or a lot of problems to deal with ▶ *I don't want to give this job to him, he's already got a lot on his plate.* ▶ *She's got enough on her plate with her mother ill and no job.*

PLAY

sth is child's play something is very easy to do or deal with ▶ *A cheap lock is child's play for a thief, so invest in a good one.*

play dirty to behave in a way that is not fair ▶ *They were accused of playing dirty in the last campaign by spreading lies and tapping telephones.*

be (all) played out to have no more energy or new ideas ▶ *Our marketing manager is all played out, so we're looking for a new one.*

play hard to get to pretend you are not interested in a romantic or business relationship with someone, in order to make them more interested ▶ *She was polite but cool to him,* which he interpreted as *playing hard to get*. ▶ *We've offered him the job, but he's playing hard to get and claiming he needs more staff and a bigger office.*

play it cool to act in a calm, careful way that does not show your feelings ▶ *Don't panic, just play it cool and nobody will know you're upset.*

play it safe not to do anything that involves risks ▶ *Let's play it safe and take the earlier train to the airport.*

a play on words an interesting or amusing way of using words or phrases so that they can have two very different meanings ▶ *In every culture, children laugh at jokes that are a play on words.*

PLUG
pull the plug on sth to prevent a plan or business from being able to continue ▶ *They pulled the plug on funding for a research laboratory.*

PLUNGE
take the plunge to finally decide to do something difficult or risky ▶ *For years, they've been talking about moving to the country, but only now have they taken the plunge.*

POCKET
dig into your pocket also **put your hand into your pocket** to pay for something expensive with your own money ▶ *He dug deep into his own pocket to pay for the professor to come over to Europe.*

be in sb's pocket to be controlled by someone, usually because they give you money ▶ *Freelance journalists are in the pockets of the big newspapers.*

out of pocket
1 having lost money ▶ *The promoters of the concert found themselves $3700 out of pocket when the singers cancelled at the last minute.*
2 (of payment) given yourself instead of coming from someone else ▶ *Because of this accident we have to pay $250 out of pocket because the insurance won't pay for counselling.*
out-of-pocket ADJ ▶ *The agents claimed a lot of out-of-pocket expenses.*

POCKETS
line your (own) pockets to make a lot of money and keep it for yourself when it should be paid out to other people ▶ *In his book, he argues that the country's corporate officials have lined their pockets at the expense of shareholders.*

POINT
sth is beside the point something is not directly connected with what we are talking about ▶ *The route we take is beside the point – what I want to know is, are you sure you can get that week off?*

(the) boiling point a point when people are very angry and likely to do something about it ▶ *The situation was clearly reaching boiling point so she decided to close the meeting.*

a jumping-off point a place, subject, style etc that you start from ▶ *We're flying to Istanbul, and using it as a jumping-off point for places around the Black Sea.* ▶ *The group used traditional jazz as a jumping-off point,* *but their performances have become steadily more original and modern.*

miss the point not to understand the main idea of something ▶ *Anyone who thinks that this book is about relationships is missing the point. It's about handling grief.*

not to put too fine a point on it also **without putting too fine a point on it** to be honest and open (used to introduce an unpleasant truth) ▶ *Not to put too fine a point on it, he doesn't find her attractive.*

the point of no return the time during a process or activity when it becomes impossible to stop or change it ▶ *By the time I realized how much it was all going to cost, we'd reached the point of no return.*

be a sore point to be a subject that will upset or annoy someone ▶ *Don't ask him how the interview went, it's rather a sore point at the moment.*

a sticking point a problem that stops you from deciding something because people cannot agree ▶ *The sticking point in these negotiations is price.*

POINTS

score points off sb to make someone seem less well informed or clever than you are ▶ *I intend to read everything I can on this subject – I'm not having her scoring points off me unnecessarily.* **point-scoring** N ▶ *The important thing now is not point-scoring but negotiating.*

score points with sb to do something that makes other people approve of or like you ▶ *The airline was one of the first to score points with passengers by banning smoking.*

POLES

be poles apart (of two people, ideas

etc) to be very different from each other ▶ *The two roles he's played on screen are poles apart – the hard-drinking soldier and the sensitive poet.*

PORT

any port in a storm I'll take any help or protection that is available when I'm in trouble ▶ *I don't like him, really; it was just any port in a storm after my divorce.*

POSSUM

play possum to pretend to be asleep or dead so that someone will not hurt or annoy you ▶ *He testified that after he was shot, he played possum until the gunman had left.*

> Possum is another word for opossum, a North American animal that protects itself from its enemies in this way.

POT

go to pot to become worse or fail ▶ *A lot of people think the legal system in this country has gone to pot.*

a melting pot a place where people from many different countries come together ▶ *The university is a melting pot of cultures and ideas from all over the world.*

the pot calling the kettle black when you are criticizing someone for the same fault as you have ▶ *In a case of the pot calling the kettle black, he accused me of spending too much money.*

take pot luck to take whatever is available ▶ *Car owners shouldn't have to take pot luck when they fill up their tank – they should know the quality of the fuel they're getting.*

This idiom comes from the time when an unexpected guest would share whatever food a family had cooking in the pot. In North America, a pot luck supper or dinner is an occasion to which each person brings one type of food and everyone shares. You do not know exactly what you might eat until you arrive.

POTATO

drop sb/sth like a hot potato to suddenly stop being involved with someone or dealing with a problem, usually because you find out something bad about them or it ▶ *If she finds out what he said to the press, she'll drop him like a hot potato.*

a hot potato a subject that a lot of people are talking or arguing about, but that nobody wants to deal with or take responsibility for ▶ *Someone in the party has to catch political hot potatoes and deal with them effectively.*

POTATOES

small potatoes something or someone that is not very big or important ▶ *As wildlife parks go, this one is pretty small potatoes, but it does give you a chance to see some exotic animals.*

POUND

take your pound of flesh also **demand your pound of flesh** to say that someone must give you what they owe you, or do something that they ought to do for you, even though it will make them suffer a lot ▶ *The banks are quite happy to take their pound of flesh from customers, even good ones who are only slightly overdrawn.*

This idiom comes from Shakespeare's play, *The Merchant of Venice,* in which Shylock demands a pound of flesh from Antonio if he cannot pay the money he owes.

POWDER

take a powder to leave a place quickly, to avoid getting into trouble ▶ *I think he decided to take a powder when he realized the police would be looking for him.*

POWDER KEG

a powder keg a very dangerous situation, in which something could go wrong at any time ▶ *Tensions in the region are increasing, and it will be a powder keg by the end of the year if nothing is done.*

POWER

more power to your elbow I agree with what you are doing, and wish you luck ▶ *"I want to work with children in distress." "More power to your elbow!"*

POWERS

the powers that be the people who have positions of authority and make important decisions ▶ *The powers that be at the gallery tend to be more interested in profit than in representing all kinds of modern art.*

PRACTICE

practice makes perfect if you do something regularly, you will become very good at it ▶ *I had a lot of trouble using this software, but maybe practice makes perfect.*

PRACTISE

practise what you preach to behave in the way that you tell others to behave ▶ *After years of telling readers to accept new technologies, the magazine has decided to practise what it preaches.*

PRAISE

damn sb with faint praise to say something about someone that sounds fairly nice, but shows that you do not really have a high opinion of them ▶ *She damned him with faint praise, saying only that he'd done what was expected of him.*

PRAISES

sing sb's praises to say how good someone or something is ▶ *The council sings the praises of the local pottery business in its new tourist booklet.*

PRESENCE

sb graces sb/sth with their presence someone comes to an event, meeting etc, although they usually think they are too important to come ▶ *It's unlike you to grace us with your presence – I thought you were too busy.* ▶ *Oh, look, the boss has decided to grace our little party with her presence!*

PRESS

get a bad press also **have a bad press** to be criticized a lot, especially in the press ▶ *Lawyers are accustomed to getting a bad press, but until recently there was no formal complaints system.* **get/have a good press** ▶ *Unlike most Hollywood actors, he has usually had a good press.*

be hot off the press to have just been printed and be available ▶ *With her new book hot off the press and already in the top ten, she has every reason to be pleased with herself.*

PRESS-GANG

press-gang sb into doing sth to force someone to do something by not giving them the chance to refuse ▶ *He press-ganged me into taking the job when I was short of money, but I've hated it from the beginning.*

A press-gang was a group of sailors who had the right to force men to join the British Navy.

PRICE

at any price whatever it costs or under any conditions ▶ *She was determined to win her freedom at any price.*

at a price in return for paying a lot of money or having to accept something unpleasant ▶ *Everything is available in this city, at a price.* ▶ *Higher train speeds have been achieved at a price – safety levels have been significantly reduced.*

everyone has their price also **every man has his price** it is possible to make anyone do what you want, if you offer them enough money or give them something they want very much ▶ *Everyone has their price, and I know we can get Jim to come and work for us if we offer him double the usual holiday.*

pay the price (for) also **pay a heavy price (for)** to be suffering because of something bad that you or someone else did ▶ *There has been a lot of petty theft from our workshops, and our customers are paying the price.* ▶ *We've paid a heavy price for promoting the wrong person.*

what price ___?
1 what is the value of (a particular thing)? ▶ *He's made more money than ever, but he's suffering from terrible stress. What price success?*
2 what are the chances of (a particular thing) happening? ▶ *The train company's on strike and the weather forecast's awful – what price a carefree holiday now?*

PRICKS

kick against the pricks to show your opposition to people in authority ▶ *She has to realize that kicking against the pricks will do her no good in this sort of organization.*

PRIDE

swallow your pride to admit that you were wrong or that you need help, even if it will embarrass you ▶ *He would never swallow his pride and say that he was sorry.* ▶ *After taking the engine to pieces, I had to swallow my pride and ask my son to help me put it back together again.*

take pride of place to be considered the best or most important thing, person, or idea ▶ *Taking pride of place in the hospital will be a CAT scanner, bought as a result of a three-year fund-raising effort.* **give sth pride of place** ▶ *He gives pride of place to a model aircraft left to him by his uncle.*

PRISONERS

sb takes no prisoners someone is

determined to succeed and will not be stopped by feelings of kindness or politeness ▶ *He's a ruthless businessman – he takes no prisoners.*

PRODUCTION

make a production (out) of sth to make something that you have to do seem more complicated, difficult, or important than is necessary ▶ *Neither of us made a big production out of splitting up – John just moved out of the flat.*

PROFILE

have/keep a high profile to be known or continue to be known as successful by the public ▶ *The company kept a high profile when other firms were doing badly.* ▶ *Like many media celebrities, she has an absurdly high profile.*

keep a low profile to try not to do anything that will make people notice you ▶ *Neighbours of the footballer say that he keeps a low profile when he's at home.* **low-profile** ADJ ▶ *The secretary of state is planning a low-profile visit next month.*

PROOF

the proof of the pudding (is in the eating) also **the proof is in the pudding** you only find out if an idea or plan is good by trying it ▶ *It may*  *sound like a crazy idea, but you know, the proof of the pudding – I'm not making up my mind yet.*

PROPHET

a prophet of doom someone who believes that bad or unpleasant things will happen ▶ *I can't agree with the prophets of doom who say the team will never get back to its former glory.*

PROVE

sb has something to prove also **sb has a lot to prove** someone has to try especially hard because people do not expect them to do well ▶ *I was happy with the band's performance, but they've still got something to prove.*
sb has nothing to prove ▶ *I've got nothing to prove by playing him again – I know I can beat him.*

P'S AND Q'S

mind your p's and q's to be very polite and well behaved ▶ *You have to mind your p's and q's when you're running a hotel, however irritating the customers may be.*

PUBLIC

in the public eye well known and interesting to the public ▶ *Her lack of experience at being in the public eye sometimes shows.* ▶ *Our aim is to keep environmental issues in the public eye.* **out of the public eye** ▶ *Since his retirement he has been out of the public eye.*

PUNCH

pack a punch to be very effective or powerful ▶ *The allure of nuclear rockets is that they pack more punch than conventional ones.*

PUNCHBAG

use sb as a punchbag also **use sb as a punching bag**

1 to criticize a person or organization publicly ▶ *I know that the fans like to*

use me as a punchbag – it's part of the job of being a football manager.*
2 to hit someone a lot ▶ *When he's drunk he tends to use his nearest drinking companion as a punchbag.*

PUNCHES

not pull any punches to say exactly what you think, even if it offends or shocks people ▶ *The documentary pulls no punches, and shows up the carelessness and complacency of the airline that allowed the crash to happen.*

roll with the punches to accept criticism or problems without being upset ▶ *Politicians have to get used to rolling with the punches.*

PURPOSES

at cross purposes (of two people or groups) not making progress because of having different aims or different ideas about a situation ▶ *I think we're talking at cross purposes – it wasn't John who asked me to come here and talk to you, it was the police.*

PURSE

hold the purse strings to control the money in a family, business

etc ▶ *You're not having a motorbike while I hold the purse strings.* **tighten/ loosen the purse strings** ▶ *Our promise to meet the deadline could help loosen the government purse strings.*

make a silk purse out of a sow's ear also **turn a sow's ear into a silk purse** to change something from being bad quality to being good quality ▶ *My*

*students try hard, but even I can't
make a silk purse out of a sow's ear.*

PUSH

be pushing it ➤ be pushing your
LUCK

when/if push comes to shove when or
if a situation becomes very difficult, or
when you finally need to take action
▶ *I have to say that if push comes to
shove, I'd rather it was me making
important decisions than any man.*
▶ *When push comes to shove, the
people will elect the person who
promises most.*

PUT

I wouldn't put it past sb (to do sth) in
my view, a particular person is quite
likely to do something ▶ *I wouldn't put
it past her to steal the money she
needs.*

put paid to sth to make it impossible
for something to happen or
continue ▶ *The torrential rain put paid
to our plans for a picnic.*

you're putting me on you're joking
▶ *"He loves the house – he wants to
buy it." "You're putting me on."*

PUTTY

be putty in sb's hands to be very
easily influenced or controlled by
another person ▶ *Inexperienced
managers are putty in the hands of a
business consultant with theories
about management psychology.*

> Putty is a soft substance that
> becomes hard when it dries, and
> is used, for example, to hold
> glass in window frames. When it
> is soft, you can make it into
> different shapes with your hands.

Qq

QUANTITY

be an unknown quantity to be someone or something whose abilities or qualities are not known, especially when these may influence a situation ▶ *His opponent tomorrow will be Chan, who is still a bit of an unknown quantity.* ▶ *The new healthcare arrangements are an unknown quantity, and may not help people with long-term illnesses.*

QUARTER

give no quarter to show no pity in a competitive situation ▶ *The new champion gives no quarter to his opponents.*

QUARTERS

at close quarters at or from a very short distance away ▶ *At close quarters the building looked older and shabbier than it had done from a distance.*

QUESTION

sth begs the question a statement or discussion causes another, more basic, question to be asked ▶ *The discussion of whether advertising is art begs the question 'What is art?'*

good question! I don't know the answer to that question ▶ *"So, why do they keep looking at houses if they can't afford to move?" "Good question!"*

out of the question not possible or not allowed ▶ *Could we have access to the students' records, or would that be out of the question?*

pop the question to ask someone to marry you ▶ *No, he didn't go down on one knee to pop the question, but it was all very romantic.*

QUICK

cut sb to the quick to upset or offend someone very much ▶ *He talked about his plans with a carelessness that cut her to the quick.*

QUITS

be/call it quits to be back in an equal relationship, or to agree to return to it, because each of you has done something for the other ▶ *He beat me on Wednesday so we're quits now.* ▶ *I paid for lunch and you paid for the theatre. Let's call it quits.*

QUOTE

quote, unquote used before or each side of a word or phrase to show that it is someone else's word or phrase, and that you do not agree with it ▶ *This is the quote, unquote charming cottage, is it? Funny, it looks like a neglected barn to me.* ▶ *I don't want to discuss his quote, apology, unquote. If that's the best he can do, then forget it.*

Q

Rr

RACE

a one-horse race a game, election etc which one competitor will definitely win ▶ *The Opposition have failed to produce a convincing candidate, so this election has turned into a one-horse race.*

a race against time a situation in which something important must be done fast ▶ *The rescue operation is a race against time, as more stormy weather is predicted for tonight.*

the rat race the usual daily life of people in business, seen as highly competitive, full of anxiety, and lacking in human values ▶ *When he decided to get out of the rat race, he opened a sailing school on the west coast.*

RACK

go to rack and ruin to be neglected, and fall into a bad condition ▶ *The house is much too big for one old lady, and it's been going to rack and ruin for years.*

RAG

sth is (like) a red rag to a bull also **sth is (like) a red rag to sb** a particular thing will make someone very angry ▶ *Defeat to Tom is like a red rag to a bull – he tries twice as hard next time.* ▶ *Any mention of the failure of their last CD is a red rag to the band.*

RAGS

(from) rags to riches from being very poor to being very rich ▶ *It is part of the American legend that anyone can* go from rags to riches. **rags-to-riches** ADJ ▶ *His life is a rags-to-riches story that is as dramatic as a Hollywood movie.*

RAGTAG

ragtag and bobtail a mixed group of people or things that seem to be without value ▶ *He bought a ragtag and bobtail collection of old warehouses and workshops at the edge of the canal.*

RAIN

it never rains but it pours also **when it rains it pours** several things of a similar kind tend to happen all at once

▶ *She wants to come and stay, but our Spanish friends will be with us that weekend – it never rains but it pours!* ▶ *When it rains it pours: I've got more work on now than I've had for four years.*

(come) rain or shine whether the weather is good or bad ▶ *She walks two miles, rain or shine, during her lunch hour.*

I'll take a rain check (on sth) I can't do something now, but I'd like to do it at another time ▶ *"Want to come over to lunch?" "Sorry, I can't today, but I'll take a rain check on it if that's OK."*

In the US, a rain check is the part of a ticket to a sports event that you keep. If it rains, and the event cannot happen, you can use that part of the ticket to go to the event when it is played again later.

RAINBOW
be chasing rainbows to be trying to get or achieve something difficult or impossible ▶ *She wants to find the perfect tango partner, but I think she's too old to go chasing rainbows all over the country.*

RAKING
sb is raking it in someone is making a lot of money ▶ *They're raking it in – have you seen the house they've bought?*

RANK
pull rank (on sb) to use your position of authority unfairly, in order to make someone do something for you ▶ *This was supposed to be a park, but one of the councillors pulled rank and had it zoned for commercial development.*

the rank and file the ordinary people in an organization, who do not have power and authority ▶ *The leadership recognizes the need to increase taxation, but knows that this will be deeply unpopular with the rank and file of the party.* **rank-and-file** ADJ ▶ *High salaries paid to the bosses will not make rank-and-file employees more willing to accept wage restraints.*

RANKS
break ranks to fail to support the group or organization that you are in, by doing something different from what you are expected to do ▶ *One*

major oil company broke ranks with the rest of the industry and supported the tough, new anti-pollution laws.

close ranks to unite more closely in a group, by supporting each other and not admitting any disagreement ▶ *Politicians of all parties are likely to close ranks against new demands for more open government.*

swell the ranks of to make a group of people larger by joining it or making people join it ▶ *Factory closures have swollen the ranks of the city's unemployed.*

RANSOM
hold sb to ransom to make a person or group do what you want, especially by threatening them ▶ *Discontented teachers were accused of holding the whole country to ransom.*

a king's ransom a very large amount of money ▶ *She might spend a king's ransom on clothes and jewellery, but she also enjoys getting a bargain in the supermarket.*

RAP
be given a rap across the knuckles also **have your knuckles rapped** to be criticized for something (usually not very important) that you have done wrong ▶ *She was given a rap across the knuckles for not turning up at the last meeting.* ▶ *I had my knuckles rapped for forgetting grandpa's birthday.*

take the rap (for) to be blamed or punished for a mistake or crime, especially for something that you did not do ▶ *It seems that he took the rap for two more crimes that he can't possibly have committed.*

RARING
be raring to go/to do sth to be very

eager to begin doing something
▶ *When are we having the competition? The kids are all raring to go.* ▶ *He's raring to get back into the team now his injury has healed.*

RASPBERRY

blow a raspberry to make a rude noise by putting out your tongue and blowing, often to show lack of respect ▶ *He responded to my plea for cooperation by blowing a raspberry in my direction.*

RAT

smell a rat to begin to think that someone is trying to deceive you, or that something about a situation is wrong ▶ *Detectives went to the hotel to meet the drug dealers, but the dealers must have smelt a rat, and they stayed away.*

RAW

in the raw in the most basic, natural, or typical state, especially when this is unpleasant ▶ *In the towns and settlements of the Gold Rush, you could see human nature in the raw.*

RAY

a ray of sunshine

1 someone or something that makes you feel happier and makes your situation seem better ▶ *The one ray of sunshine during those months was a letter from Kate promising that she would visit me in April.*

2 (used humorously) someone who makes you feel less happy and makes your situation seem worse
▶ *"Nobody's going to want to buy our house." "You're a right little ray of sunshine, aren't you?"*

REACTION

a knee-jerk reaction an action or answer that someone does or gives too quickly, without thinking first ▶ *Judo teaches you a rational response to being attacked, not just a knee-jerk reaction.*

READ

read too much into sth to think that something has more meaning or importance than it really has ▶ *Analysts warned against reading too much into the low unemployment figures.*

READY

be ready to roll to be ready to start doing something ▶ *By 5 o'clock next morning, all of the bus crews were down at the depot and ready to roll.*

REAL

sb/sth is for real someone is or does exactly what they say, or something is true ▶ *When the old man had finished his speech, Jo turned to me and whispered, "Is this guy for real?"*

REAP

you reap what you sow also **as you sow, so shall you reap** ▶ You will get the results you deserve ▶ *You reap what you sow, and you may eventually regret your behaviour in Friday's game.*

REAR

bring up the rear to be last ▶ *A group of children brought up the rear of the procession.*

REARGUARD

fight a rearguard action to make a determined effort to prevent something from happening, even though you think it is too late to succeed ▶ *The family have been fighting a rearguard action to prevent their home from being destroyed by developers.*

REASON

it stands to reason it is sensible and easy to understand ▶ *It stands to reason that you'll be more enthusiastic about studying English if you know it's going to help you in your career.*

RECIPE

be a recipe for ___ to be very likely to have a particular result ▶ *Relying on commercial organizations to provide a proper health service may be a recipe for disaster.* ▶ *If your sister's anything to go by, work hard and play hard seems like a recipe for success.*

RECORD

(just) for the record
1 said when you want to make something clear, or to be sure that it has been recorded correctly ▶ *I need a 'yes' or 'no' from you, just for the record.*
2 said when you are giving information that may interest people, though it is not the main thing you are talking about ▶ *Just for the record, the picture was taken with a Nikon F5, fitted with a 600 mm lens.*

off the record said when you are not making an official statement, and do not want the public to know about it ▶ *His remarks about the policy were made during a conversation that he thought was off the record.* **off-the-record** ADJ ▶ *At an off-the-record meeting with reporters, the police chief outlined his concerns about terrorist activity.*

set the record straight also **put the record straight** to tell people the true facts about a situation, when you think that they have a wrong idea about it ▶ *He was anxious to set the record straight about his involvement with drug companies.* ▶ *Let me put the record straight by correcting the mistakes you made in your speech.*

RED

in the red owing money, especially to a bank ▶ *I'm afraid the business will be in the red this year.*

REIN

give sb (a) free rein also **allow sb (a) free rein** to give someone the freedom to do what they want ▶ *The hotel has a brilliant young chef who is given free rein with the menu.*

give free rein to sth to let something be fully expressed, without controls or limits ▶ *I use this exercise to help students become less self-conscious and give free rein to their imagination.*

keep a tight rein on sb/sth also **keep sb/sth on a tight rein** to control someone or something  very strictly ▶ *It is impossible to be competitive in business today without keeping a tight rein on costs.* ▶ *The head of department kept the teachers on a tight rein, and did not allow them to design their own courses.*

REINS

take over the reins also **take (up) the**

reins to take control (of a country or organization) ➤ *The vice-president took over the reins when the president died.*

Reins are long narrow bands of leather that are fastened around a horse's head to control it.

REMAIN

who shall remain nameless *also* **who will remain nameless** who I do not want to name because I am saying something bad about them (but who is almost certainly known to listeners) ➤ *A certain person, who shall remain nameless, left all the heaters on.*

REST

give it a rest stop talking about that subject because you are boring or annoying me ➤ *"Maybe I shouldn't have said what I thought." "Give it a rest, there's nothing you can do about it now."*

no rest for the wicked even though I'm tired, I have to keep working ➤ *Do you need a clean shirt for tomorrow? Oh, well, no rest for the wicked.*

RETREAT

beat a (hasty) retreat to leave a place quickly ➤ *Finding themselves surrounded by large men with kitchen knives, the health inspectors beat a hasty retreat.*

RETURNS

many happy returns (of the day) may you have a long and happy life (said on someone's birthday) ➤ *All right, I won't ask how old you are, but many happy returns, anyway.*

RHYME

without rhyme or reason *also* **there is no rhyme or reason (to sth)** with no

clear cause or explanation ➤ *They decided to take the house off the market, without apparent rhyme or reason.* ➤ *There's no rhyme or reason to these changes in government policy.*

RICH

that's rich (coming from sb) *also* **it's a bit rich (for sb) to do sth** what someone has said or done is surprising and not reasonable ➤ *"John said I'll never get a job if I don't try harder." "That's rich coming from him – he spends half the day in bed."* ➤ *It's a bit rich for the minister to accuse us of a casual attitude, when he's only bothered to attend one of the meetings.*

RIDE

give sb a free ride
1 to give someone the advantages of a situation which other people are paying for, or in which other people are doing most of the work ➤ *The proposed tax changes will give the rich a free ride, while the poor pay the penalty.*
2 to allow someone to do what they want, without criticism ➤ *The opposition were in no mood to give the minister a free ride.* **get a free ride** ➤ *Why should people who are too lazy to support their families be getting a free ride at our expense?*

go/be along for the ride to go somewhere or do something with other people just for fun or interest ➤ *We're all serious musicians – except Helen, who's along for the ride.* ➤ *I don't mind what we do, I'm just along for the ride.*

ride roughshod over to treat with no respect; to ignore ➤ *Changes to the* law must concentrate on the victim's evidence without riding roughshod over the defendant's right to a fair trial.

be riding high to be very confident and successful ▶ *The president is riding high on her foreign policy successes.*

a rough ride also **a bumpy ride** a time when there are a lot of difficulties and problems ▶ *Investors face a rough ride as the market continues to react to political developments.* ▶ *The policy has had a bumpy ride, but we're beginning to see the benefits now.*

a smooth ride ▶ *Party leaders are predicting a smooth ride for their policy changes next week.*

take sb for a ride to trick someone ▶ *A couple tried to take the mayor for a ride last week when they claimed to be important foreign visitors.*

RIGHT

Mr/Miss Right the perfect man or woman for you to marry ▶ *He's very nice, but I don't really think he's Mr Right.*

RIGHTS

put sth/sb to rights also **set sth/sb to rights** to put something right or correct someone ▶ *One of the great things about university is being able to sit up late, talking and setting the world to rights.* ▶ *I was starting out in completely the wrong direction until that chap put me to rights.*

RING

ring hollow also **have a hollow ring** to seem false or insincere ▶ *His promise rings hollow to me – I shouldn't count on him being there.* ▶ *Her enthusiastic praise for the organizers had a hollow*

ring, given what she said about them yesterday.

ring true to seem completely true and easy to believe ▶ *The description of a Jewish community in 1930s New York rings completely true.*

RINGER

be a dead ringer for sb to look exactly like another person ▶ *My kid sister is a dead ringer for their lead singer.*

RINGS

run rings around sb to be able to defeat someone easily because you are more intelligent or

skilful than they are ▶ *The smugglers have been running rings round our officers because we simply haven't got enough trained people.*

RIOT

sb/sth is a riot someone or something is very funny ▶ *Sam's a riot when he's had a few drinks.* ▶ *The show we put on for the children was a riot and we all had a great time.*

read (sb) the riot act to give someone a strong warning that they must stop doing something that you do not like ▶ *She opened the classroom door and read the girls the riot act.*

> In nineteenth-century Britain, reading the Riot Act to a crowd of people was an official warning that they were causing trouble and must separate and leave. If they did not do this, they were breaking the law.

R

RISE

get a rise out of sb to make someone show that they are annoyed or embarrassed ▶ *We used to try to get a rise out of the physics teacher – and it worked every time.*

rise and shine! wake up and get out of bed! ▶ *Wake up, rise and shine, it's a beautiful morning!*

RIVER

sell sb down the river to do something that harms someone who trusted you, in order to get an advantage for yourself ▶ *The company sold us down the river, lying to us about how well they were doing and then cutting jobs when it suited them.*

ROAD

down the road ➤ down the LINE

hit the road to begin a journey ▶ *No, I won't have any more coffee, thanks; it's time to hit the road.*

ROCK

(caught) between a rock and a hard place in a difficult situation, in which any choice that you make will have bad results ▶ *Of course we don't really want to go on strike – we're caught between a rock and a hard place.*

(as) solid as a rock
1 strong and firm ▶ *The table was made of oak, a hundred years old and solid as a rock.*
2 able to be trusted ▶ *The company has remained as solid as a rock during the years of financial turmoil.*

ROCKER

be/go off your rocker also **be/go off your trolley** to be or become crazy ▶ *He's off his rocker – have you heard his weird ideas?* ▶ *He's going off his trolley with boredom.*

ROCKET

sth isn't rocket science something is not very difficult or complicated ▶ *This computer program isn't rocket science – you can learn it in an hour or two.*

ROCKS

on the rocks
1 with ice ▶ *She ordered two vodkas on the rocks and a lager.*
2 failing or about to fail ▶ *I got the impression that their marriage was on the rocks.* ▶ *Her company is well and truly on the rocks.*

ROD

rule sb with a rod of iron also **run sth with a rod of iron** to control a person, group, or organization so strictly that they are too frightened to disobey you ▶ *The general ruled his men with a rod of iron, but he was always fair.* ▶ *His mother was a tough old woman who had run her family with a rod of iron for 40 years.*

ROLL

be on a roll to be going through a very successful stage ▶ *The company's on a roll at the moment – we're having to employ more staff to keep up with the work.*

ROLLING

be rolling (in it) to have a lot of money ▶ *People assume that just because you've made a hit record you*

must be rolling in it. ▶ *He's not just rich, he's rolling.*

ROME

Rome wasn't built in a day what you want to happen will take a long time (said to encourage someone to be patient) ▶ *People complain that new towns lack entertainment facilities, but after all, Rome wasn't built in a day.*

when in Rome (do as the Romans do) it is best to behave in the same way as the people around you in a situation, even if you would not normally do so ▶ *None of the women were drinking alcohol, so I thought, when in Rome, and took an orange juice.*

ROOF

go through the roof also **go through the ceiling**
1 to become much higher, more expensive, or more extreme ▶ *Beer sales have gone through the roof because of the recent spell of hot weather.*
2 to become very angry ▶ *She'll go through the roof when she sees what you've done to her dress.*

hit the roof also **hit the ceiling** to become very angry ▶ *Dad hit the ceiling when he saw the mess in the bathroom.*

ROOFTOPS

shout sth from the rooftops also **shout sth from the housetops** to try to tell everyone about something ▶ *I agree with your point of view, but you don't have to shout it from the rooftops.*

ROOST

rule the roost to be the most important thing ▶ *Politics, not finance, clearly rules the roost in this country.* ▶ *In many countries, women rule the roost at home.*

ROOT

take root (of an idea) to become accepted or established ▶ *In the last couple of days, a sense of confidence has begun to take root among investors.*

ROOTS

put down roots to begin living in a place and decide that you are going to live there for a long time ▶ *Most new arrivals put down roots in their new country, but a few never settle down.*

ROPE

give sb enough rope (and they'll hang themselves) if you let someone do what they want, they will probably make mistakes and fail to achieve anything good ▶ *She's very arrogant, but her boss is going on the principle of give her enough rope and she'll hang herself.*

give sb a lot of rope to give someone freedom to do what they want ▶ *I was given a lot of rope at the newspaper, which annoyed some of the older journalists.*

ROPES

know/learn the ropes to know or learn how to do a particular job or how to behave in a particular situation ▶ *Keep quiet and stay in the background until you know the ropes.* ▶ *I don't think he would be a good manager – he hasn't had time to learn the ropes yet.*

This idiom comes from the time when sailors (=men who work on ships) had to know how to deal with the ropes on ships.

on the ropes doing badly or about to fail ► *Two mediocre films put his career back on the ropes, and he didn't work again for three years.*

show sb the ropes also ***teach sb the ropes*** to show someone how to do a particular job, or how to behave in a particular situation ► *They brought in an engineer and he showed us the ropes, but after that we were left to get on with it.*

ROSES

everything's/it's coming up roses everything or a particular thing is happening exactly as it is supposed to, and there are no problems ► *It was a time when everything was coming up roses for her.*

come up smelling of roses also ***come up smelling like roses*** to get an advantage from a situation, when you ought to be blamed, criticized, or harmed by it ► *Everyone loved her and she always came up smelling of roses, however many mistakes she made.*

ROUGH

rough and ready simple and basic, or made or done very quickly without much preparation ► *School exams are only a rough and ready guide to a pupil's potential.* ► *I can offer you a rough and ready lunch if you've got time.*

take the rough with the smooth to be willing to accept the unpleasant parts of a situation with the pleasant parts ► *I needed the press as much as they* needed me, so I was polite to journalists and was happy to take the rough with the smooth.

ROUTE

go down the ___ route to follow a particular course of action ► *Britain may end up going down the European route, and introducing changes to the law.*

RUB

rub it in to remind someone of a mistake they have made or something bad they have done ► *"I've never been so drunk I couldn't find my key." "OK, don't rub it in!"*

there's the rub also ***therein lies the rub*** that is the problem that makes a situation difficult ► *The manual is very thorough, but there's the rub – will busy managers have time to read it all?*

This idiom is from a line in Shakespeare's play, *Hamlet*.

RUG

pull the rug (out) from under sb to stop supporting someone suddenly, or take away something that they

depend on for success ► *I'd just outlined my proposal when he pulled the rug from under me by announcing they'd already made their decision.*

RULE

the golden rule the most important rule or principle ▶ *The golden rule is to begin gently and not to plunge into an exacting schedule of vigorous exercise.*

a rule of thumb a piece of advice or general rule which is usually true ▶ *The general rule of thumb is not to apply oil-based paint over latex paint.*

> Brewers (=people who make beer) used to test the temperature of beer with their thumb to see if it was ready.

work to rule to protest by only doing exactly what your job contract says and no more ▶ *The ambulance staff were working to rule, and only answering emergency calls.*

RUMOUR

rumour has it (that) people are saying (that) ▶ *Rumour has it that the company's in trouble.*

RUN

give sb a run for his/her money to do very well in competition with a particular person or group, even if you don't win ▶ *I won the first set and gave the champion a good run for her money.*

go on a ___ run to go to buy something ▶ *Could one of you kids go on a milk run, please?*

in the long run also **in the long term** over a long period of time ▶ *A house is a pretty safe investment in the long run.* **In the short run/term** ▶ *A crash diet will make you lose weight in the short term, but you're unlikely to keep it off.*

run amok to start behaving in a violent, extreme, or crazy way ▶ *The place looked as though drunken students had run amok with spray cans.*

run deep also **go deep** to be very strong for a long time ▶ *Many farmers are suspicious of government help, and this lack of trust runs very deep.* ▶ *Feelings about the death of a parent are bound to go deep.*

run sb ragged to make someone very tired by giving them too much work or too many problems ▶ *Managing the business on his own is running him ragged.*

run riot to be wild and free of control ▶ *This is a place where children can run riot and enjoy themselves.* ▶ *She had let her imagination run riot on the costume designs for the play.* ▶ *The virus will run riot and the animal will die within a few days.*

run with it to do as much as you can to develop an idea, be imaginative in a job etc ▶ *If someone gives you the chance of a job like that, you take it and run with it.*

RUN-AROUND

give sb the run-around to avoid giving someone a definite answer ▶ *Everyone in your office is giving me the run-around – is there any way of talking to someone who will take responsibility?* **get the run-around** ▶ *I'm tired of getting the run-around and I want answers to my questions.*

RUNES

read the runes to examine a situation and understand it because of your special experience and skill ▶ *Those who are skilled in reading the runes predict that the rebels will make an offer of peace talks.*

R

RUNG

the bottom rung of the ladder *also* **the first rung of the ladder** the lowest level or position in a system or organization ▶ *I started on the bottom rung of the ladder as a messenger.* **the top/highest rung of the ladder** ▶ *Do human beings really occupy the highest rung of the evolutionary ladder?*

RUN-IN

have a run-in with sb to have an argument or disagreement with someone ▶ *She had a run-in with the chairman recently over the new sales campaign.*

RUNNING

be in the running (for sth) to have a good chance of getting (a job, prize etc) ▶ *Both players are in the running to play in Saturday's game.*

RUT

get (stuck) into a rut *also* **be (stuck) in a rut** to become or be bored because you seem to be living or working in a situation that never changes ▶ *In the last few years I've got into a rut – I need to apply for a more challenging job.* ▶ *She's worried she's going to get stuck in a rut.*

Ss

SACK

get the sack to be dismissed from your job ▶ *If I don't finish this by Friday, I'll get the sack.*

hit the sack also **hit the hay** to go to bed and sleep ▶ *I guess we'd better hit the sack – we've got to get going early tomorrow.*

SAID

that's/it's easier said than done it will be difficult to do what someone has suggested ▶ *"Try to forget him." "Yes, well, that's easier said than done."*

SAILS

trim your sails (to sth) to change your behaviour, especially to spend less money, in order to deal with a difficult situation ▶ *The company has had to trim its sails to the present decline in the economy.*

SALAD

sb's salad days the time when someone was young and did not have much experience of life ▶ *His later music is very different from the precise, classically-based works of his salad days.*

SALT

no ___ worth his/her salt would do sth also **any ___ worth his/her salt would do sth** nobody/someone who is good at their job would do a particular thing ▶ *No government organization worth its salt would negotiate with terrorists.* ▶ *Any woman worth her salt would refuse to work on those terms.*

In ancient Rome, soldiers were paid in salt instead of money.

rub salt in sb's wounds also **rub salt in the wound** to do something that makes someone feel even more upset about their situation than they already do ▶ *Not only has he treated her like dirt, but he's rubbing salt in her wounds by bringing Joanne to her party.*

Sailors (=men who work on ships) were punished in the past by being beaten with a rope. Salt was put on their wounds because people thought it would help them get better but, of course, it just made them hurt more.

the salt of the earth a person or group of people you admire because they are ordinary, good, and honest ▶ *The couple who run our local shop are the salt of the earth; they'd always help you out in an emergency.*
salt-of-the-earth ADJ ▶ *We like our politicians to be salt-of-the-earth types.*

SAND

be built on sand to be established without having enough money, support, trust etc to be completely safe ▶ *The bank had lent too much to private corporations built on sand.* ▶ *I'm not surprised about the divorce – the whole marriage was built on sand.*

SANDWICH

one sandwich short of a picnic very stupid or slightly crazy ▶ *He's a nice old man, but I think he's one sandwich short of a picnic.*

S

SAUCE

(what's) sauce for the goose (is sauce for the gander) if one person is treated in a particular way then you should treat other people in the same situation in the same way ▶ *Let your boyfriend have some fun, Jan – sauce for the goose, you know!*

SAY

as they say used to show that what you are saying is a well-known and ordinary phrase ▶ *Shares in the film company have reached an all-time low, but that, as they say, is show business.*

I'll say! yes, I agree! ▶ *"Kit's an aggressive driver." "I'll say!"*

you can say that again I agree with what you have just said ▶ *"I've eaten way too much." "You can say that again – I cooked enough for six!"*

you said it! what you have just said is true, but I didn't like to say it myself ▶ *"I think I was a bit rude to her." "You said it."*

SCENE

set the scene (for) ➤ set the STAGE (for)

SCENES

behind the scenes privately, not in public ▶ *There'll be a special programme on what goes on behind the scenes of the World Cup.*

SCENT

put sb off the scent also **throw sb off the scent** to prevent someone from finding out something by telling lies or giving them something else to do ▶ *On the day of the surprise party, Tom put her off the scent by taking her to an early film.*

SCHEME

in the (grand) scheme of things when you compare something to larger problems or events ▶ *Really, in the grand scheme of things, my housing situation is pretty unimportant.*

SCIENCE

blind sb with science to tell someone something in a complicated and technical way ▶ *The computer specialists tend to blind us with science instead of explaining very simply how to operate the software.*

SCORE

know the score to know all the facts of a situation ▶ *We'll know the score when we see who's running the new project.*

settle an old score to do something to harm or upset someone because they have harmed or upset you in the past ▶ *Terry started the fight because he wanted to settle an old score with John.*

SCRATCH

be/come up to scratch to be or become good enough ▶ *He wanted to play, but his health's not up to scratch yet.* **get/bring sth up to scratch** ▶ *We've got to get the gardens up to scratch before the open day.*

from scratch from the very beginning ▶ *Her mother still makes pasta from scratch with special flour – it takes ages, but it tastes wonderful.*

S

SCREW

have a screw loose to be slightly crazy
▶ *He's shouting at all the passers-by – has he got a screw loose?*

SCREWS

put the screws on sb to force someone to do what you want, often by threats ▶ *He's well-known for putting the screws on his competitors.*

SCRUFF

take sth by the scruff of the neck to take determined action to deal with a difficult problem ▶ *The government has taken the education system by the scruff of the neck and introduced some radical reforms.*

SCUM

the scum of the earth the worst people you can imagine ▶ *The charity helps people living on the streets – those that society considers the scum of the earth.*

SEA

a sea change a complete change in a situation or in people's opinions
▶ *Technological developments in the past few years have caused a sea change in the way we communicate.*

be (all) at sea to be very confused
▶ *She was all at sea when she*

suddenly had to step in and chair the meeting.

SEAMS

be bursting at the seams also **be bulging at the seams** to be extremely full ▶ *The restaurant's always bursting at the seams on Fridays and Saturdays.*

come apart at the seams also **fall apart at the seams**
1 to start to go wrong and be very likely to fail ▶ *The company came apart at the seams when Johnson left.* ▶ *Her arguments in favour of the scheme fell apart at the seams when we questioned her.*
2 to become very upset or anxious
▶ *At exam time, Kim would come apart at the seams.*

SEARCH

search me! I don't know the answer
▶ *"Which is bigger, London or New York?" "Search me."*

SEASON

open season on ___ a time when it is acceptable to criticize something or someone ▶ *After that documentary, it seemed to be open season on doctors.*

> Open season is the time each year in the US when it is legal to kill particular animals or fish.

SEAT

back seat driver someone who likes to give the driver of a car advice about how to drive ▶ *My husband is a terrible back seat driver – he can't bear anyone else to be in charge.*

fly by the seat of your pants to use your natural ability and intelligence to do something instead of learning and preparing it ▶ *We often have to fly by the seat of our pants because there's seldom time to prepare lessons before*

S

class. **seat-of-the-pants** ADJ ▶ *She has a refreshing, seat-of-the-pants approach to business.*

be in the driving seat also **be in the driver's seat** to be in control ▶ *The unions are putting us under a lot of pressure, but we're still in the driving seat for the moment.*

in the hot seat in a situation where you have to deal with difficult problems ▶ *The salon manager is in the hot seat, having to deal with the most troublesome clients as well as keeping the staff happy.*

take a back seat (to) to become less important or influential ▶ *I had to take a back seat in the production of this film, and it was sometimes difficult not to give my opinion.* ▶ *Housing, health, and social services would have to take a back seat if the government spent what is needed on education.*

SECURITY

a security blanket something that makes you feel safer or more confident ▶ *Some people treat their favourite business suit as a security blanket because they feel at ease doing business in it.*

SEE

see red to become very angry suddenly ▶ *When he threatened to end their affair, she saw red and punched him.*

see what sb is (really) made of also **find out what sb is (really) made of** to find out how strong, determined, or skilful someone is by watching them ▶ *They won easily last week, but in today's game we'll find out what they're really made of.* **show sb what you're (really) made of** ▶ *It wasn't till*

I started work that I could show my parents what I was made of.

SEED

go to seed also **run to seed** to start to look old and neglected ▶ *The city centre had gone to seed over the years.* ▶ *The photo was of a sad-looking man who had run to seed.*

> This idiom comes from plants that should be picked before the seeds form, for example so that the young leaves can be eaten.

SEEDS

sow the seeds (of sth) to start a process that will have a particular result ▶ *Stopping trade with these countries is just sowing the seeds of disaster.* ▶ *The seeds of his acting career were sown while he was at school.*

SELL

the hard sell trying to persuade someone to buy something or do something by putting a lot of pressure on them ▶ *He's been doing the hard sell on this biography, telling people there's stuff in it that no one has even guessed at before.*

sell sb/sth short not to give someone or something the treatment that they deserve ▶ *Museums should be learning environments, and to settle for popularity alone is to sell them short.*

SEND

send sb packing to make someone leave ▶ *Her life changed dramatically when she sent her lazy husband packing.*

SENSES

come to your senses to realize that you are doing the wrong thing, and

start behaving in a reasonable way
▶ *After a few years trying to make a living as a singer he came to his senses and went back to college.*

bring sb (back) to his/her senses
▶ *Mum threatened to leave Dad, and I think it brought him to his senses.*

take leave of your senses to start to behave in an unreasonable or silly way
▶ *Have you taken leave of your senses? How can we possibly afford a car like that?*

SERVE

(it) serves sb right someone deserves something bad that has happened to them ▶ *"I've got a parking fine." "Serves you right for being too lazy to walk from the car park."*

SET

set sb straight to correct someone or tell them the truth ▶ *Mum thought it was my fault that the computer broke down – can you set her straight?* ▶ *She was starting to add water to the scrambled eggs until I set her straight.*

SHADE

put sb/sth in the shade also *leave sb/sth in the shade* to be so good or impressive that other things or people seem less impressive in comparison
▶ *Ginny, elegantly dressed as usual, put the other women in the shade.*
▶ *Their new sports car left its rivals in the shade at this year's show.*

SHADES

shades of ___ that reminds me of (something) ▶ *"I got drunk and was thrown in the fountain." "Shades of your graduation party!"*

SHADOW

beyond a shadow of (a) doubt also *without a shadow of a doubt*

definitely and without any doubt at all
▶ *We proved it was suicide, beyond a shadow of doubt.*

cast a shadow over sth to make something seem less good or more difficult to enjoy ▶ *The feelings of tension between my father and my brother cast a shadow over our wedding day.*

sb is a shadow of his/her former self also *sth is a shadow of its former self* someone or something is less strong, healthy, or important than in the past
▶ *After the accident, he became a shadow of his former self.* ▶ *Today, the capital remains a shadow of its former self, its beautiful buildings now in ruins.*

be scared of your own shadow to be extremely shy or nervous ▶ *The boy was scared of his own shadow. He'd certainly never argue with anyone in authority.*

SHAKES

no great shakes not very good
▶ *"How's the new restaurant?" "No great shakes."* ▶ *He was no great shakes as a pianist, but he really enjoyed playing.*

SHAPE

knock sb/sth into shape also *lick sb/sth into shape* to get someone or something into the right condition
▶ *The army reckons it takes at least six months to knock raw recruits into shape.* ▶ *Can you lick that presentation into shape by this afternoon?*

the shape of things to come how things will be in the future ▶ *Are out-of-town shopping malls and empty town centres an indication of the shape of things to come?*

S

SHARE
the lion's share of sth the biggest part of something ▶ *When we buy a bottle of wine for dinner he usually gets the lion's share.*

SHAVE
a close shave ➤ a close CALL

SHEEP
the black sheep of the family someone who a family or group is ashamed of because they are less successful or more immoral than the rest ▶ *My uncle ran away from home and joined the circus – he was definitely the black sheep of the family.*

separate the sheep from the goats to find out which of a group of people or things have the qualities that you want, and which do not ▶ *The aim of the application form is to separate the sheep from the goats, so that only the best people are interviewed.*

SHELL
come out of your shell to become less shy and more confident ▶ *She*

always comes out of her shell when she's had a glass of wine. **bring sb out of his/her shell** ▶ *Jack's very good at bringing the new students out of their shells.*

SHINE
take the shine off sth to spoil a pleasant or successful occasion by making it seem less good or special ▶ *Tiredness and depression may take the shine off your first days with a new baby.*

take a shine to to decide that you like someone as soon as you first meet or see them ▶ *My dad's taken quite a shine to you – come and see us again.*

SHIP
leave a sinking ship also **jump ship** to leave a company, place etc because you believe it is in trouble ▶ *The company did very badly that year, and he wasn't the only person to leave a sinking ship.* ▶ *When the first signs of unrest came, several businesses jumped ship.*

when your ship comes in when you become rich ▶ *When our ship comes in, we'll get a nice, modern kitchen.*

> This idiom comes from a time when business people and the wives of sailors (=men who work on ships) waited for ships to return so that they could be paid for their goods that were sold abroad, or use the money their husbands brought home.

SHIRT
have the shirt off sb's back to take a lot of someone else's money ▶ *If you go to those lawyers, they'll have the shirt off your back and you'll get nothing out of it.*

keep your shirt on be calm and patient! ▶ *"Hurry up, we'll miss the train!" "Keep your shirt on – there's plenty of time."*

lose your shirt to lose a lot of money ▶ *He's stopped going to the races since he lost his shirt last year.*

sb would give you the shirt off his/ her back someone is very generous and helpful ▶ *He's the kind of man who'd give you the shirt off his back.*

SHIVERS

give you the shivers to make you feel afraid or anxious ▶ *I don't like being alone in the house at night, it gives me the shivers.*

send shivers (up and) down your spine also **send a shiver down your spine** to make you feel frightened or excited ▶ *That music sends shivers up and down my spine.* ▶ *The sound of gunfire sent a shiver down his spine.*

SHOES

be in sb's shoes to be in someone else's situation ▶ *If I were in your shoes, I'd find out everything I could about the company.* ▶ *It was the right choice, and anyone in her shoes would have done the same thing.*

put yourself in sb's shoes to try to understand what someone else's situation is like ▶ *It's easy to be critical, but put yourself in her shoes – what else could she have done?*

step into sb's shoes also **fill sb's shoes** to do the job that someone else has been doing ▶ *There are plenty of eager young managers waiting to step into my shoes.* ▶ *I think it'll be difficult for her to fill Katy's shoes.*

SHOESTRING

on a shoestring with very little money to spend ▶ *As students, we used to go travelling on a shoestring.*

SHOP

set up shop to start a business or activity ▶ *She decided to set up shop as a computer consultant.*

shut up shop to close a business or stop an activity ▶ *The company has been forced to shut up shop, owing to lack of demand for its superb, but rather specialized, books.*

talk shop to talk about your work with someone else who is involved in it ▶ *The two girls were talking shop all evening while we watched TV.* **shop talk** N ▶ *She doesn't like shop talk at the dinner table.*

SHORT

short and sweet shorter than you expected, especially when you are pleased by this ▶ *We have one other item of business before lunch, and I'll try to keep it short and sweet because we've all worked hard this morning.*

SHOT

a big shot an important or powerful person ▶ *His mother is a big shot in local politics.* **big-shot** ADJ ▶ *I don't like him – he acts like some big-shot movie star.*

sth is a cheap shot a remark or joke about someone which is unfair or unkind ▶ *"His clients may be willing to lose his services for a week – indeed they may be glad to." "That's a cheap shot."*

like a shot very quickly ▶ *If your mum thought you were in trouble, she'd be round here like a shot.*

S

be a long shot to be worth trying, even though you think it is not likely to succeed ▶ *We could advertise for volunteers. It's a long shot, but it might work.*

not... by a long shot not at all ▶ *He's won the case, but his problems aren't over by a long shot.*

a/sb's parting shot a final remark that warns or criticizes the person someone is talking to ▶ *He left with a vicious parting shot: "You'll never get a penny of that money."*

a shot across the bows also **a warning shot (across sb's bows)** something that you do or say in order to warn someone you oppose what they are doing and will try to stop them ▶ *We must regard the outcome of this case as a shot across our bows.*

> The bows are the front part of a ship. This idiom comes from a fighting ship firing towards another ship to warn it that it may attack.

a shot in the dark a complete guess ▶ *It's just a shot in the dark, but could there be an oil leak?*

SHOTS

call the shots also **call the tune** to make the decisions in a situation ▶ *We have taken over full responsibility, which means we call the shots and we pay the bills.*

SHOULDER

give sb the cold shoulder to be unfriendly to someone ▶ *I tried to sort things out with Jean, but she gave me the cold shoulder.* **cold-shoulder** v ▶ *He cold-shouldered all the opposing candidates.*

sb is looking over his/her shoulder someone is worried or being careful in case something dangerous or unpleasant happens to them ▶ *Employees are looking over their shoulders, wondering if they will be the next to lose their jobs.*

sb is looking over your shoulder someone is checking and judging what you are doing because they do not trust you ▶ *Even if I get this promotion, I'll still have Sam looking over my shoulder.*

put your shoulder to the wheel to start to work with great effort and determination ▶ *You can get a good degree if you decide to put your shoulder to the wheel.*

a shoulder to cry on someone whom you can talk to about your problems ▶ *My office is at the end of* *the corridor – come and see me if you need a shoulder to cry on.*

SHOULDERS

rub shoulders with sb to meet and spend time with people who are different from you, especially people who are famous or important ▶ *In the hotel industry you often have the chance to rub shoulders with the stars.*

SHOW

get/keep the show on the road to start or continue an activity ▶ *Now the* contract's been signed we can get the show on the road. ▶ *In spite of illness and bad luck, they managed to keep the show on the road for another year.*

steal the show to get more attention than anyone else ▶ *An audience of politically-aware students almost succeeded in stealing the show from the official speakers.*

SHREDS

tear sb/sth to shreds also ***tear sb/sth to pieces*** to criticize someone or something very unkindly and severely ▶ *When he appeared on the chat show, the interviewer tore him to shreds.* ▶ *I thought I'd proved something new, but the tutor just tore my essay to pieces.*

SHRIFT

get short shrift also ***be given short shrift*** to receive very little attention, consideration, or sympathy ▶ *Evidently, women employees are getting short shrift in spite of the council's equal opportunities policy.*

give sth short shrift ▶ *Any argument in favour of private education was given short shrift.*

SIDE

the flip side a different or opposite side of something ▶ *The flip side of the farmers' success story is the destruction of wildlife by pesticides.*

get on the wrong side of sb to annoy someone or make them angry ▶ *If you get on the wrong side of her, you might as well start looking for another job straightaway.*

have sth on your side something is an advantage to you ▶ *He did not have much experience in politics, but he had youth and enthusiasm on his side.*

sth is on your side ▶ *It will be a hard*

struggle, but justice is on our side.

keep on the right side of sb to be careful not to annoy someone ▶ *We kept on the right side of the English teacher, who was known for his biting sarcasm.*

be on the side of the angels to be doing something good and morally right ▶ *Don't get angry with the farmers, they're on the side of the angels in this dispute.*

be on the wrong/right side of 40 etc to be older/younger than a particular age ▶ *He's boring and on the wrong side of 60, but she loves him.* ▶ *I want to have kids while I'm still on the right side of 40.*

the other side of the coin a different or opposite side of a situation, problem, idea etc ▶ *It was a very unpleasant experience – but on the other side of the coin, I did learn a lot.*

the other side of the tracks also ***the wrong side of the tracks*** a poor part of a town or of society ▶ *The twins were from the other side of the tracks, and we weren't allowed to play with them.*

SIDES

play both sides against the middle to be friendly with people on both sides of an argument, in order to gain an advantage ▶ *Since my parents' divorce, I have become expert at playing both sides against the middle.*

be two sides of the same coin (of two problems or situations) to be so closely related that they are really just two parts of the same thing ▶ *It is often true that social deprivation and poor school performance are two sides of the same coin.*

SIGHT

lose sight of sth to forget something

important that you should bear in mind ▶ *We were starting to make money, but we were losing sight of our original purpose, which was to serve the public.* ▶ *He decided when he was eight that he wanted to be an actor, and he never lost sight of that goal.*

out of sight, out of mind when you do not see someone or something, you do not think or care about them ▶ *As soon as I've left he'll forget all about me. It's out of sight, out of mind with him.*

not a pretty sight
unpleasant to look at ▶ *He'd stayed in the sun too long, and his back wasn't a pretty sight.*

be a sight for sore eyes to be very welcoming or attractive to look at ▶ *The friendly lights of the pub were a sight for sore eyes after our long, wet journey.*

SIGHTS

have sb/sth in your sights to decide that you will try to win or get something, or defeat someone ▶ *After yesterday's success, she has the Open Championship in her sights.* ▶ *She made a good start to the race, with her chief rival firmly in her sights.*

> This idiom comes from shooting. You look along the sights on the top of a gun when you are aiming it at something.

set your sights on sth to decide that you really want something and will try to get it ▶ *During his last year at*

school, he had set his sights on becoming a lawyer.

SIGN

a sign of the times something that you think is typical of the present state of society ▶ *It's a sign of the times, I suppose – it takes two seconds to phone a company on the other side of the world, and ten minutes for them to find someone who can deal with your enquiry.*

signed, sealed, and delivered also **signed and sealed** (of an agreement) made, completed, and not able to be changed ▶ *Everything is signed, sealed, and delivered; the two companies have merged under the new name.* ▶ *We can move into the new house as soon as it's all signed and sealed.*

SINK

sink or swim to succeed by your own efforts without help from anyone else ▶ *Surviving financially at university is difficult, but it prepares students for the world of work in which they must sink or swim.*

SIT

sit tight to wait without doing anything until the situation changes ▶ *We are advising our clients to sit tight at the moment, and not to buy or sell until the market becomes more stable.*

be sitting pretty to be in a good situation with many advantages ▶ *We're sitting pretty now. I've paid off the mortgage and there's money left over to repair and paint the house as well.*

SIXES

be at sixes and sevens to be in a

confused state ▶ *Please excuse the mess, I'm all at sixes and sevens this morning.*

SIZE

cut sb down to size to criticize or insult someone in order to make them feel that they are not as successful or important as they thought they were ▶ *Many journalists are attracted by the chance to cut famous people down to size.*

that's about the size of it that's a reasonable judgment of the situation ▶ *"He seems like a stupid kid who's got into trouble, not a criminal." "That's about the size of it." ▶ "We've done our best and now we've got to wait and see – that's about the size of it."*

try sth (on) for size to try something and see if it is suitable for you ▶ *The only problem with this shop is that you can't try the clothes on for size until you get them home. ▶ I like your marketing ideas, and I'll get the committee to try them for size next week.*

SKATES

get your skates on to hurry up ▶ *We'll have to get our skates on if we want to book a decent holiday this year.*

SKIDS

be on the skids to be in a bad situation that is getting worse ▶ *By the end of that month I realized that my business was on the skids.*

SKIN

by the skin of your teeth only just; with very little time, space etc left over ▶ *I caught the plane by the skin of my teeth. ▶ He had survived the recession by the skin of his teeth.*

get under sb's skin
1 to understand what someone thinks and feels ▶ *An actor must understand his characters and get under their skin.*
2 to cause someone to become annoyed or angry ▶ *The way he sucks his teeth is really beginning to get under my skin.*
3 to attract someone ▶ *Somehow in those two weeks she had got under my skin, and I hated the idea of leaving.*

have (a) thick skin to stay relaxed when people criticize you or do not like you ▶ *It is good to have a thick skin if you are appointed as head of a department with instructions to sort it out.*

it's no skin off my/your etc nose also **it's no skin off my/your etc back** someone doesn't care because it doesn't affect them ▶ *It's no skin off our nose if they raise prices – we'll just raise ours. ▶ It's all right for him, it's no skin off his back if we lose this game.*

make your skin crawl to make you feel frightened or sick ▶ *He loves horror movies that make your skin crawl.* ▶ *She can't bear him to touch her; she says it makes her skin crawl.*

nearly jump out of your skin to be so surprised or shocked that you make a sudden movement ▶ *When I tapped Jim on the shoulder he nearly jumped out of his skin.*

save your/sb's skin to save yourself or

S

someone else ▶ *He realized that the only way to save his skin was to make a deal with the police.*

skin sb alive to be very angry with someone ▶ *I'm late again, and I know my mother will skin me alive this time.*

SKINFUL

have had a skinful to have drunk a lot of alcohol ▶ *You've had a skinful – you'd better stay here tonight.*

SKIP

skip it I don't want to continue talking about that ▶ *"Do you really like her?" "Who?" "Ah, skip it, forget I asked."*

SKULL

bored out of your skull ➤ bored out of your MIND

SKY

the sky's the limit there are no limits to what someone can do, achieve, spend, or earn ▶ *Now he's joined a professional team the sky's the limit.*

SLAP

be (like) a slap in the face (of a decision, answer etc) to be very disappointing or insulting ▶ *His refusal of help was like a slap in the face.* ▶ *The government's cutback of funding was a cruel slap in the face to our national museums.*

a slap on the wrist a punishment or criticism that you do not think has been serious or severe enough ▶ *Many corrupt government officials were being let off with a slap on the wrist.* **be/get slapped on the wrist** ▶ *If young offenders simply get slapped on the wrist, they will offend again.*

SLATE

a clean slate a new situation in which past mistakes or crimes do not stop

you succeeding ▶ *Employers who join the scheme have to guarantee that ex-criminals can start with a clean slate.*

> A slate is a small, smooth board that children used to write on at school in the past. When they had finished one piece of work they would rub the writing off and start again.

wipe the slate clean to agree to forget about past mistakes, arguments, or crimes ▶ *Chris and his wife agreed to wipe the slate clean and start all over again.*

SLEEP

sb can do sth in his/her sleep someone can do something very easily ▶ *Don't worry, I've driven to the hospital so many times I could do it in my sleep.*

not lose any sleep over sth not to worry or be anxious about something ▶ *He thinks he may be out of a job in the New Year, but he's not losing any sleep over it.*

sleep on it to delay making a decision until the next day so that you have more time to think about it ▶ *"I don't really know if I want the job." "Go home and sleep on it, and give me a call in the morning."*

SLEEVE

have sth up your sleeve also **have an ace up your sleeve** to have a secret plan, advantage, or argument that you can use ▶ *If that medicine doesn't* work, I've got some other ways of treating you up my sleeve. ▶ He had an ace up his sleeve, but he wasn't sure whether to tell them yet.

This idiom comes from card games, in which someone could cheat by hiding a card in his sleeve (=the part of a shirt, coat etc that covers your arm) until he needed it.

sb is laughing up his/her sleeve someone is secretly laughing ▶ Is he serious about his art, or is he laughing up his sleeve at the people who are paying huge sums of money for those ridiculous sculptures?

SLEEVES
roll up your sleeves to get ready to work hard ▶ It's time for students to roll up their sleeves and start revising for their final exams.

SLICE
a slice of the cake also **a piece of the pie** a part of something, often an amount of money, that one person gets when several people are each getting a part of it ▶ The actors who appear in these films are now demanding a bigger slice of the cake. ▶ Old people have seen their piece of the national pie grow smaller every year.

SLIP
a Freudian slip something you say that is different from what you intended to say, and is supposed to show your hidden emotions or thoughts, especially about sex ▶ She called him Michael without even realizing it – obviously a Freudian slip.

This phrase comes from Sigmund Freud's ideas about the way the human mind works.

a slip of the tongue something that you have said by mistake ▶ "Eight thousand? I thought you said it would cost six thousand." "Yes, sorry, slip of the tongue, of course I meant six."

SLOPE
be on a/the slippery slope to be starting an unpleasant process that will get worse and more difficult to control

▶ Grandma thinks that if I occasionally have a beer I'm on the slippery slope towards a life of drunkenness.

SLUM
slum it to spend time in worse conditions than the ones you are used to ▶ Poor Joe had to slum it in business class instead of first class!

SLY
do sth on the sly to do something secretly ▶ Although our parents had forbidden it, Anita and I continued to meet on the sly.

SMILES
wreathed in smiles smiling a lot ▶ He was wreathed in smiles as he received the award.

SMOKE
go up in smoke to fail completely because the situation has changed ▶ When he got ill, the family's holiday plans went up in smoke.

S

(there's) no smoke without fire if people are saying something unpleasant or shocking, it is probably based on truth ▶ *You can't believe everything the children say about the school, but there's no smoke without fire, and it's worth asking the head.*

SNAKE

a snake in the grass someone who pretends to be your friend but does something to harm you ▶ *Don't listen to her flattery – she's a snake in the grass and she means you harm.*

SNAP

snap out of it to stop yourself thinking or behaving in a particular way ▶ *Oh, snap out of it – you're not a little girl any more and you can't get what you want by screaming.*

SNEEZE

sth is not to be sneezed at something is impressive ▶ *An event that attracts participants from 35 nations is not to be sneezed at.*

SNOW

a snow job lies and tricks that someone uses to make people believe something that is untrue ▶ *The whole story is a major snow job, if you ask me. He would rather have us think he's insane.*

SO

so and so also **so-and-so**
1 a particular person, when you do not give their name ▶ *She'd point someone out and say 'That's so and so', but I never remembered their names.*
2 someone unpleasant or difficult to deal with ▶ *I've warned him, but he's such an obstinate so-and-so, he won't be told.*

so far, so good up to now, everything is going well ▶ *I held my breath and climbed onto the saddle. So far, so good – and then the horse started to move.*

so near (and) yet so far something has almost been achieved, but it seems you are just as far from achieving it as before ▶ *We were winning in the final until the last minute – so near and yet so far.*

so what? what has just been mentioned is unimportant to you ▶ *"You were on the phone for an hour!" "Yeah, so what?"*

SOAPBOX

get on your soapbox to express strong opinions about something, and try to persuade other people that you are right ▶ *I don't want to be here when she gets on her soapbox about animal rights.*

This idiom comes from a time when people made informal speeches standing on strong wooden boxes used for packing soap in.

SOCK

put a sock in it! stop talking, or doing something annoying ▶ *"Mum, he's tickling me!" "If you two don't put a sock in it, I'm going to stop the car."*
sock it to sb also **sock it to 'em!** to do something that surprises, shocks, or impresses someone ▶ *I'm glad the government's started socking it to tax dodgers.* ▶ *Get on that stage and sock it to 'em!*

SOCKS

knock sb's socks off also **blow sb's socks off** to surprise or impress someone a lot ▶ *Here's a recipe for fish curry that will knock your socks off.*

S

pull your socks up to work harder and improve your standard ▶ *Ruth is a very intelligent girl, but she needs to pull her socks up and pay more attention in class.*

work/laugh etc your socks off to work very hard, laugh a lot etc ▶ *I worked my socks off on that report.* ▶ *Her feeble excuses always made me laugh my socks off.*

SOLD
be sold on sth to like something very much ▶ *"Which shirt do you like the best?" "To be truthful I'm not really sold on any of them."*

SONG
make a song and dance about sth to complain or talk a lot about something so that it seems more important or difficult than it is ▶ *I've done a lot of extra work for you and I don't expect you to make a big song and dance about my taking one long lunch break.* ▶ *He always used his money to help other people, but he never made a song and dance about it.*

SORROWS
drown your sorrows to drink a lot of alcohol in order to try and forget about a problem ▶ *Whenever they had an argument, he would drown his sorrows in several large whiskies.*

SORTS
feel out of sorts to feel slightly ill or upset ▶ *In this stormy weather, even the dog feels out of sorts.*

SOUL
bare your soul to tell someone your most private feelings and thoughts ▶ *It's strange how people who have kept secrets from their families for years choose to bare their souls on television chat shows.*

sell your soul (to) to be willing to do anything (in order to get or achieve something) ▶ *She would have sold her soul for a chance to appear on the show.*

be the soul of ___ to have a lot of a good quality ▶ *His mother, although a little strict, was the soul of kindness and hospitality.*

SOUR
turn sour to stop working well and begin to fail ▶ *The communal farm was an experiment that turned very sour.*

SPACE
some breathing space a short time when you stop doing something difficult or tiring, so that you can think about the situation ▶ *The relationship counsellor advised us to get some breathing space and come back again after the weekend.*

watch this space to expect more interesting news about a subject ▶ *He's been seen dining out with a certain TV presenter – watch this space!*

SPADES
in spades to a great degree or in a great amount ▶ *Chris was lazy, and his brother's the same in spades!* ▶ *She's had bad luck in spades since the film came out.*

SPARKS

make (the) sparks fly also **send sparks flying** to cause arguments, excitement, or the expression of strong emotions ▶ *Her decision to oppose the policy made the sparks fly at head office.*

SPEAK

speak for yourself that may be true for you, but not for me ▶ *"The food was good, there were lots of single men – we all had a great time." "Speak for yourself. I had a lousy time."*

SPEED

up to speed
1 working as well as possible after a bad time ▶ *If work on the magnetic train is stopped, it will take us at least five years to get up to speed on a new project.*
2 understanding as much about a situation, process, subject etc as most people who know about it ▶ *After our reorganization we ran seminars to bring our area staff up to speed.*

SPELL

be/fall under sb's spell to be or become very attracted to someone ▶ *Everyone who has seen her performance has fallen under her spell.*

SPENDERS

(the) last of the big spenders
someone who is always worried about money and tries not to spend much ▶ *You know Darren, the last of the big spenders – he sometimes has two cups of coffee with his lunch.*

SPICK

spick and span extremely clean and tidy ▶ *Their place is always spick and span, more like a hotel than a home.*

SPIRIT

if/when the spirit moves you if/when you want to do it ▶ *I only clean up if the spirit moves me.* ▶ *When the spirit moved him, he would take off and not come back for a month.*

the spirit is willing but the flesh is weak you want to do something, but you are too tired or weak to do it ▶ *I couldn't possibly climb up that mountain – the spirit is willing but the flesh is definitely weak.*

the spirit of the law the intended or general meaning of the law, rather than the exact words ▶ *Luckily for me the policeman kept to the spirit of the law, as he could see I'd made a genuine mistake in picking up the wrong bag.*

SPLASH

make a splash to do something that makes a lot of people notice you ▶ *The band made a big splash with their second video.*

SPLEEN

vent your spleen to express what has been making you angry for a long time ▶ *Protesters were given the chance to vent their spleen in a meeting with the directors.*

SPOKEN

be spoken for to be no longer available ▶ *Most of my salary is spoken for, and I have very little left for holidays.* ▶ *I'm forever falling in love with my co-stars – but they're always married or spoken for.*

SPOON

sb was born with a silver spoon in his/her mouth someone has a lot of advantages because their parents were rich ▶ *He was born with a silver spoon in his mouth, so his life has never been a struggle.*

SPOT

a blind spot (of sb's) something that a person refuses to deal with, or accept ▶ *Researchers usually ignore religion in their studies; it's a blind spot that all of the social sciences have.* ▶ *I have to admit my children are my blind spot – they're all wonderful.*

do sth on the spot to do something immediately, often without thinking about it very carefully ▶ *Most questions coming into the press office can be answered on the spot.*

have a soft spot for to like someone or something very much ▶ *I think she has a soft spot for you, Tom.* ▶ *He loves his food and has a particularly soft spot for prawn curry.*

hit the spot to be exactly what you wanted, or exactly right ▶ *I feel better now – that bag of fish and chips really hit the spot.* ▶ *Their review hit the*

spot – *'a bad film, well made'.*

a hot spot
1 a place where trouble or fighting is likely to happen ▶ *The report identifies eight pollution hot spots at the mouths of British rivers.*
2 a place that is very popular for a particular type of entertainment ▶ *They regularly played at London's leading hot spots.*

in a tight spot in a difficult or dangerous situation ▶ *I can pay off what I borrowed, but if they want the interest too, I'll be in a very tight spot.*

be on the spot to be in the place where something is happening ▶ *Luckily, the police were on the spot when the accident occurred.* **on-the-spot** ADJ ▶ *In some countries the police will make you pay an on-the-spot fine for speeding.*

put sb on the spot to put someone in a difficult situation by asking them hard or embarrassing questions ▶ *That interviewer put me on the spot – she asked me what I'd do first to improve the company.*

rooted to the spot not moving, especially because of fear or surprise ▶ *She stood rooted to the spot, staring at the snake as though hypnotized.*

SPOTLIGHT

in the spotlight suddenly getting a lot of attention from newspapers, television etc ▶ *The latest court case has put the university's drug problems back in the spotlight again.* **out of the spotlight** ▶ *The boy was kept out of the spotlight in accordance with his father's wishes.*

SPREAD

spread yourself too thin to try to do

S

too many things at the same time so that you are unable to do any of them well ▶ *Even the largest companies can lose their competitive edge if they spread themselves too thin.* ▶ *I work better when I can focus on one project at a time instead of spreading myself too thin.*

SPUR

do sth on the spur of the moment to do something quickly without thinking about it ▶ *I decided, on the spur of the moment, to take a few days' holiday.*
spur-of-the-moment ADJ ▶ *I don't know why I bought that coat. It was a spur-of-the-moment decision.*

SQUARE

be back at square one to be in exactly the same situation that you started from ▶ *The murder hunt team are now back at square one after having arrested and released 27 men.* **go back to square one** ▶ *We've had to abandon that design and go back to square one.*

SQUEEZE

put the squeeze on to try to limit something, or limit someone in what they can do ▶ *The government is trying to put the squeeze on spending.* ▶ *Increased competition in the international marketplace is putting the squeeze on coffee producers.*

SQUIB

a damp squib something that you expect to be interesting or impressive, but is not ▶ *The show turned out to be a damp squib, and half the audience left at the interval.*

STAB

have a stab at to try ▶ *Have a stab at writing down your first impressions and then I'll check your work.*

STAGE

set the stage (for) also **set the scene (for)** to do something which allows or helps certain things to happen afterwards ▶ *The mishandling of the crisis set the stage for another confrontation between farmers and the government.* ▶ *The report set the scene for dramatic reform of the prison service.*

STAND UP

stand up and be counted to make your opinion clear ▶ *A lot of people say they want things done, but they are reluctant to stand up and be counted.*

STARS

have stars in your eyes to be very hopeful that you will become famous in the future
▶ *Young*

people who have stars in their eyes flock to Hollywood from all parts of the world.

thank your lucky stars to be grateful or feel very fortunate ▶ *I just thank my lucky stars the police got here so quickly.* ▶ *You should thank your lucky stars that you've got a job to go to.*

START

get off to a flying start to be very successful when you start something ▶ *They got off to a flying start with a three-goal lead after just 20 minutes.*
give sb/sth a flying start ▶ *A rich investor gave the company a flying start ten years ago.*

STATE

state of the art also **state-of-the-art**
using the most modern and recently
developed ideas, systems, or materials
▶ *The baggage handling system may
have been state of the art, but the
public address system certainly wasn't.*
▶ *This great new game uses state-of-
the-art computer graphics.*

the state of play what is happening
now ▶ *What's the state of play with
the rebuilding project?* **state-of-play**
ADJ ▶ *What I really need is a state-of-
play report every Monday morning to
keep me in touch.*

STAY

stay put to remain in one place and
not move ▶ *Just stay put and we'll
send a car around for you.*

STEAD

stand sb in good stead to be very
useful to you in the future ▶ *Learn to
speak in public: it will stand you in
good stead for the rest of your life.*

STEAM

**be/get
steamed up**
to be or
become
excited and
angry or
worried ▶ *It's
not worth*
getting steamed up about these
extreme fashions that teenagers like,
it'll only make them worse.*

full steam ahead moving something
forward with a lot of energy ▶ *We've
decided to go full steam ahead with
our plans to move house.* ▶ *It's full
steam ahead for the renovation of the
hotel.*

Some of the 'steam' idioms come
from the time when ships
operated by steam power. If a
ship travelled **full steam ahead** it
was going as fast as it could. A
ship could also travel **under its
own steam**, or be pulled by
smaller boats, for example
through a narrow place.

let off steam to get rid of your anger,
anxiety, or excitement by doing
something active ▶ *I love going to the
gym – it helps me let off steam.*

pick up steam to become more
successful and run better ▶ *Interest in
recycling has slowly picked up steam
over the last decade.*

run out of steam to begin to lose
energy; to become slower or weaker
▶ *I began to run out of steam before I
was halfway round the field.*

We get this idiom and several
others from the time when
railway engines operated by
steam power. An engine could
run out of steam if the fire
became low, or it did not have
enough water, and would have to
let off steam if the pressure of
steam became too high.

under your own steam alone, without
anyone else's help ▶ *Would you like a
lift tonight or can you get there under
your own steam?*

STEP

be out of step (with) not to agree
(with); be different (from) ▶ *The
existing law is out of step with what is
actually happening in the community.*

keep in step (with) also *be in step
(with)* to advance or develop in the
same way (as) ▶ *I've kept in step with*

S

my business partner all the way through. ▶ *Computerization means that payroll and personnel data are always in step.*

one step ahead (of) better prepared, or knowing more (than) ▶ *In his first year as a lecturer he managed to keep one step ahead of the students.*

a step in the right direction an action that brings you nearer to what you want to achieve ▶ *Any initiative which helps to prevent crime has got to be a step in the right direction.*

step on it to hurry up ▶ *If you don't step on it, we're going to miss the plane.*

watch your step to be careful ▶ *The adder is poisonous, but it usually only bites in self-defence – all you need to do is watch your step.* ▶ *"We can't take any more risks." "Don't worry, I'll watch my step."*

STEPS

take steps to do sth to do the things that are necessary to achieve something ▶ *Local authorities are taking steps to stop vandalism on the railways.*

STICK

the big stick a way of making someone do what you want by threats or violence ▶ *The protest would have been peaceful if the authorities had used gentle persuasion instead of the big stick.*

more ___ than you can shake a stick at a lot of something ▶ *She's hosted more dinner parties than you can shake a stick at.*

stick-in-the-mud also **stick in the mud** someone boring or old-fashioned ▶ *"I don't go to nightclubs any more."*

"Come on, don't be such a stick-in-the-mud."

STING

a sting in the tail a part of something that is unexpected and unpleasant

▶ *The budget was welcomed by most sectors of society, but there was a sting in the tail for pensioners.*

take the sting out of to make an unpleasant thing less upsetting and easier to accept ▶ *More firms are trying to take the sting out of redundancy by offering employees counselling and retraining packages.*

STINK

kick up a stink to complain loudly ▶ *There are lots of businesses kicking up a stink about interest rates.*

STIR

cause a stir to make everyone interested and excited ▶ *One of the protesters caused a stir by arriving on horseback dressed head to foot in black robes.*

STITCH

a stitch in time (saves nine) if you spend a little time or effort dealing with a small problem when it first appears, you will stop it turning into a big problem ▶ *A stitch in time saves nine: we should have mended the roof last year when there were only a few tiles missing.*

STITCHES

in stitches laughing a lot ▶ *Her quick wit kept the audience in stitches throughout the show.*

STOMACH

find sth hard to stomach to find it difficult to accept an action, situation, or attitude ▶ *The public will find it very hard to stomach another increase in petrol prices.*

not have the stomach for sth/to do sth to have no desire for something or to do something ▶ *I don't know how anyone has the stomach to work in a slaughterhouse.*

turn your stomach to make you feel angry, upset, or sick ▶ *The smell in the room was bad enough to turn the strongest stomach.*

STONE

leave no stone unturned to do everything possible in order to find or achieve something ▶ *She said the union would leave no stone unturned in its efforts to save the factory.*

be set in stone also **be carved in stone** (of a plan) to be completely fixed and not able to be changed ▶ *Here are a few ideas for the campaign, but nothing's set in stone yet, so let's have your suggestions.*

STOPS

pull out (all) the stops to do everything possible in order to achieve something ▶ *The vote is going to be really close, so it's vital that we pull out all the stops in the next week or two.*

This idiom comes from the organ, a large musical instrument in which the sound is made by air passing through pipes. The stops control the flow of air, and if you pull out all the stops, the organ makes as loud a sound as it can.

STORE

set (great) store by to think that something is important or valuable ▶ *He respected his superiors highly, and set great store by their good opinion of him.*

STORM

the calm before the storm also **the lull before the storm** a short time when things are calm before a time when there is a lot of trouble, noise, or activity ▶ *We'd cut all the sandwiches and made the tea – it was the calm before the storm, as the coach party would arrive any minute.*

take sth by storm to be extremely successful or popular in a particular place or with a particular group ▶ *The all-girl band took pre-teen Britain by storm.*

weather the storm also **ride (out) the storm** to continue through a difficult situation without being too badly affected by it ▶ *So far the company has weathered the storm of criticism by environmental protesters.*

STORY

to cut a long story short I am only going to give you the most important facts ▶ *"Why did you break up with your previous girlfriend?" "Well, to cut a long story short, her parents didn't like me."*

STOVE

be slaving over a hot stove to be spending a lot of time cooking ▶ *If you'd rather not spend your valuable evenings slaving over a hot stove, buy a microwave.*

STRAIGHT

get sth straight to make sure that everyone understands the truth about

S

a situation ▶ *Let's get this straight –* *you're picking up Carol and I'm going to the meeting with Rob.* ▶ *Can we get one thing straight? I'm not interested in buying insurance.*

keep sb on the straight and narrow to make someone live in an honest or moral way ▶ *He says it was the support of his wife that kept him on the straight and narrow.* **stray/slip from the straight and narrow** *She's not the only politician who's ever slipped from the straight and narrow.*

STRAITS

be in dire straits to be in a very serious and difficult situation, especially a financial one ▶ *The hill people are still in dire straits a year after the famine.*

STRANGER

sb is no stranger to sth someone has often experienced a particular situation ▶ *She is no stranger to life in the country, since she was brought up on a farm.*

STRAW

draw the short straw to have to do something unpleasant, especially because you were chosen by chance ▶ *Three women have drawn the short straw for Christmas duty at the traffic information centre.*

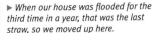

the last straw also **the final straw** the final one in a series of difficulties, especially if it makes you change or leave the situation that you are in

▶ *When our house was flooded for the third time in a year, that was the last straw, so we moved up here.*

be the straw that breaks the camel's back to be the problem that finally makes someone unable to deal with a situation ▶ *In her fragile state, even a mild criticism can be the straw that breaks the camel's back.*

STRAWS

be clutching at straws to be willing to try anything to get out of a bad situation ▶ *The doctors admit they're clutching at straws with this new treatment.*

STREET

be right up sb's street ➤ be right up sb's ALLEY

___ is a two-way street this process or activity must include the opinions and feelings of both sets of people involved ▶ *The interview is a two-way street – it gives you a chance to see what you think of us, as well as helping us to make a decision about you.*

the man/woman in the street an ordinary man or woman ▶ *These are the sort of reforms that the woman in the street is hoping for.*

STRENGTH

give me strength! I need to be stronger or more patient to bear this ▶ *"She says she won't do it. You'll have to do it yourself." "Give me strength!"*

go from strength to strength to keep getting better or more and more successful ▶ *Started in 1990, the organization has gone from strength to strength and now has over ten million members.*

STRETCH

not by any stretch of the imagination not in any way ▶ *Now the Palace Hotel was many things, but it was not, by any stretch of the imagination, a palace.*

STRIDE

get into your stride also **hit (your) stride** to start doing something well and confidently, as you continue doing it ▶ *Just as the speaker was getting into her stride, the whole school was plunged in darkness.*

put sb off their stride also **put sb off their stroke** to spoil the smooth progress of someone's speech or actions ▶ *A noisy interruption from the audience put the speaker off his stride.*

take sth in (your) stride to deal with something in a calm and efficient way, without needing to make a special effort ▶ *Mum takes change in her stride, but Dad gets anxious about everything.*

STRIKE

strike (it) lucky to suddenly have good luck ▶ *We really struck lucky with our hotel – it was beautiful.*

strike it rich to become very rich or very successful ▶ *Two contestants struck it rich on the TV quiz show yesterday.*

STRINGS

pull (some) strings to use secret influence with important people in order to gain an advantage ▶ *He must have pulled strings to get that job in Paris.* **string-pulling** N ▶ *She knew that she would never get a job in TV without some serious string-pulling.*

pull the/sb's strings to control another person or an organization ▶ *There is a suspicion that big business and not the*

elected government pulls the strings in this country.

> This idiom comes from a puppet (=a model of a person or animal with strings attached to parts of its body). The person who pulls the strings controls the movement of the puppet.

with no strings (attached) also **without strings** with no unpleasant or unexpected conditions ▶ *He's offered me a job as a model, with no strings attached.*

STRIPES

earn your stripes to do something that shows that you deserve your job, position, or rank ▶ *He knows the company well, having earned his stripes as assistant to the managing director.*

STROKE

at a stroke suddenly, with one action or event ▶ *Two thousand jobs will be created at a stroke by the building of the new car plant.*

put sb off their stroke ➤ put sb off their STRIDE

STUFF

the hard stuff strong alcoholic drinks ▶ *There were about a dozen writers in* *the pub, most of them busy knocking back the hard stuff.*

sb is made of sterner stuff someone has a stronger character than other people ► *We expected the children to be scared by the special effects, but they seemed to be made of sterner stuff.*

strut your stuff to do something that you think you do well, usually in a proud way ► *We had to watch some mediocre dancers strutting their stuff before the band came on.*

STYLE

cramp sb's style to limit someone's freedom or make them feel uncomfortable, especially by being with them ► *I go out when his girlfriend comes over; I don't want to cramp his style.*

do sth like it's going out of style ► do sth like it's going out of FASHION

SUCH

such as it is said just after you mention something to show that it is not very good ► *The play, such as it is, is a tedious tirade against men.*

SUCKER

be a sucker for sth to like someone or enjoy something a lot, especially if you are a little embarrassed by it ► *I have to admit that I'm a sucker for an old-fashioned romance.*

SUIT

follow suit to do the same thing that someone else has just done ► *The bank has already set up childcare facilities at its headquarters, and other branches are expected to follow suit.*

A suit is one of four types of playing cards. Your 'strong suit' is the one you have most of in your hand (=group of cards you are holding). In some games you have to 'follow suit' (play the same type of card as the last player).

___ is sb's strong suit someone is very good at a particular thing or knows a lot about it ► *Making polite conversation has never been his strong suit.*

SUMMER

an Indian summer
1 a period of time in autumn when the weather is warm and sunny ► *An Indian summer leads to extra-ripe grapes with a higher sugar content.*
2 a happy or successful period of time when you are older or near the end of your working life ► *Bands that came to fame 30 years ago seem to be enjoying an Indian summer of popularity.*

SURFACE

scratch the surface (of sth) to deal with only a very small part of an important subject ► *We like to think we know quite a lot about schizophrenia, but actually we've only scratched the surface.*

SUSPICION

have a sneaking suspicion to think that something may be true, without having any definite proof ► *She thinks the company's in trouble, and I have a sneaking suspicion she may be right.*

SWALLOW

sth is hard to swallow *also* **sth isn't easy to swallow** something is difficult to believe or accept ▶ *I found some of his stories rather hard to swallow.* ▶ *It wasn't easy to swallow criticism from someone like her.*

one swallow doesn't make a summer you should not be too hopeful just because one good thing happens ▶ *We've had a big order in from Japan, but we should all remember that one swallow doesn't make a summer.*

swallow sth whole to believe or accept something completely without asking any questions ▶ *He's always turning up late with some fantastic excuse, expecting me to swallow it whole!*

SWEAT

by the sweat of your brow by your hard work or effort ▶ *Whatever I've got in life I've had to earn by the sweat of my brow.*

get into a sweat (about sth) *also* **break out into a cold sweat (about sth)** to become nervous or frightened about something ▶ *Come on, there's no point getting into a sweat about it; I'm sure you'll do fine.* ▶ *I break out into a cold sweat just thinking about flying.*

no sweat I can do something easily ▶ *"Are you sure you can carry that bag?" "No sweat."*

sweat it out to wait or be patient until something unpleasant ends ▶ *I sat there in the courtroom, sweating it out and trying to be positive.*

SWEEP

a clean sweep
1 a complete victory for one group ▶ *The school had a clean sweep in the regional championships, getting all ten gold medals.*
2 a complete change in a country or organization, made by getting rid of a lot of people or things ▶ *We made a clean sweep when we took over, then appointed five new staff.*

SWIM

be/keep in the swim (of things) to be or stay interested in exciting or fashionable activities ▶ *She moved to London because she likes to be in the swim of things.* ▶ *I may not be young, but I do try to keep in the swim.*

SWING

get into the swing (of sth) to start doing something well and enjoying it ▶ *I think you'll enjoy the work, once you get into the swing of it.*

in full swing in progress, with a lot happening ▶ *An aerobics class was in full swing on the floor below.*

swing it to find a way to deal with a difficult problem, often by doing something wrong ▶ *Work visas are very difficult to get. Even with your friend's help you may not be able to swing it.*

S

SWINGS

it's swings and roundabouts a situation or decision has both advantages and disadvantages ▶ *The train is faster, but the bus is cheaper – it's swings and roundabouts, really.*

SWIPE

take a swipe at sb to criticize someone or something, especially in public ▶ *In its more serious scenes, the film takes a swipe at political corruption.*

SWOOP

in one fell swoop also **at one fell swoop** all at the same time, with one action ▶ *Someone had pressed the wrong key and deleted all the files in one fell swoop.*

This idiom comes from a line in Shakespeare's play *Macbeth*.

SWORD

be a double-edged sword something that may bring success, but could also harm you ▶ *His appointment is a double-edged sword – it brings him status and money but also very difficult problems to solve.*

the sword of Damocles something bad that may affect you at any time ▶ *Since my illness was diagnosed, I have lived with the sword of Damocles hanging over my head.*

SWORDS

cross swords (with) to argue (with) ▶ *It isn't the first time he and I have crossed swords over his teaching methods.*

SYSTEM

beat the system to achieve what you want even though society's rules or powerful organizations do not allow it or approve of it ▶ *Theoretically, she wasn't eligible for a loan for her degree course, but she managed to beat the system.*

buck the system to oppose the rules of society ▶ *When I became one of the first few women managers, I was seen as a rebel who had bucked the system.*

get sb/sth out of your system also **get it out of your system** to do something that helps you to stop feeling angry, unhappy etc ▶ *I had such a bad day at the office – I went for a swim to get it out of my system.* ▶ *I've tried to get her out of my system – I've gone out with other girls but it's no good.*

SYSTEMS

(it's) all systems go a plan or process is ready to start ▶ *It's all systems go for this year's spectacular airshow.*

S

Tt

TAB
pick up the tab (for) to pay (for something) ▶ *The garages can charge what they want, and the insurance companies pick up the tab.*

TABLE
drink sb under the table to drink a lot more alcohol than someone else ▶ *He was well known for his ability to drink nearly everyone under the table.*

on the table being considered and discussed in a formal way ▶ *The possibility of an arms embargo is still on the table.* ▶ *We put a very fair bid on the table, and we are not prepared to go any higher.*

TABLES
turn the tables (on sb) to gain an advantage over someone who has been in a stronger position than you ▶ *Students get a chance to turn the tables on the lecturers in the annual teaching assessments.*

TABS
keep tabs on to watch someone or something carefully ▶ *The company is keeping tabs on the number of phone calls employees make.*

TACK
change tack also **try a different tack** to try a different job, topic, or way of dealing with something ▶ *After her business failed, she changed tack and became a consultant for a big company.* ▶ *I decided to try a different tack – she might be more interested in sport than in cinema.*

TACKS
get down to brass tacks to start talking about the things that are important ▶ *Let's get down to brass tacks. Can you guarantee this quality of product all year round?*

TAIL
be chasing your (own) tail to spend time and energy trying to do something, with little success ▶ *At first I was always chasing my tail and being late for everything, but I gradually got more organized.*

be on sb's tail to be chasing or following someone very closely ▶ *She spoke hurriedly and kept checking all the time that there was no one on her tail.*

the tail wags the dog a small or unimportant part of something is controlling or affecting the whole of a situation or process ▶ *Often the tail wags the dog, and a new software product boosts the sales of a particular computer.*

turn tail to leave a difficult situation; to run away ▶ *The rebels turned tail and ran in the face of the army offensive last week.*

with your tail between your legs ashamed, embarrassed, or unhappy because you have failed or been defeated ▶ *When she came back a week after her wedding with her tail between her legs, her parents didn't ask awkward questions.*

When a dog is afraid or unhappy it puts its tail between its legs.

T

TAKE

do a double take to look at something again, just after you have seen it for the first time, because it surprises you ▶ *I walked by him and did a double take because he looked just like my grandfather.*

be on the take to be accepting money for doing something wrong ▶ *I knew he was on the take, but I never had enough evidence to show the police.*

take it as read to accept that something is true or correct because it is not necessary to have any proof ▶ *Let's take it as read that most students will never have studied medieval history.*

take it easy also **take things easy** to relax and not do very much ▶ *Why don't you take it easy tonight? I'll cook supper.* ▶ *Let's just stay at home and take things easy this weekend.*

take it from me believe me, because I know ▶ *Take it from me, she has no idea that you're interested in her.*

take it or leave it say yes or no, but there can be no discussion ▶ *I can offer £5000 for the car, take it or leave it.*

take sb/sth for granted also **take it for granted that** to be so sure of something or someone that you do not pay attention to it or them ▶ *I just took it for granted that my parents would support me through university.* ▶ *He expects me to be there with a meal cooked every evening – he's always taken me for granted.*

take sth hard to become sad because of something that happens ▶ *Jake took his brother's death very hard; they'd always been so close.*

not take sth lying down not to accept being treated badly ▶ *The company has treated me unfairly and I'm not going to take it lying down.*

be taken with to like or be attracted by ▶ *My brother seems quite taken with you!* ▶ *I was particularly taken with the pottery on show in the gallery.*

sth takes some doing something is difficult and needs a lot of effort, skill, or determination ▶ *With the two of us working so hard, finding time for holidays together can take some doing.*

you can't take sb anywhere said when someone who is with you is annoying or embarrassing you or other people ▶ *Look at my wife, arguing again – I can't take her anywhere.* ▶ *You've got chocolate all over the chair – I can't take you anywhere!*

TALE

live to tell the tale to be alive and well after a dangerous or (humorously) after an unusual experience ▶ *He lived among beggars, drunks, and drug users, and lived to tell the tale.* ▶ *She worked for Mr Smith and lived to tell the tale – so he can't be that bad!*

an old wives' tale a piece of advice that people believed in former times, but that most people now think is not true ▶ *My granny used to say that it's bad luck to look at the new moon through glass, but I think that's an old wives' tale.*

TALES

tell tales to tell a lie, or say something unpleasant about another person, especially to someone in authority ▶ *I'm not supposed to tell tales, but some of the kids have been bullying Mark.*

TALK

I'm/we're talking ___ I'm/we're emphasizing how much money something costs or someone has ▶ *It's going to cost a fortune. You're talking £100 for labour alone.* ▶ *Is she rich? Oh, yes, we're talking serious money here.*

sb is all talk (and no action) someone is always talking about doing something, but never actually does anything ▶ *Politicians are all talk – they never keep their promises.*

look who's talking! also **you can/can't talk** you have faults or problems that are similar to the ones you are criticizing ▶ *"Cathy worries too much about her children." "Look who's talking – you take Robbie to the doctor for the least little thing."* ▶ *"Wayne didn't like my report." "He can't talk – his reports are full of mistakes!"*

talk about ___ there is a lot of something, or something has a lot of a quality ▶ *Talk about crowds – I've never seen anything like it!* ▶ *I went down to the cellar – talk about scary, I was shaking when I came up again.*

be the talk of the town to be talked about by a lot of people ▶ *When the minister's son was seen with that film star he became the talk of the town.*

walk your talk to do what you say you will or what you tell other people to do ▶ *You can't just tell your kids to be polite and respectful, you have to walk your talk.* ▶ *He really walks his talk and lives up to his political ideals.*

TANGENT

go off at a tangent also **fly off at a tangent** to start thinking or talking about a completely different subject ▶ *Our discussion on fund-raising went off at a tangent, and we spent half the morning talking about political correctness.*

TAP

on tap available and ready to be used when you need it ▶ *With the Internet you have travel information on tap 24 hours a day.*

TAPE

have (got) sth taped to understand something completely and to know how to deal with it ▶ *After three months, I thought I had everything taped, but they said they were getting complaints about my work.*

red tape official rules or processes that prevent things from being done quickly and easily ▶ *You have to go through a lot of red tape if you want to start a business in this country.*

> Government officials used to tie their papers together with red tape (=a long, thin piece of material like string).

TASK

take sb to task to criticize someone for a particular thing ▶ *The report takes teachers to task for failing to give children self-confidence.*

TASTE

an acquired taste something that people only begin to like after they have tried it a few times ▶ *For most children, olives are an acquired taste.* ▶ *I love early Celtic music, but I suppose it's an acquired taste.*

T

leave a bad taste in the mouth also **leave a nasty taste in the mouth** to be something so upsetting or unpleasant that you remember it for some time ▶ *Knowing that so many respected people avoid paying their taxes leaves a very bad taste in the mouth.*

there's no accounting for taste it's difficult to understand why people like or don't like certain things ▶ *My sister loves seventies dance music – there's no accounting for taste, I suppose.* ▶ *"She's going out with Dan." "Oh, well, there's no accounting for taste, is there?"*

TEARS

not shed tears (over) to feel glad that someone or something has gone or stopped ▶ *After that awful meal we had there on our anniversary, I didn't shed any tears when the restaurant closed.* ▶ *"Cathy's finally handed in her resignation." "Nobody will shed tears over that."*

TEE/T

...to a tee also **...to a T** exactly ▶ *They wanted a Russian-speaking English graduate, so I suited them to a tee.* ▶ *She said she'd rather have the money? That's our Eileen to a T!*

> In this idiom, 'tee' or 'T' comes from a tool called a T-square, which is used to make sure that the corners of something are cut to exactly the right angle.

TEETH

be armed to the teeth to possess a lot of weapons ▶ *Both sides are armed to the teeth and the chances of peace appear remote.*

cut your teeth on sth to do something as the first work that you do, that helps you learn ▶ *Joe had a summer job in a law firm, which gave him the chance to cut his teeth on a few simple legal problems.*

> We say that a baby is cutting its teeth when they begin to appear in its mouth for the first time.

get your teeth into sth to begin working hard at something that interests you ▶ *This new research*

project would give me something to get my teeth into.

(wail and) gnash your teeth to be very angry and upset, often because you feel sorry about something that has happened ▶ *It's no use wailing and gnashing your teeth now, you should have been nicer to Anne when you were still married.*

grit your teeth to be determined to remain calm and in control of yourself while something unpleasant is happening ▶ *She gritted her teeth as the nurse gave her the injections.*

in the teeth of working against ▶ *They married in the teeth of opposition from both sets of parents.* ▶ *We had to walk to work in the teeth of the gale.*

sb lies through his/her teeth someone is lying, without being embarrassed or ashamed ▶ *She claims she isn't seeing him any more, but I know she's lying through her teeth.*

set your teeth on edge to give you an uncomfortable feeling that you cannot bear ▶ *The unripe mangoes were so sour they set our teeth on edge.* ▶ *He spoke with an insincere politeness that set my teeth on edge.*

show your teeth to let someone see your anger or strength, in order to warn them not to start an argument or fight ▶ *If people feel they are unjustly treated, they will start to show their teeth.*

TEETHING

teething problems small problems that a company, product, system etc has at the beginning ▶ *Inevitably, the new computer system has had its teething problems.*

TELL

I can't tell you how/what I want to emphasize how/what ▶ *I can't tell you how wonderful it was to be out in the sunshine.* ▶ *I can't tell you what problems we've had with the drains.*

(I) tell you what... I'd like to suggest or emphasize something ▶ *Tell you what – give me your number, and I'll try to organize something.* ▶ *I tell you what, when we finally landed I was ready to kiss the ground.*

tell it like it is to say exactly what you think or what is true, without hiding anything ▶ *The author tells it like it is, which may embarrass a lot of people.*

tell me about it I understand because I have experienced what you're talking about ▶ *"They said they couldn't get replacement parts for this machine because it's too old." "Tell me about it!"*

tell sb where to go to speak to someone angrily because you feel what they have just said is insulting, unreasonable, or unfair ▶ *He asked me to work late again, but I told him where to go.*

that would be telling I cannot tell you something because it is a secret ▶ *"And does he get together with the girl in the end?" "Well, that would be telling."*

there's no telling also **there's no knowing** it is impossible to know or find out ▶ *We'll have new examiners next year, and there's no telling what they'll be like.* ▶ *The books have been promised for next week, but there's no knowing whether they'll arrive in time or not.*

you're telling me! I know, and I agree with you ▶ *"It takes a lot of work to cook a three-course meal." "You're telling me!"*

TEN

ten to one it's very likely ▶ *You spend hours in the shop choosing the paint, and ten to one it doesn't go with the chair covers.*

TENTERHOOKS

be on tenterhooks to be nervous and excited because you are waiting for something ▶ *He was on tenterhooks waiting for the exam results.*

> Tenterhooks are used to stretch cloth tightly when it has just been woven.

TERM

in the long term ➤ in the long **RUN**

TERMS

come to terms with sth to accept

something after a long time, and deal with it successfully ▶ *We try to help people come to terms with retirement.* ▶ *She's never come to terms with Bill's death.*

in no uncertain terms in a clear, firm, and often angry way ▶ *He told her in no uncertain terms that she had made his life a misery for the last ten years.*

TERRITORY

sth comes with the territory something, especially a problem, is a usual part of a particular situation ▶ *There are always last-minute crises when you're organizing a banquet – it comes with the territory.*

TEST

put sth to the test to test or find out how good something is, or how true a statement or idea is ▶ *My resolution to drink less was immediately put to the test when I was invited to a party.*

sth will stand the test of time something is so good that people will continue to like it, use it etc for a long time ▶ *Certain key products have stood the test of time, and are still as much in demand as ever.*

THANKS

no thanks to sb/sth someone or something did not help you, or tried to prevent you from doing what you wanted ▶ *"Did you get home OK last night?" "Yes, no thanks to you."* ▶ *I finally finished writing the article – no thanks to the cat, who decided to give birth to eight kittens last week.*

THAT

that does it! that's the final and most

annoying thing, and I refuse to deal with it any more ▶ *"Mum, the handle's come off again!" "That does it! I'm going straight out to buy a new frying pan."*

that's sb all over also ***that's sb for you*** a particular way of behaving is typical of someone, or of a group ▶ *"He's blaming me, and it was his fault!" "Yeah, that's Adam all over."* ▶ *It's our wedding anniversary and he wants to take me to a football match! That's men for you.*

that's more like it! I'm satisfied with an improvement that has been made ▶ *"I've made 20 more contacts today for possible sales." "Ah, that's more like it!"*

...(and) that's that that's finished, and there's no more discussion ▶ *I'm not typing your homework for you and that's that!*

(now) that's what I call ___ I think that is very good, attractive, interesting etc ▶ *Thank you, dear, that's what I call a nice cup of tea.* ▶ *Now that's what I call a kitchen – it's got everything you could possibly want!*

that's what you think I know that what you have just said is wrong ▶ *"She doesn't even like Jack." "That's what you think!"*

that's where sb/sth comes in also ***that's where sb/sth comes into it*** this is how someone or something has a place in that situation ▶ *You look at a house, make an offer and it's accepted, and that's where the solicitors come in.* ▶ *I had a bad morning, but a fabulous afternoon, and that's where Jack came into it.*

THEM

them and us two groups who feel that they are very different, and cannot work together ▶ *Do you feel there's a*

them and us attitude between the arts and the business world? ▶ *"Why is it that workers and managers find it so hard to compromise?" "It's them and us, isn't it?"*

THERE

be there for sb to be ready to help someone or be kind to them when they have problems ▶ *Jeff knows I'll always be there for him, whatever kind of trouble he gets into.*

there you are also **there you go**
1 (said when you give someone something) here it is ▶ *There you are – will that be enough for the train fare?*
2 what has just happened is just what I would have expected, or proves what I have said ▶ *"Kath says she can't pay me back for two months." "There you are, you see, I said you shouldn't lend her the money."* ▶ *"You were right about waiting to buy our tickets – they're reduced this week." "Well, there you go."*

you've got me there I do not know the answer ▶ *"What other sort of work would give me the variety I have now?" "Well, you've got me there."*

THICK

do sth through thick and thin to keep doing something in spite of difficulties or problems ▶ *The local merchants*

have supported this community through thick and thin.

be in the thick of sth also **be in the thick of it** to be involved in the most active, most dangerous etc part of a situation ▶ *He threw himself into the thick of the action.* ▶ *The recession affected all industries, and theatre was right in the thick of it.*

thick and fast (happening or coming) in large amounts or numbers ▶ *Criticisms of the policy are coming thick and fast from all sections of society.*

THIEVES

be (as) thick as thieves (of two people) to be very friendly and share a lot of secrets ▶ *Those two girls are as thick as thieves; you never see them apart.*

THING

be the done thing to be the socially correct way of behaving ▶ *In their country it isn't the done thing to accept an invitation the first time it's offered.*

do your own thing to do what you want to do ▶ *You can join a tour, learn a water sport, or just do your own thing.*

for one thing to give one important reason ▶ *We can't go – for one thing, the tickets are £200, which is too expensive for me.*

have a good thing going to be in a situation in which you will earn a lot of money, gain a lot of advantages etc ▶ *A schoolboy had a good thing going by charging his classmates a huge amount for using his mobile phone.*

have a thing about to like or dislike someone or something so much that it is unusual ▶ *He's got a thing about*

T

Marilyn Monroe – he's bought all her films on video. ▶ *I know I didn't sound confident enough; it's because I've got a thing about being too pushy.*

be just the thing to be exactly what is needed ▶ *Her designs are just the thing to wear for casual events or relaxing at home.*

know a thing or two about sth to have a lot of knowledge about something ▶ *Anyone who knows a thing or two about poetry will be fascinated by this new collection.* ▶ *She knows a thing or two about divorce – she's been married six times.*

not know the first thing about not to know anything about ▶ *Sorry, I can't help you – I don't know the first thing about horses.*

one thing led to another a situation developed in a way that most people understand ▶ *"What happened with Luke last night?" "Well, I invited him back for coffee and, you know, one thing led to another. We're seeing each other again tonight."*

be onto a good thing to have found a situation that is helpful for you, especially a way of getting money ▶ *He knew he was onto a good thing when three separate newspapers made him an offer for the story.*

the thing is... the disadvantage or the problem is ▶ *The thing is, he's not interested in her, but she doesn't seem to realize.* ▶ *The salary is good, but the thing is, I'd have to learn German.*

what with one thing and another for several reasons ▶ *Sam burnt the rice and they began arguing, and what with one thing and another, I began to wish we'd stayed at home.*

THINGS

all good things (must) come to an end you have to accept it when something good ends ▶ *It's been a great party, but I really must go – all good things come to an end.*

all (other) things being equal unless the situation changes in an unexpected way ▶ *All other things being equal, you'll just need a blood test every six months.*

be all things to all men also **be all things to all people** to please or be useful to all types of people ▶ *The show's a mixture of everything – it tries to be all things to all men and ends up pleasing nobody.*

This idiom comes from I Corinthians in the Bible.

first things first the most important things must be dealt with first ▶ *OK, first things first, can I have your name and address?*

it's (just) one of those things it's something that I could not prevent or change ▶ *We couldn't meet the deadline because too many people were away – it's just one of those things.*

of all things I am surprised by this thing ▶ *One of my mates was injured by a beer barrel, of all things, when it fell on top of him.*

things that go bump in the night things that frighten you, especially at night ▶ *Allowing children to handle bats is a good way to conquer* *their fear of things that go bump in the night.*

things go from bad to worse a situation that is already bad is getting worse ▶ *Things at the school are going from bad to worse – my daughter's missed three weeks because of staff shortages.*

THINK

sb has got another think coming what someone is expecting will not happen ▶ *If he thinks I'm going to start serving him breakfast in bed he's got another think coming!*

not think straight to be unable to think properly ▶ *Shut up a moment – I can't think straight with you shouting in my ear.*

think twice (about) to think carefully before doing something (and probably not do it) ▶ *Good locks and lighting will make a burglar think twice.* ▶ *Most companies would think twice about recruiting someone who is still involved in a dispute with their previous firm.*

not think twice (about) not to think carefully about or pay attention to something ▶ *People who wouldn't think twice about going to a doctor for a burn on the hand refuse to go for something psychological.* ▶ *She didn't think twice about giving up her job for a chance to sail round the world.*

wishful thinking believing or hoping that something is true because it is what you want ▶ *He seemed to be flirting with me at the party or is that just wishful thinking?*

THIS

this and that several different things but nothing very important ▶ *"What did you do today?" "Oh, this and that."*

this, that and the other (thing) several things of different kinds ▶ *Every magazine you read tells you you shouldn't have too much fat, too much sugar, too much of this, that and the other.*

THORN

a thorn in sb's side someone or something that keeps causing problems ▶ *The office administrator has been a thorn in our side for two years – thank goodness she's leaving.*

THOUGHTS

have second thoughts (about sth) to change your mind or feel sorry (about a decision you have made) ▶ *Did you ever have any second thoughts about joining the army?*

on second thoughts having changed my mind ▶ *I'll have a glass of wine – no, on second thoughts, make that a whisky.*

THREAD

be hanging by a thread to be in danger of ending or failing ▶ *For six months after he was born, our son's life hung by a thread.* ▶ *He was called into the*  *manager's office and told that his job was hanging by a thread.*

THROAT

sb is cutting his/her own throat someone is making a decision that

T

may damage or destroy them ▶ *She may have cut her own throat by speaking to the press so openly.*

have something rammed down your throat *also* **have sth shoved down your throat** to be forced to accept something that someone thinks is very good, although you do not agree ▶ *Though the play has a political message, it is not rammed down our throats, but suggested to us by the action.* **ram/shove sth down sb's throat** ▶ *The government can't shove tax increases down our throats and expect us to like it.*

jump down sb's throat to criticize or get angry with someone as soon as they say something ▶ *I suggested that he should see a counsellor and he jumped right down my throat.*

sth sticks in sb's throat something is very difficult for someone to accept ▶ *Paying extra for facilities we haven't used sticks in my throat.*

THROATS
be at each other's throats to be fighting or arguing ▶ *They're at each other's throats all the time, and they're nowhere near an agreement.*

THROES
be in the throes of (doing) sth to be dealing with something that is difficult or takes a long time ▶ *We're in the throes of organizing a seminar on genetic engineering.*

THROUGH
through and through definitely and completely ▶ *He was a romantic through and through, as you can tell from his poetry.* ▶ *Politicians are wasting their time trying to improve a system that is rotten through and through.*

THROW
(just) a stone's throw away very close ▶ *The hotel is just a stone's throw away from a beautiful sandy beach.*

THROWBACK
a throwback to (a time when) *also* **a throwback to the 50s etc** something that is unusual now, but like something that happened or existed in the past ▶ *His new film is a throwback to the romantic comedies of the 30s and 40s.*

THUMB
stick out like a sore thumb *also* **stand out like a sore thumb** to be very easy to see, and especially to look wrong or strange ▶ *We live in a village where any foreigner would stick out like a sore thumb.* ▶ *That ugly office block stands out like a sore thumb.*

under sb's thumb completely controlled by someone ▶ *She's got you totally under her thumb – you do everything she tells you.*

THUMBS
give sth/sb the thumbs up to show that you approve of something or somebody ▶ *The council gave the thumbs up to a* *plan to redesign the city centre.* ▶ *The critics hated the comedian, but the public seems to have given her the thumbs up.* **get the thumbs up** ▶ *Plans for the stadium got the thumbs up from officials and fans today.* **give sth/sb the thumbs down** ▶ *Schoolchildren have given the latest educational software the thumbs down.* **get the thumbs down** ▶ *My*

project got the thumbs down – they said it would cost too much.

twiddle your thumbs to do nothing ▶ *We can't just sit around twiddling our thumbs until the management produce an offer.* ▶ *Basically, he's getting paid to sit in an office and twiddle his thumbs.*

THUNDER
steal sb's thunder to get praise and attention that someone else deserves or expects ▶ *The speaker before me stole my thunder by using three of my jokes.*

TICKET
be a one-way ticket to sth to be sure to produce a particular result that cannot be changed ▶ *Using hard drugs is a one-way ticket to self-destruction.*

TICKLED
be tickled pink also **be tickled to death** to be very pleased ▶ *She was tickled pink that her daughter was finally getting married.* ▶ *He'll be tickled to death when I tell him he's won.*

TIDE
stem the tide (of) to stop a flow of people, things, or ideas ▶ *Tighter quality controls have been introduced to stem the tide of complaints.*

swim against the tide also **go against the tide** to have opinions or ideas on a particular subject that are the opposite of most people's at the time ▶ *He was a sensitive headmaster, who swam against the tide at a time when schools thought that academic success was everything.* **swim/drift with the tide** ▶ *He was not the kind of man to swim with the tide just because it was convenient.*

the tide turns people's opinions have started to change in a particular way ▶ *With the growth of environmental awareness, the tide has turned against big road-building projects.*

turn back the tide to stop a change in people's opinions or behaviour ▶ *Many doctors are trying to turn back the tide of popular support for alternative therapies.*

TIGHTROPE
walk a tightrope to be in a situation where you must be very careful to stay balanced ▶ *Parents today have to walk a tightrope between protecting their children and encouraging independence.*

TILL
be caught with your hand in the till also **be caught with your fingers in the till** to be caught stealing money from the place where you work ▶ *He was not the only boss to be caught with his hand in the till.*

TILT
(at) full tilt very fast or with lots of energy ▶ *She wasn't looking where*

she was going, and ran full tilt into a tall stranger. ▶ *The debate was going at full tilt when we arrived.*

TIME
ahead of her/its etc time having or using very modern ideas ▶ *He was*

ahead of his time in realizing that a craving for alcohol was a disease.
▶ *The light, airy factory was way ahead of its time.*

all in good time be patient; what you want will happen or be dealt with later ▶ *"Any news? I can't wait to hear." "All in good time. We're still waiting for Mick and Jeff."*

bide your time to wait patiently for the right moment to do something ▶ *She bided her time, reading a magazine, until the secretary left her desk for a moment.*

big time in an extreme or serious way ▶ *She had been borrowing money, big time.*

the big time the highest level of a job, especially if it involves fame and money ▶ *She hit the big time when she became a producer for a radio station. He has been itching for a chance to get back into the big time of Formula One racing.*

do sth in your own time
1 to do something when you are ready to do it ▶ *The minister promised to deal with both points in his own way and in his own time.* ▶ *Knowing Bob, he'll tell us his plans in his own good time.*
2 to do something outside the hours you are paid to work, or outside the time that you spend in school ▶ *She did the course in her own time while she was working for Taylors.*

do time to spend time in prison ▶ *You're not going to do time just to protect her, are you?*

for the time being for a short time, but not permanently ▶ *She can stay with us for the time being, until she finds a place of her own.* ▶ *Let's leave the question of cost for the time being,*

and concentrate on the advantages of the system.

from time to time sometimes, but not regularly or very often ▶ *I still think of him from time to time, although I know we'll never get back together.*

give sb a hard time to criticize someone a lot or cause problems for them ▶ *When we couldn't supply the toy for Christmas, our customers gave us a really hard time.*

not give sb the time of day to refuse to talk to someone ▶ *I'm surprised that you do business with him – I wouldn't give him the time of day.*

have all the time in the world to have as much time as you want ▶ *Although he's busy, the doctor gives the impression he has all the time in the world for his patients.*

have no time for to dislike someone or something and not to waste time dealing with them or it ▶ *My father had no time for writers and academics – he valued practical skills.* ▶ *Like most scientists, she had no time for astrology.*

have the time of your life to enjoy yourself a lot ▶ *I really am having the time of my life – this is a wonderful holiday.*

have time on your hands to have more time than you can fill in a useful way ▶ *There's a cinema showing continuous cartoons for people with time on their hands.*

have time on your side *also* **time is on your side** to have plenty of time to do what you want ▶ *Don't worry if you don't get this job; you're only 22, so you've got time on your side.*

in no time (at all) very quickly or very soon ▶ *It isn't far to York – we'll be* *there in no time.* ▸ *Children seem to learn video games in no time at all.*

it's about time *also* **it's high time** something should happen soon or should already have happened ▸ *I think it's about time management started to listen to the nurses.* ▸ *It's high time that something was done about the state of our roads.*

kill time to do something that is not very useful or interesting because you are waiting for something ▸ *I occasionally dropped into the library to kill time between classes.*

let time take its course ➤ let NATURE take its course

be living on borrowed time
1 to be likely to die soon ▸ *He's been living on borrowed time since his illness was diagnosed.*
2 to be at risk of losing your job, or of failing ▸ *She's made too many mistakes – she's living on borrowed time now.* ▸ *The small shops have been living on borrowed time since the new shopping centre was built.*

long time no see I haven't seen you for a long time ▸ *Hello, Charles. Long time no see. Fancy a drink?*

make good time to make progress as fast as or faster than expected ▸ *There were no problems on the roads so we made good time.*

make up for lost time to experience something as much as you can because you could not do it before ▸ *He didn't travel much as a young man, but he's made up for lost time recently.*

be marking time to spend time not doing or achieving very much ▸ *When I decided to start working part-time, I accepted that I might be marking time in my career.*

When soldiers mark time, they move their legs as if they were marching, but stay in the same place.

(there's) no time like the present if something must be done, it's best to do it now rather than later ▸ *You need a holiday so why don't you come back with us today? There's no time like the present.*

(there's) no time to lose something must be done now, or quickly ▸ *He knew he had to get her to the hospital – there was no time to lose.*

pass the time of day (with sb) to have a conversation about unimportant things (with someone) ▸ *My hairdresser's always happy to pass the time of day with her clients.*

play for time to try to delay something so that you have more time to think or plan ▸ *"Did you get the letter? "Did I what?" I said, playing for time until I knew exactly what she was talking about.*

the time is ripe (for) conditions are right (for something to happen) ▸ *I'll apply for another job when the time's ripe, but I'm quite happy here at the moment.*

(only) time will tell something will become clear at some time in the future ▸ *Only time will tell if he's the right man for the job.*

TIMES

at the best of times when conditions are most favourable ▸ *Running an airline is an expensive business at the best of times; during a recession it can be a way of using up money very quickly.*

fall on hard times *also* **hit hard times** to become poorer and less

T

successful ► *His old friend had fallen on hard times and was looking for work.* ► *The coal industry hit hard times in the 1960s.*

for old times' sake to remember happy times in the past ► *One day, just for old times' sake, I paid a visit to my junior school.*

move with the times to change things in order to stay modern ► *Until recently, the hotel showed few signs of moving with the times.*

TIP

sth is on the tip of your tongue you cannot remember something, but you think you will soon ► *What was the name of that awful teacher? Wait, it's on the tip of my tongue. Something like Hammond – no, Hallett!*

(just) the tip of the iceberg the smallest sign of a larger problem ► *He*

couldn't pay me back this week, but that's just the tip of the iceberg – he owes everyone money.

TIT

tit for tat also **tit-for-tat** something done in return for something unpleasant ► *Chris insulted me so I didn't invite him to the wedding – it's just tit for tat!*

TODAY

here today, gone tomorrow here for only a very short time ► *There's no job security nowadays – you can be here today, gone tomorrow.*

TOE

dip a toe in the water to start doing a new activity in a small way to see if it works ► *They were the first company to dip a toe in the water of genetic engineering.*

TOES

keep sb on their toes to keep someone paying attention and stop them from relaxing ► *Having three kids under five keeps me on my toes all day.* **be/stay on your toes** ► *As a security guard, you need to be on your toes all the time.*

make your toes curl to give you an uncomfortable feeling of dislike or embarrassment ► *When I think about what I said to her, it makes my toes curl.*

tread on sb's toes also **step on sb's toes** to offend or annoy someone

► *I don't want to tread on anybody's toes, but I'm going to have to rewrite this report.*

TOKEN
by the same token in the same way (used to connect two statements) ▶ *Any doctor with Aids should inform their patients. By the same token, patients with Aids have an obligation to tell their doctor.*

TOLL
take its toll (on sth/sb) also *take a heavy toll (on sth/sb)* to cause harm or damage (to someone or something) ▶ *Heavy workloads are taking their toll on nurses' health.* ▶ *The old man looked exhausted; the long journey had taken a heavy toll.*

TOM
every Tom, Dick, and Harry also *any Tom, Dick, or Harry* everyone and anyone ▶ *We can't audition every Tom, Dick, and Harry who wants to be a singer.*

TOMORROW
do sth like there's no tomorrow to be doing something a lot, or too much ▶ *After her divorce, she started spending money like there was no tomorrow.*

TON
come down on sb like a ton of bricks to criticize or punish someone severely ▶ *I made the mistake of laughing at her son and she came down on me like a ton of bricks.*

TONGUE
bite your tongue to stop yourself from saying something ▶ *When parents tell me they're too busy to come and discuss their children's work I just have to bite my tongue.*

find your tongue to start speaking after you have been quiet for a while

▶ *Before Lucy could find her tongue, he had left the room, slamming the door behind him.*

loosen sb's tongue to make someone say something that they would not normally say ▶ *The wine had loosened her tongue, and she found herself telling him her life story.*

sb speaks with (a) forked tongue someone is speaking dishonestly, especially by saying two opposite things at different times or to two different groups ▶ *The management has been speaking with a forked tongue, promising pay rises, but privately agreeing to do nothing.*

(with) tongue in cheek as a joke ▶ *He claims that his remarks were made tongue in cheek, and he's sorry if people found them so offensive.*
tongue-in-cheek ADJ ▶ *They're making a tongue-in-cheek horror movie.*

> Pushing out your cheek with your tongue while someone was talking was used in former times as a sign to another person that you thought the speaker was not telling the truth.

watch your tongue also *watch your mouth* to stop talking about something, or to stop being rude ▶ *If you don't learn to watch your tongue, you're going to end up in trouble one of these days.*

TONGUES
set tongues wagging to make people start talking ▶ *The tiny bikini she was wearing set a few tongues wagging.*

TOOTH
fight tooth and nail to fight very hard ▶ *Local residents will fight tooth and*

T

nail to save the sports ground. ► He fought tooth and nail for the right to see his daughter.

have a sweet tooth to like sweet food ► I'd love some chocolate – I've got a very sweet tooth, you know.

long in the tooth
old, or too old
► At the age of 45 I felt rather long in the tooth to be a trainee.

TOP
blow your top
to get so angry that you lose control ► She blew her top after she was dropped from the team.

come out on top to win or succeed ► Don's very upset – it's the first time in his career he hasn't come out on top.

sth gets on top of you something makes you upset or anxious ► She needs a rest: her work's been getting on top of her recently.

go thin on top to be losing a lot of hair from your head ► He's going a bit thin on top, but he doesn't look 50.

on top of sth
1 in addition to something ► It was the lack of privacy on top of the strict discipline that made me decide to leave the army. ► As a waiter, you get tips on top of your basic salary.
2 dealing with something successfully ► I've managed my time much better this term, and I'm on top of my revision.

over the top also **OTT** too extreme ► The film starts well but the ending's really over the top. ► I think I went a

bit OTT when we were arguing last night.

the top of the heap also **the top of the pile** the highest, most powerful, or richest positions in society ► He was a self-made man who climbed his way up to the top of the heap. **the bottom of the heap/pile** ► Their aim is to improve the lives of those at the bottom of the pile.

to top it all (off) this is the last in a series of annoying, unpleasant, or funny events ► She fainted, fell, and broke her ankle, and then, to top it all off, her house got flooded.

TORCH
carry a torch for sb to feel love for someone when you cannot have a relationship with them ► He's been carrying a torch for your aunt since they were at college together.

carry the torch to support an idea publicly ► He's one of the old-style politicians, still carrying the torch of land reform.

pass the torch also **hand on the torch** to give someone else the knowledge or opportunity that you have had, so that they can continue what you were doing ► I've spent 20 happy years reading the news, and now I feel it's time to pass the torch. ► She's handing on the torch of exceptional management to her friend and deputy.

The torch in the idioms **carry the torch** and **pass the torch** was the flame that was carried by several runners, one after another, to a place where games would be held in Ancient Greece. This was an important religious ceremony, and today something like it is done before the Olympic Games.

TOUCH

the common touch the ability of a famous or powerful person to talk to and be friendly with ordinary people ▶ *Old-style aristocrats who lack the common touch are not being chosen as party candidates.*

be in touch (with) also **keep in touch (with)**
1 to continue to communicate (with someone) ▶ *Are you still in touch with him?* ▶ *We haven't actually seen each other for years but we keep in touch.*
2 to be or stay familiar (with something) ▶ *It is vitally important for people in government to stay in touch with public opinion.* **get in touch (with sb/sth)** ▶ *Police have asked anyone who saw the robbery to get in touch with them.* ▶ *She says she needs to get in touch with her feelings.*

it is touch and go it is a dangerous, uncertain, or risky situation ▶ *Rehearsals went so badly, it was touch and go whether I'd still be in the play by the end of the afternoon.* ▶ *I'm afraid your father's very ill – it's touch and go.*

lose touch (with)
1 to stop communicating (with someone), usually by mistake ▶ *We were very close at school, but we lost touch when I went to college.* ▶ *NASA is trying to find out why the spacecraft keeps losing touch with earth.*
2 to stop being familiar (with something) ▶ *Critics say that the radical environmental pressure groups have lost touch with the wishes of local people.*

be out of touch (with)
1 to be no longer communicating (with someone) ▶ *My sister and I have been out of touch for ages.*
2 to be no longer familiar (with something) ▶ *I haven't worked in a hospital for about 20 years. I'm completely out of touch with modern nursing methods.*

a soft touch also **an easy touch** someone who you can get to do what you want, or give you what you want ▶ *Dad's a soft touch, I'll get him to lend me the money.* ▶ *The charity is not an easy touch; we carry out rigorous checks on who gets help.*

TOUCHES

put the finishing touches to to do the last few things that complete something ▶ *She's just putting the finishing touches to your portrait – you can see it in a moment.*

TOWEL

throw in the towel to stop trying to achieve something because it has been too difficult ▶ *His children tried to persuade him to throw in the towel, but he refused to give up his job.*

TOWER

a tower of strength someone who is always there to give you help, sympathy, and support ▶ *When my wife left me, my mother was a tower of strength.*

TOWN

go to town to do something with a lot of enthusiasm, often spending a lot of money ▶ *They're going to town on the Christmas decorations this year, aren't they?*

a one-horse town a small, boring town ▶ *I grew up in a one-horse town and couldn't wait to leave.*

paint the town red to go out and enjoy yourself in bars, clubs etc ▶ *Finals are*

T

over – tonight we're going out to paint the town red.

TRACK

have the inside track also **be on the inside track** to have an advantage or information that makes you most likely to succeed ▶ *He knew that other candidates were more experienced, but felt that he had the inside track because of his background.*
▶ *According to people who are on the inside track, the property market is set to go up again.*

keep track of to know what is happening to (someone or something) ▶ *Our telephone banking service helps small businesses keep track of their cash flow.* ▶ *We must keep track of time – I want to get home before dark.*

lose track of ▶ *Don't lose track of what you're spending.*

off the beaten track in a place that is quiet and far from a lot of people ▶ *We found a tiny beach right off the beaten track.*

on the fast track (to sth)
1 likely to be successful quickly ▶ *He joined the firm at the same time as me, but he's on the fast track.*
2 likely to be dealt with quickly ▶ *A biography of the former prime minister has been put on the fast track for publication.* **fast-track** ADJ ▶ *May plays a fast-track airline executive.*

be on the right track to be working towards the right result ▶ *I think I know the method to use – can you tell me if I'm on the right track?* **be on the wrong track** ▶ *No, a graphologist's nothing to do with geology – you're on the wrong track there.*

TRACKS

cover your tracks to hide something

that you have done so that no one finds out ▶ *Phelps tried to cover his tracks by growing a beard and using a false passport.*

make tracks to leave a place ▶ *I think we'd better be making tracks.*

stop (dead) in your tracks to stop suddenly ▶ *I stopped (dead) in my tracks as a car screeched round the corner.*

stop sb/sth in its tracks ▶ *We have received new information that could stop the deal in its tracks.*

TRAIL

blaze a trail to be the first to do something new ▶ *She blazed a trail for female physicists.* **trail-blazing** ADJ ▶ *The trail-blazing magazine is celebrating its 50th anniversary this year.*

be hot on the trail of to be close to finding someone or something you want ▶ *Police are hot on the trail of the thief who stole several cars in the past month.*

TRAP

fall into the trap (of) to make the common mistake (of) ▶ *Don't fall into the trap of thinking everything you do is equally important – set priorities.*
▶ *Advertisers always show us ideal families buying their products and thousands of gullible people fall into the trap.*

keep your trap shut to say nothing ▶ *Keep your trap shut about the party when we get to Dave's.*

TREAT

go down a treat to be enjoyed very much ▶ *"Fancy a cup of tea?" "That would go down a treat."*

TREE

sb is barking up the wrong tree someone has the wrong idea about

something ▶ *If they think I'll support that crazy scheme, they're barking up the wrong tree.*

TRICK

do the trick to solve a problem or provide what is needed ▶ *If you take these pills and drink plenty of water, that will probably do the trick.*

sb doesn't miss a trick someone is quick to notice what is happening and gets advantages from every situation ▶ *When it comes to saving money, he doesn't miss a trick.*

TRICKS

sb is up to his/her old tricks used in order to show that you disapprove because someone is behaving badly in a way that they have done before ▶ *He's up to his old tricks again – he's taken another two-hour lunch break.*

tricks of the trade clever methods that are used in a particular job or activity ▶ *She learned the tricks of the trade by watching and listening to the experienced reporters.*

TRIP

an ego trip when you do something because it makes you feel important ▶ *This film is not even entertaining; it's just an ego trip for the director.*

TROLLEY

be/go off your trolley ➤ be/go off your ROCKER

TROUBLE

go to a lot of trouble to make a special effort to do something properly ▶ *My family went to a lot of trouble to give me a wonderful birthday.*

TROUSERS

(she) wears the trousers it is the woman and not the man who makes decisions in the family ▶ *He may be in charge at work, but his wife wears the trousers at home.*

TRUMPET

blow your own trumpet to praise yourself for your achievements in a

proud way ▶ *Success hasn't changed him, and he can never be accused of blowing his own trumpet.*

TRUST

not trust sb as far as you could throw him/her also **not trust sb farther than you could throw him/her** not to trust someone at all ▶ *I'm sorry that he's* *going out with Lisa – I wouldn't trust her as far as I could throw her.*

TRUTH

to tell you the truth to be open and honest with you (used to introduce a statement) ➤ *To tell you the truth, I'm amazed that they gave him the job in the first place.*

TUBES

go down the tubes ➤ go down the DRAIN

TUNE

call the tune ➤ call the SHOTS

sb (has) changed his/her tune someone has changed their mind, or the way they are talking about something ➤ *Schools that had refused to admit students with special needs quickly changed their tune when government grants became available.*

in tune with understanding, agreeing with, or right for ➤ *These new houses are designed to be in tune with the environment.* ➤ *His speech was in tune with the general philosophy of the company.* **out of tune with** ➤ *Her public appeal for donations to charity was out of tune with her usual meanness.*

sing a different tune to completely change the opinions you have expressed before ➤ *Since being elected, he's singing a different tune about wage cuts for politicians.*

to the tune of involving the sum of (a large amount of money) ➤ *They are subsidized to the tune of £4 million a year.*

TURKEY

go cold turkey to stop doing something that is a habit, such as

taking a strong drug, completely and immediately ➤ *The most frightening inmates of the prison are the addicts – especially when they are going cold turkey.* **cold-turkey treatment** ➤ *I told him to try the cold-turkey treatment with Jan and never to see her or speak to her again.*

TURN

at every turn all the time, in all conditions ➤ *The new legislation has been influenced at every turn by the very banks that it is supposed to control.*

do sb a good turn to do something that helps another person ➤ *You did me a good turn suggesting me for the job – I love it.*

one good turn deserves another if someone helps you, you should do something nice to thank them ➤ *She was wonderful when I was ill, and one good turn deserves another, so I'm glad to be able to give her this holiday.*

speak out of turn to say something that is unsuitable or wrong at a particular time ➤ *I think the minister spoke out of turn when he criticized the police.*

take a turn for the better/worse to get much better or worse suddenly ➤ *Relationships between the two countries took a turn for the better last year.*

turn round and do sth to do the opposite of what someone expects ➤ *They ordered this meal specially; they can't just turn round and say they don't want it.*

turn sth inside out also **turn sth upside down**
1 to search something in a thorough

way ▶ *The thieves had turned the kitchen inside out looking for cash.* ▶ *I turned the house upside down, but I never found the earrings.*
2 to change something completely ▶ *The fire turned our lives inside out.* ▶ *The new managing director plans to turn the company upside down.*

TURN-UP
a turn-up for the books an unexpected and surprising event, especially a pleasant one ▶ *"Sam was on time for once." "Well, there's a turn-up for the books."*

TWINKLING
in the twinkling of an eye very quickly ▶ *In the twinkling of an eye, her life had changed and she was no longer certain of anything.*

TWIST
drive sb round the twist ➤ drive sb round the BEND

TWO
it takes two to tango if a situation involves two people, they are both equally responsible for it ▶ *You can't just blame her for flirting with your boyfriend – it takes two to tango.*

put two and two together to guess the meaning of something you have heard or seen ▶ *He'd been on several business trips, and he kept bringing me flowers, so I put two and two together.* ▶ *When John saw us whispering, he put two and two together and unfortunately made five.*

that makes two of us I agree with you and feel the same way ▶ *"I'd like to work in Hawaii." "Mmm, that makes two of us."*

T

Uu

UNDERGROUND

go underground to start doing something secretly or hide in a secret place ▶ *She stayed in the country, going underground when the invading army tried to force her to work for their newspaper.*

UP

it's/that's up to you you should make the decision yourself ▶ *"Shall we have dinner before we go?" "I don't mind; you're the cook, it's up to you."*

be on an up to feel happy and cheerful ▶ *It seemed that whenever I was on an up, he felt down.*

be on the up (and up) something is improving or increasing ▶ *Experts say that the standard of university teaching is on the up.*

be up and down to be well, happy, or good sometimes and ill, unhappy, or bad at other times ▶ *Dad's been up and down since his last operation.* ▶ *The business has been up and down this year, but on the whole I think we're doing all right.*

be up and running to be working well ▶ *I'm afraid we can't accept any orders until the new machines are up and running.*

be up on sth to know a lot about a particular subject ▶ *Dad won't be much help – he's not really up on pop music.*

not be up to sth not to have the energy, interest, or ability for something ▶ *You never do any exercise, so you certainly won't be up to trekking in the mountains.* ▶ *I'm afraid she just isn't up to the job.*

UPS

ups and downs a mixture of good and bad experiences ▶ *Any marriage has plenty of ups and downs.*

U-TURN

do a U-turn to have a complete change of ideas, plans etc ▶ *The government has been accused of doing U-turns on a number of election promises.*

> If a car does a U-turn, it turns around completely in the road and drives back the way that it was coming from. In Britain, this idiom is almost always used about politicians or political parties who do the opposite of what they have promised to do.

U

Vv

VACUUM

in a vacuum existing completely separately from other things ▶ *Like any social problem, drug abuse does not exist in a vacuum.*

VARIETY

variety is the spice of life doing many different things is what makes life interesting ▶ *I like to play a different sport each season – variety is the spice of life.*

VENGEANCE

with a vengeance a great deal ▶ *She began drinking with a vengeance when she lost her job.*

VERGE

on the verge of (doing) sth just going to, or likely to do something ▶ *Problems with her career left her on the verge of a nervous breakdown.*

VIEW

a bird's-eye view (of sth) a view of a place from a high position ▶ *From his office he had a bird's-eye view of the whole city.*

do sth with a view to (doing) sth to do something for a particular purpose ▶ *He is trying to save some money with a view to taking a university course next year.*

take a dim view of to think that something is bad ▶ *Her family took a dim view of her decision to go into acting.*

a worm's-eye view (of sth) an idea of what is happening, seen from a low position ▶ *The office messenger had a worm's-eye view of the whole organization.*

VINE

wither on the vine also *die on the vine* (of an idea, plan etc) to fail early before having a chance to develop ▶ *We don't want to see reform of the system just wither on the vine.*

VIRTUE

by virtue of because of ▶ *Women outnumber men in retirement homes by virtue of the fact that they live longer.*

make a virtue of necessity to get an advantage out of something that you have to do ▶ *Because we have such a small garden, we've made a virtue of necessity and concentrated on miniature plants.*

VISIONS

have visions of (doing) sth to think or imagine (doing) something ▶ *I had visions of the wobbly stage collapsing and taking us with it.*

VOICE

give voice to to express your feelings or opinions ▶ *Our party gives voice to the reasonable people caught between the two extremes.*

speak with one voice to express one opinion ▶ *I think we all speak with one voice when we say that something must be done to improve matters.*

V

a voice (crying) in the wilderness
someone who is going against popular
or expert opinion ▶ *For a long time,*
scientists warning against global
warming were merely voices crying in
the wilderness.

VOLUMES
speak volumes (about) to express
something very clearly without using
words ▶ *She said it didn't matter, but*
her enraged expression spoke
volumes.

V

Ww

WAGON

go on the wagon to decide not to drink any alcohol ▶ *Sometimes I go on the wagon for a few days, just to prove to myself that I can do it.* **fall/ come off the wagon** ▶ *It was at Rick's stag night that I really fell off the wagon.*

WAIFS

waifs and strays people or animals who do not have anywhere to live ▶ *Here at the animal sanctuary we take in all sorts of waifs and strays.*

WAIT

wait and see be patient! ▶ *"What's your wedding dress like?" "Sorry, you'll have to wait and see."*

WAKE

(leave/bring sth) in its wake ▶ *High volumes of traffic bring several health problems in their wake.*

in the wake of sth after something, and often as a result of it ▶ *People here are still cleaning up in the wake of the floods.*

WALK

from all walks of life also **from every walk of life** from many different types of job, family background etc ▶ *Stress is a common complaint in every walk of life.*

walk all over sb to treat someone with no respect ▶ *Don't be too soft with him, or he'll end up walking all over you.*

WALL

come up against a brick wall also **hit a brick wall** to be blocked from doing

or continuing something ▶ *We can give you some tips on tracing your family tree, and what to do when you come up against a brick wall.*

drive sb up the wall to annoy someone a lot ▶ *I can't remember his name and it's driving me up the wall!*

go to the wall
1 to fail, usually because there is no more money ▶ *Thousands of companies went to the wall when the stock market crashed.*
2 to be so sure that what you believe in is right, that you are ready to suffer because you support it ▶ *Do you believe the boy's story? Would you go to the wall for it?*

hit the wall to reach a point where it is difficult to achieve any more ▶ *Everyone talks about hitting the wall at the 24-mile mark when you run the marathon, and that's just what happened to me.*

nail sb to the wall to punish someone and make them suffer ▶ *She really dislikes him – she can't wait to nail him to the wall for some breach of the rules.*

off the wall unusual or slightly crazy ▶ *Those new furniture designs are completely off the wall.* ▶ *It was only when he talked about politics that you realized he was off the wall.* **off-the-wall** ADJ ▶ *We're looking for exciting, off-the-wall ideas.*

WALLS

be climbing the walls to be very impatient and annoyed ▶ *After waiting* *for three hours in the departure lounge, we were climbing the walls.*

WAND

you can't wave a magic wand you cannot solve a problem immediately ▶ *We have to be realistic; the government can't wave a magic wand and get rid of the housing problem.*

WANE

on the wane becoming smaller, weaker, or less common ▶ *Police say that violent crime is on the wane in the city.*

WAR

wage war on to start to fight or destroy someone or something ▶ *The president promised to wage war on domestic poverty.*

a war of words a very angry or serious argument ▶ *The war of words between the two countries over fishing rights reached new heights last week.*

WARM

you're getting warm you have nearly guessed something ▶ *"Has he got me a camera?" "No, but you're getting warm – it is something that you would be able to use on holiday."*

WARPATH

be on the warpath to be very angry and determined to deal with a situation ▶ *Parents' associations are on the warpath about the cuts in the education budget.* ▶ *Mum's on the warpath – she's just seen what you've done to your bedroom wall!*

WARS

sb has been in the wars someone has had a lot of problems ▶ *Poor thing, you've really been in the wars, haven't you? Let me put a bandage on for you.*

WARTS

warts and all including the bad parts as well as the good parts ▶ *This biography of Beethoven aims to depict him as he really was, warts and all.*

A wart is a small, hard, raised spot on your skin. This idiom comes from the 17th-century British politician, Oliver Cromwell, who told a painter to paint a picture of him and include his warts and anything else that made him look ugly.

WASH

sth doesn't wash (with sb) something is impossible to believe ▶ *His claim that he wasn't even there doesn't wash with me.*

WASHED UP

be (all) washed up to fail or be ruined ▶ *For the first time he realized that their marriage was all washed up.*

WASTE

lay waste (to) sth to destroy something completely ▶ *Dogs and rats have laid waste to much of the native Caribbean wildlife.*

WATER

blow sth out of the water to destroy completely ▶ *Assertions that these foods are completely safe have been blown out of the water by a number of recent scandals.*

be dead in the water to have failed completely or have no chance of

W

succeeding ▶ *The peace initiative looks dead in the water now that the ceasefire has been broken.*

not hold water (of a plan, argument, or idea) not to work; to be false ▶ *The argument sounds logical, but doesn't hold water when you actually look at the facts.*

in/into deep water in or into difficulties ▶ *Psychologists can get into deep water trying to explain everything in terms of childhood experiences.*

in/into hot water in or into trouble ▶ *I'm afraid this is not the first time that she's been in hot water with the committee.*

sth is (like) water off a duck's back something has no effect on someone ▶ *He couldn't upset her, however hard he tried; his subtle rudeness and game-playing tactics were like water off a duck's back.*

it's/that's (all) water under the bridge something is in the past and is best forgotten ▶ *Can't you forgive him? After all, it's water under the bridge now.*

a lot of water has flowed under the bridge since a lot of time has passed and a situation has changed a lot since a particular event ▶ *A lot of water has flowed under the bridge since we met, but we're still good friends.*

a ____ of the first water someone or something is an extreme example of a particular type of person or thing ▶ *He hardly knew anyone at the party; only Barbara, and she was a bore of the first water.*

pour cold water on sth to say you do not like or agree with something, and try to stop people being excited about it ▶ *There will always be someone pouring cold water on new ideas, but don't let them discourage you.*

test the water also **test the waters** to find out what reaction people would have to a plan or idea before you use it ▶ *I'd like to test the water before we put in a formal request for a new sports hall.*

be treading water to have stopped developing or becoming more successful ▶ *Some companies can afford to tread water, but there is usually pressure to expand.*

> Treading water is a way of swimming that lets you float and look around without moving forward.

WATERS

muddy the waters to make a situation confusing ▶ *Many of us are prepared to learn about computers, but the jargon muddies the waters.*

still waters run deep someone who seems quiet or calm has hidden emotions and qualities ▶ *He hardly says a word in the office, but still waters run deep, so maybe he's got a passionate love life.*

W

WAVELENGTH

be on the same/on sb's wavelength to have similar ideas, opinions, and attitudes to another person ▶ *She and I work well together – we're on the same wavelength.* **be on a (totally) different wavelength** ▶ *I just couldn't talk to those arty people, I felt I was on a totally different wavelength.*

WAVES

make waves to cause problems for people by doing something new ▶ *The new minister is already making waves with his proposal to make people work for their unemployment benefit.*

WAY

any way you slice it also **whichever way you slice it** however you think about it ▶ *Any way you slice it, it is clear that we have to pay more taxes if we want tougher environmental laws.*

be behind sb all the way also **be with sb all the way** to support someone completely ▶ *Go and tell Mike about your idea; we're behind you all the way.*

by the way used before or after you say something that is not directly connected to what you are talking about, for example something that you meant to say earlier ▶ *Make sure that your notes are written up neatly and, by the way, there'll be a test next Friday.*

sth could swing either way you cannot tell in advance which of two results something will have ▶ *The match could have swung either way in the thrilling last ten minutes.*

every which way in all directions at the same time ▶ *I heard a crash and looked up – glass was flying every which way.*

get/be under way to start to happen

or be happening ▶ *There were problems even before work on the building got under way.* ▶ *The project to clean up the river is well under way.*

go back a long way also **go way back** to have known each other for a long time ▶ *She goes back a long way with the company – she joined us ten years ago.* ▶ *Sam and I go way back – we sat next to each other on our first day at school.*

go out of your way to do sth to make a special effort to do something ▶ *Dave was very kind to the new students and went out of his way to help them settle in.*

be going sb's way to be happening in the way that someone wants or hopes ▶ *Things don't seem to be going my way today – I think I'll go home.*

go the way of to behave or be treated in the same way as someone or something else ▶ *I'm afraid old-style typists have gone the way of other out-of-date office equipment.* ▶ *She's likely to go the way of her sister, who became an alcoholic.*

go your own way to do what you want to do ▶ *Your children grow up and go their own way, and you have to find other interests.*

have come a long way to have improved or changed a lot ▶ *Diesel engines may have come a long way, but they are still rather noisy.*

have a long way to go to need to improve a lot ▶ *He has a long way to go, but he's got the right attitude – he could be a good runner.*

have a way with to be good at dealing with ▶ *He had a way with the older people at the centre – they all liked him.* ▶ *He was a shy, quiet man who had a remarkable way with numbers.*

not have much in the way of sth not to have much of that sort of thing ▶ *We don't have much in the way of vegetables, but I could get some frozen peas.* **What have you got in the way of...?** ▶ *What have you got in the way of picture frames?*

be in a bad way to be ill, very upset, or in a bad situation ▶ *She was in a very bad way after the accident – they think that's why she lost the baby.*

in a big way a lot ▶ *European companies are putting their money into the region in a big way.*

not know which way to turn to be confused and unable to make a decision ▶ *I've got so many things to do before the wedding, I don't know which way to turn.*

be laughing all the way to the bank to be very happy because you are making a lot of money

▶ *She inherited three decaying old houses in the centre of town, and now she's laughing all the way to the bank.*

learn sth the hard way also **discover sth the hard way** to learn something by having an unpleasant experience ▶ *I learned how to look after a car the hard way – my first one was always breaking down.*

look the other way to ignore something that is illegal or not allowed ▶ *Very often people prefer to look the other way instead of reporting suspicious incidents involving their neighbours.*

make way for to allow someone or something to pass or go into an empty place, by moving or being moved ▶ *Please can you make way for the wheelchair?* ▶ *A number of paintings will be put in storage to make way for an exhibition of Flemish sculptures.* ▶ *Oranges have made way for high-tech industry in California's Silicon Valley.*

no way no, not at all ▶ *"Can I have a bite of your pizza?" "No way – get your own."* ▶ *"She called and asked me out last night." "No way, really?"*

pave the way for also **smooth the way for** to make something easier by preparing the situation ▶ *This case could pave the way for a major reform of the fraud laws.*

see your way (clear) to to agree to ▶ *Do you think you could see your way clear to lending me a few quid?*

take the easy way out to choose the easiest solution, which is not always the best one ▶ *Too many parents take the easy way out by letting their kids eat what they want instead of insisting on a good diet.*

take sth the wrong way to be offended by something someone has said or done, even though there was no intention to offend ▶ *Now please don't take this the wrong way, but I've asked Heather to submit the report instead of you.*

there's more than one way to skin a cat there is more than one way of achieving something ▶ *There's more than one way to skin a cat, so don't give up if your first idea fails.*

way to go! well done! ▶ *Are you done? Way to go. It looks great!* ▶ *"I got 80% on the test!" "Way to go!"*

WAYS

sth cuts both ways something has two

W

different or opposite effects ▶ *We should remember that forensic evidence cuts both ways – it clears the innocent as well as implicating the guilty.*

mend your ways also ***change your ways*** to improve your behaviour or performance ▶ *We're trying to mend our ways by keeping the public better informed.* ▶ *I've learned my lesson, and changed my ways. I just hope you can forgive me.*

no two ways about it that is certainly true ▶ *With that haircut you look ten years younger, no two ways about it.*

a parting of the ways a decision by two people or groups to live or work separately ▶ *After we left university there was a natural parting of the ways: Jo got a job in London and I went overseas.*

be set in your ways to be unable or unwilling to change your habits and opinions ▶ *Employers used to believe that younger employees would be less set in their ways, but a recent survey challenges this view.*

there are ways and means (of doing sth) there are effective methods of achieving something, although they may be secret or illegal ▶ *The company has ways and means of finding out what the competition are up to.*

you can't have it both ways you should choose one course of action or one opinion, and accept the results ▶ *You can't have it both ways – if we tell children not to talk to strangers, we can't blame them for being rude to people who talk to them in the street.*

WAYSIDE
fall by the wayside
1 to leave or stop doing something

▶ *The course is very tough, and more than half of the trainees fall by the wayside every year.*
2 to fail ▶ *The project fell by the wayside because there wasn't enough interest in keeping it going.*

WEAR
be/look none the worse for wear also **be/look no worse for wear** to be or look quite well, even after being in a bad situation ▶ *The cat had bruised ears and a broken claw, but was otherwise none the worse for wear.* **be/look the worse for wear** ▶ *She arrived at the press conference looking a little the worse for wear, having just flown in from Moscow.*

wear thin (of something that was amusing or pleasant at first) to be no longer good or enjoyable ▶ *He says 'I'm Jolly by name and jolly by nature' to every new person he meets and it's beginning to wear thin.* ▶ *Snakes make unusual pets, but require a lot of work and are often abandoned once the novelty wears thin.*

WEATHER
keep a weather eye on to keep your attention on a situation, so that you will notice any changes that may cause problems ▶ *The government is keeping a weather eye on inflation.*

be/feel under the weather to be or feel slightly ill ▶ *I'm feeling a bit under the weather this morning.*

WEB
a tangled web a very complicated situation ▶ *The heroine of the novel finds herself in a tangled web of conspiracy and lies when she picks up the wrong bag at the airport.*

This idiom comes from a line in Sir Walter Scott's poem, *Marmion*: O what a tangled web we weave, When first we practise to deceive.

WEDGE
drive a wedge between to cause anger or disagreement between two people or groups ▶ *Arguments about how to spend the school fund continue to drive a wedge between the sports staff and the academic staff.*

WEEK
it's not my week ➤ it's not my DAY
week in, week out ➤ DAY in, day out

WEIGHT
carry weight to have a lot of influence ▶ *Expert opinions carry quite a lot of weight with the jury.*
(a) dead weight someone or something that does not add any advantage to an organization ▶ *Too many members of the school team are simply dead weight.*

A dead weight is someone or something that is very heavy to carry, especially someone who is unconscious or not helping you to carry them.

have the weight of the world on your shoulders to feel very worried and unhappy because of your problems

▶ *What's wrong with her? She looks as if she's got the weight of the world on her shoulders.*

pull your weight to work as hard as other people ▶ *Everyone is expected to pull their weight in this department.*
throw your weight around to show people in a proud way how powerful and important you are ▶ *Just because he trained in the London office doesn't mean he can throw his weight around here.*
throw your weight behind sb/sth to show that you strongly support someone or something ▶ *He threw his weight firmly behind the environmentalists who were campaigning for traffic restrictions.*

worth his/ her weight in gold extremely valuable, helpful, or useful ▶ *Any secretary who can read my notes is worth her weight in gold.*

WELCOME
outstay your welcome to stay in a place that you are visiting for too long ▶ *She ordered the news crews out of her house, saying that they had outstayed their welcome.*

WHALE
have a whale of a time to enjoy yourself very much ▶ *You seem to be having a whale of a time with Lou.*

WHAMMY
a double whammy when someone is unlucky because two bad things happen at the same time ▶ *This is a double whammy for the poor – higher taxes combined with welfare and education cuts.*

WHAT

...and/or what have you and/or other things of the same kind ▶ *If a community has some shortage – a water shortage, a gas shortage, or what have you – you would expect people to try to help by saving.*

for what it's worth my opinion may not be very important, but here it is anyway ▶ *For what it's worth, I think this report is wildly optimistic, and I disagree with these figures.*

know what's what also **understand what's what** to understand what the situation is or how a system works ▶ *I'm new, and I still don't really know what's what around here.*

...or what? used after a question, which is usually a criticism of someone or something ▶ *I'm thinking, is she stupid or what? She gives up a career in fashion to work here! ▶ Are you going to tell him or what? You said you would!*

what about it? also **what of it?** what does that matter? ▶ *"That's the third plate you've broken this month." "Yeah, what about it?" ▶ "Are you going to see Rebecca again?" "Yes, what of it?"*

what do you know! said when you are surprised and happy about something you have just heard or seen ▶ *"I think I've fixed it." "Well, what do you know – we've got a mechanic in the family."*

what goes around comes around if you are nice, good things will happen to you, and if you are bad, then bad things will happen to you ▶ *He did nasty things to other people, and what goes around comes around. Nobody cares that they tried to kill him.*

what got into sb? why is someone

behaving like that? ▶ *What's got into Molly? She actually smiled at me just now! ▶ I don't know what got into me – I just got so upset.*

what makes sb tick the thoughts, desires, opinions etc that make someone behave in the way that they do ▶ *I've always been interested in what makes people tick, which is probably why I became a journalist.*

what's eating him/her? why does he/she seem annoyed, upset etc? ▶ *What's eating Martin? He's been snapping at everyone all day.*

what's it worth (to sb)? what will you do for someone if they do what you want? ▶ *What's it worth to you to have the tapes destroyed?*

what's up? (with sb/sth) what's the matter? ▶ *What's up? Are you OK? ▶ What's up with the CD player? I can't make it work.*

what's with sb? what is wrong with someone? ▶ *What's with Mike? He's in a foul mood.*

what's with sth? what is a particular thing for? ▶ *What's with the microphone? Are you recording us?*

WHATEVER

whatever turns you on you have the right to like a particular thing, but I don't like it ▶ *I just can't stand musicals, but whatever turns you on, I suppose.*

WHEAT

sort (out) the wheat from the chaff also **separate the wheat from the chaff** to choose the good or useful things or people and get rid of the rest ▶ *After years of experience, antique dealers have no difficulty sorting the wheat from the chaff.*

WHEEL

a/the big wheel ➤ a/the big **CHEESE**

reinvent the wheel to work on something that you think is new and different, but that has already been done by someone else ▶ *With so many different groups working on new software, there is a real danger of reinventing the wheel.*

the squeaky wheel (gets the grease) the person who complains the most is the one who gets what they want ▶ *Pete was the squeaky wheel in the department who got promotion first.*

wheel and deal to do clever but possibly dishonest things to get what you want ▶ *They've got to wheel and deal to get the players they want.* **wheeling and dealing** N ▶ *You wouldn't believe the wheeling and dealing that's going on to get the film started.* **wheeler-dealer** N ▶ *I think Dave's parents know he's a bit of a wheeler-dealer, but they're not going to report him to the police, are they?*

the wheel has come full circle something has now come back to the state or situation it was in at the beginning ▶ *The wheel has come full circle since the expansion of the universities and now they're facing cuts in funding again.*

WHEELS

oil the wheels to help something happen by talking to people and making them like you ▶ *He's difficult to talk to, but I'm taking Jill along to oil the wheels.*

set the wheels in motion to do what is necessary to make something begin ▶ *Why did the police wait so long before setting the wheels in motion to track down the killer?*

set/keep the wheels turning to make something work or continue to work properly ▶ *They explained what they needed to get the wheels turning again.*

wheels within wheels lots of influences that make a situation complicated ▶ *"How did you get involved in all this?" "Oh, well, wheels within wheels. I happened to know someone who was very useful to them."*

WHEN

when all is said and done after all; in the end ▶ *He had his problems like everyone else, but when all is said and done, he was a great man who did a lot for this community.*

WHERE

where sb is coming from why someone behaves or thinks the way they do ▶ *I spent years trying to get close to him, trying to work out where he was coming from.*

where it's at a place or activity that is very popular, exciting, and fashionable ▶ *If you're interested in great food, Paris is where it's at.*

WHILE

be worth your while the advantage you get from something is worth the money, time, or effort you use to do it ▶ *I don't think it's worth my while waiting for him – he might be hours yet.*

make it worth sb's while to give someone money for doing something for you ▶ *I'd like you to help me with that article – I'd make it worth your while.*

WHIP

crack the whip to control people and force them to work harder ▶ He tends

to crack the whip a bit too often for my taste.

WHIRL

give sth a whirl to try something new ▶ I've no idea how to ski, but I'm longing to give it a whirl.

be in a whirl to feel very excited or confused ▶ Her mind was in a whirl as she considered his suggestion.

WHISKER

by a whisker by a very small amount of time, space etc ▶ He ran well in the heats, but failed to qualify by a whisker.

be within a whisker of (doing) sth to be very close to doing something

▶ The two companies were within a whisker of agreeing on a deal when disaster struck.

WHISTLE

blow the whistle (on) to tell someone about something that is wrong or illegal because you think it should be stopped ▶ The former oil-rig worker was dismissed after blowing the whistle on safety violations by his drilling company. **whistle-blower** N ▶ Depending on whose version you believe, she was either a principled whistle-blower or a bitter ex-employee.

WHOOP

whoop it up to have a lot of fun with a group of friends ▶ I found an old photo of us whooping it up on the day we left college.

WHYS

the whys and wherefores (of sth) the reasons and explanations (for something) ▶ As a good journalist, I don't only want to know the story, I want to know the whys and wherefores.

WIDE

be wide open (of a competition or race) to be able to be won by any of the competitors ▶ When the favourite horse fell at the first fence, the race was suddenly wide open.

WIDOW

a golf/football etc widow a woman whose husband leaves her alone to spend time playing or watching sport ▶ I used to hate being a golf widow every weekend, but it pushed me into taking art classes, which I love.

WIGGLE

get a wiggle on to do something more quickly ▶ You guys will have to get a wiggle on!

W

WILL

where there's a will there's a way if you really want to do something, you will find a way to do it ▶ *I've finally saved enough money to travel for a month – where there's a will, there's a way.*

WILLIES

give sb the willies to make someone feel nervous, frightened, or worried ▶ *Barney said somebody died here, but don't tell the kids – it'll just give them the willies.*

WIN

a no-win situation a solution to a problem that gives nobody an advantage ▶ *If we sell the flat now, we have to sell at a loss, and if we wait, we'll lose the house we want – it's a no-win situation.*

win-win also ***a win-win situation*** a solution to a problem that gives both people an advantage instead of one winning and one losing ▶ *Instead of fighting over the land, they formed a partnership to develop it and then sold it for thousands – a case of win-win.*

WIND

get wind of sth to find out about something that other people wanted to be secret ▶ *Let's get out of here before the press get wind of what's happened.*

get your second wind also ***catch your second wind*** to have a new flow of energy or improvement of natural skills ▶ *I got my second wind and wrote the conclusion of my report in 15 minutes.*

sth is in the wind something is being planned or considered, usually secretly ▶ *By the end of May we knew that there were some changes in the wind.*

it's an ill wind (that blows no good) also ***it's an ill wind that blows nobody any good*** every problem or bad situation brings advantages for someone ▶ *Furniture shops had a record year after the floods – it's an ill wind.*

sail close to the wind to take a risk by doing something that may be dishonest or illegal ▶ *Some of these travel companies have a reputation for sailing close to the wind.*

see/know which way the wind is blowing also ***see/know which way the wind blows*** to find out or know what is likely to happen or what people think, before you decide what to do ▶ *In this business you have to see which way the wind is blowing – what's in fashion and what isn't.*

take the wind out of sb's sails to make someone feel much less confident or proud ▶ *He often boasted about his tennis, but he had the wind taken right out of his sails when I took the first set 6-0.*

WINDMILLS

be tilting at windmills to be attacking imaginary enemies or wrongs ▶ *She blames our company for all the problems in this area, but she's tilting at windmills.*

WINDOW

sth goes out (of) the window something is ignored or forgotten completely ▶ *All my good intentions to stick to my diet went out the window when I saw the fantastic meal he'd made.*

a window of opportunity a period of

time in which you can do something
▶ *The collapse of the national
corporation opened a window of
opportunity for the smaller companies
in the area.*

WINE

wine and dine sb to try to impress
someone by giving them expensive
meals ▶ *He went to a lot of trouble to
wine and dine the clients, and finally
agreed the deal.*

WING

do sth on a wing and a prayer to start
a new activity hoping that things will
go well and trusting to luck ▶ *Joss set
off round the world on a wing and a
prayer, with little more than the
clothes he was wearing.*

take sb under your wing to help and
protect someone ▶ *Sam took me
under his wing when I started working
here, which helped me a lot.*

under the wing of controlled or
protected by ▶ *Accountants operate
under the wing of their professional
institute.*

wing it to do something without
planning or preparing ▶ *Have you
thought out some answers to likely
questions, or are you going to wing it?*

sth wings its way to something is sent
somewhere quickly ▶ *A bottle of
champagne will be winging its way to
the lucky winner of today's
competition.*

WINGS

clip sb's wings to limit someone's
freedom or power ▶ *Many national
governments feel that the Internet is a
threat, and they want to clip its wings
before it gets too powerful.*

be (waiting) in the wings to be

waiting ▶ *Other firms are waiting in
the wings, ready to step in with their
own bids.*

spread your wings to do something
new, exciting, or brave ▶ *I can
understand it – she's 18 and she's
determined to spread her wings.*

**try your
wings**
to try to do
something
new ▶ *Having
to organize
the trip has
given him a
chance to try
his wings and see how he gets on.*

WINK

not sleep a wink also **not get a wink
of sleep** not to be able to sleep at all
▶ *He got up feeling as if he hadn't
slept a wink.* ▶ *I don't get a wink of
sleep until I know they're home safely.*

WINNER

be onto a winner to be selling,
producing or doing something that is
likely to be very successful ▶ *He's set
himself up as the sole importer of
these new bikes, and thinks he's onto
a winner.*

WIRE

sth goes (right) down to the wire the
time when something will end or be
decided is very close ▶ *The
negotiations went right down to the
wire, but we reached an agreement
just before the deadline.* **down-to-the-
wire** ADJ ▶ *They won a down-to-the-
wire victory yesterday.*

sb is a live wire someone is very
cheerful and funny, and has a lot of
energy ▶ *Their son's a live wire, isn't
he?*

W

WIRES

have/get your wires crossed to be or become confused and wrong about what someone wants, or has

said ▶ *Someone had got their wires crossed and double-booked the villa.* ▶ *I think we've got a lot of wires crossed and we need to have a talk to sort it out.*

WISE

get wise to sb/sth to realize that someone is doing something that is not right or honest ▶ *She used to meet him secretly, until her parents got wise to what was going on.*

be none the wiser also **not be any the wiser** to know or understand nothing, even if you have had the opportunity to know or understand ▶ *She gave me some long explanation for why she hadn't turned up but in the end I was none the wiser.* ▶ *He could easily have phoned her, and we wouldn't have been any the wiser.*

WISH

I/you wish! I/you wish that was true, but it isn't ▶ *"You look as if you've lost some weight." "I wish!"* ▶ *"I might win and then I'll be off to the Caribbean!" "You wish!"*

your wish is my command! I am ready to do anything you ask me to do ▶ *Where would you like me to take you tonight? Your wish is my command.*

WITH

be with it to feel intelligent and organized ▶ *I'm sorry, I don't know what's the matter with me – I'm just not with it this morning.*

WITS

gather your wits also **collect your wits** to control yourself and think clearly and calmly ▶ *By the time I had gathered my wits to reply, she had put the phone down.*

keep your wits about you to be ready to think clearly and quickly in a difficult situation ▶ *You had to keep your wits about you when you played poker with my father and Uncle Charlie.*

pit your wits against sb/sth to use all your intelligence to try and beat someone or something ▶ *The school chess champion will have a chance to pit his wits against the best players in the region.*

scare sb out of their wits also **scare the wits out of sb** to make someone very frightened ▶ *What did you do that for? You scared me out of my wits!*

WOE

woe betide sb someone will have trouble ▶ *When I was at school, we had a spelling test every day, and woe betide you if you got three or more wrong.* ▶ *The superintendent was a very fair man, but woe betide any officer who disobeyed him.*

WOLF

cry wolf to keep saying that there is a problem or danger when there is not, so that when there is a problem, no one believes you ▶ *She had cried wolf so often that nobody realized she was really ill until she ended up in hospital.*

W

This idiom comes from an old story about a boy who was looking after sheep and, as a joke, called out that a wolf (=an animal like a large dog) was coming. His friends ran to help him, but when a wolf really came, they thought his cry for help was another joke, and they did not come.

keep the wolf from the door to earn enough money to buy enough to live on, but no more ▶ *I'm working part-time just to keep the wolf from the door.*

a lone wolf someone who prefers to spend time alone ▶ *He's not an easy person to make friends with – a bit of a lone wolf, I'd say.*

be a wolf in sheep's clothing to seem nicer or better than is really true ▶ *You shouldn't trust Lew, he's a wolf in sheep's clothing – he'll borrow money and never pay you back.*

WOLVES

throw sb to the wolves to let someone be attacked or criticized in order to gain an advantage for yourself ▶ *He has been cleared of stealing, but has been thrown to the wolves to show the public that the system is effective.*

WOMAN

be as ____ as the next woman ➤ be as ____ as the next MAN

if you want..., sb is your woman ➤ if you want..., sb is your MAN

make an honest woman (out) of sb to marry a particular woman ▶ *At last he's made an honest woman of his partner of ten years.*

sb's right-hand woman ➤ sb's right-hand MAN

you can't keep a good woman down ➤ you can't keep a good MAN down

be your own woman ➤ be your own MAN

WONDER

I don't wonder (that) I'm not surprised ▶ *I don't wonder you're cold, you haven't even got a coat on.*

(it's) no wonder also **(it's) small wonder** it's not surprising ▶ *No wonder you're tired if you walked all that way.* ▶ *When doctors have to work such long hours it's little wonder that mistakes are made.*

a one-hit wonder a singer or band that only makes one successful record ▶ *Do you remember any of the one-hit wonders of the past ten years?*

WONDERS

do wonders (for) also **work wonders (for)** to be surprisingly effective for someone or something ▶ *Taking exercise can work wonders for your mood.* ▶ *Her new boyfriend has done wonders for her – she looks so happy.*

wonders will never cease that is very surprising ▶ *Nick had done all the ironing when I got home. Wonders will never cease!* ▶ *Some local lawyers are donating their time free. Will wonders never cease?*

WOOD

sb can't see the wood for the trees someone can't see what is important about a situation because they are paying too much attention to its small details ▶ *Planning officials can't see the wood for the trees, worrying about a barn door instead of blocking a new petrol station.*

dead wood people in an organization who are no longer useful or needed

▶ *The new chairman of a public company can dispose of dead wood and bring in fresh talent.*

touch wood also **knock (on) wood** said when you want your good luck to continue ▶ *I haven't had a serious illness in my life, touch wood.*

WOODS

not be out of the woods (yet) to be in a difficult situation still ▶ *She's much better, but she isn't out of the woods yet.*

WOODWORK

come out of the woodwork to appear suddenly, especially from an unknown place

▶ *Once they saw how slim she was, volunteers for the diet started coming out of the woodwork! ▶ Art dealers are eager to see if any more of these portraits come out of the woodwork.*

WOOL

pull the wool over sb's eyes to deceive someone ▶ *He's pulling the wool over your eyes – can't you see he's never going to pay back that money?*

WORD

be as good as your word to do exactly what you have promised to do ▶ *She said she'd get everything organized, and she was as good as her word.*

not breathe a word also **not say a word** not to tell anyone anything ▶ *You can trust me. I won't breathe a word to anyone. ▶ She had to promise that she*

wouldn't say a word about the new designs.

by word of mouth (of information) heard directly from people you know ▶ *The most reliable way to choose a language school is by word of mouth.*

from the word go from the beginning ▶ *The marriage was a disaster from the word go.*

not get a word in edgeways not to get a chance to speak because someone else is talking too much ▶ *Once he starts talking about politics, no one else gets a word in edgeways.*

give sb your word (that) to promise someone very seriously (that) ▶ *I'd like to tell you, but you have to give me your word you won't tell anyone else.*

hang on sb's every word also **hang on sb's words** to listen very carefully to everything someone says ▶ *She's a brilliant speaker and the audience were hanging on her every word.*

sb has the last word someone is the person who makes the final decision about something, or the final point in an argument ▶ *She took a deep breath, determined that she would not let him have the last word.*

have a word (with sb) to talk to someone, usually privately ▶ *I'd like to see you in my office, I need to have a word with you about that survey. ▶ Good morning, Mr Hughes. Could I have a quick word, please?*

in a word ___ used to introduce one word that expresses everything you want to say ▶ *The show was well directed, well acted, full of colour and life – in a word, sensational.*

sth is a dirty word a particular activity or quality is not generally approved of ▶ *Politics is a dirty word among the young people in this country.*

W

___ isn't the word for it a particular word is not strong enough to describe something ▸ *Disappointment wasn't the word for it. I felt completely devastated.*

keep your word to do what you promised ▸ *We have kept our word since the last election – taxes have not risen.*

be the last word in ___ to be the best, most modern thing of its type ▸ *First prize in our competition is a deep-pile carpet – the last word in luxury.*

a man/woman of his/her word someone who always does what they have promised to do ▸ *I've always found him to be a man of his word.*

mum's the word don't tell anyone about this ▸ *Remember, mum's the word – I don't want anyone else to know until I'm certain.*

put in a (good) word for sb to say good things about someone to help them get something ▸ *I'm not promising anything, but I'll put in a good word for you at the meeting.*

(just) say the word just ask and I'll do what you want ▸ *Hey, if you want any help with that, just say the word.*

take sb at his/her word to believe what someone says ▸ *Lou promised he'd pay me back on Friday, and I took him at his word.*

take my word for it believe me ▸ *You don't have to take my word for it, you can check with any of the other members of staff.*

sb's word is law everyone always obeys a particular person ▸ *Mum was kind and fair-minded, but her word was law.*

word for word
1 in exactly the same words as before ▸ *She told me, almost word for word,* *the same story as Rob did.*
2 translating the meaning of each single word instead of translating the meaning of a whole phrase or sentence ▸ *It is often completely misleading to translate the text word for word.*

the word (on the street) is that *also* **word has it that** the news is that ▸ *The word on the street is that stripes are making a comeback.* ▸ *The word is that morale is low among university teachers, primarily because of lack of funding.* ▸ *Word has it that the prisoner will be released early tomorrow.*

WORDS

(be forced to) eat your words to admit that what you said was wrong ▸ *He was forced to eat his words at an angry meeting of European finance ministers.*

famous last words that is likely to be the last thing you say before something happens to prove it wrong ▸ *"Don't worry, I can see where I'm going." Famous last words, I thought, as I heard her stumble into the dustbin.*

have words (with sb) to argue with or speak angrily to someone ▸ *I had words with Mark's teacher about that letter.*

in so many words (said) very clearly, directly, and usually rudely ▸ *My boss told me, in so many words, to quit my job.*

not in so many words not clearly or directly, but having a particular meaning ▸ *"Did he admit he did it?" "Not in so many words, but I'm pretty sure that's what he was getting at."*

lost for words *also* **at a loss for words**
unable to say anything because you are surprised,

shocked, unhappy etc ▶ *She was lost for words when her friends sprang a surprise party for her 70th birthday.*
▶ *His rudeness left me at a loss for words.*

(you) mark my words pay attention to what I'm saying ▶ *We haven't heard the last of him, you mark my words.*
▶ *Mark my words, that marriage won't last.*

not mince (your) words to say exactly what you think ▶ *Believe me, you'll know if she's angry. She doesn't mince her words.*

put words in(to) sb's mouth to say that someone said something that they did not actually say, or suggest that they are going to say something that they do not intend to say ▶ *I did not say you were lazy! Don't you dare put words into my mouth!* ▶ *Ask your daughter what happened, and try not to put words into her mouth.*

words fail me I don't know what to say ▶ *The way that man just drove right in front of me – well, words fail me.*

you took the words (right) out of my mouth you said exactly what I was going to say ▶ *"What a waste of time that was!" "You took the words right out of my mouth."*

WORK

(it's) all in a day's work it's what I do every day, so it's usual for me
▶ *Dealing with dead animals is all in a day's work for zoo staff.*

all work and no play (makes Jack a dull boy) it is not good for you to work too hard; you need to relax too ▶ *Why don't you go for a swim? All work and no play, you know.*

do sb's dirty work to do the unpleasant or dishonest things that someone else does not want to do
▶ *He's rich enough to pay other people to do his dirty work for him.*

have your work cut out (for you) you will have to work very hard ▶ *She has her work cut out for her keeping those kids amused.*

make short work of sth to finish something quickly and easily ▶ *He made short work of the huge plate of fish and chips.*

nice work if you can get it your work is very good, easy, or enjoyable

▶ *Researchers for the book had to visit pubs, play darts and drink with the lads. Nice work if you can get it.*

WORKS

the (whole) works everything ▶ *Jeff was really sorry – he apologized with flowers, chocolates, the whole works.*

WORLD

brave new world a new time that is starting after great changes have happened ▶ *Do any kids still enjoy reading in this brave, new, high-tech world where the computer game is king?* ▶ *Welcome to the brave new world of college football!*

W

This phrase comes from a line in Shakespeare's play *The Tempest*. It was also used by Aldous Huxley as the title of a book about a time in the future when everything is controlled using science, and people can make no choices for themselves.

dead to the world very deeply asleep ▶ *Didn't you hear the phone ring? You must have been dead to the world.*

come up in the world to become richer or more successful ▶ *She's come up in the world since the days when she had to pay publishers to print her books.* **come/go down in the world** ▶ *The family had clearly come down in the world since their grandfather's time.*

do sb the world of good to make someone feel much better ▶ *A holiday in the sun would do you the world of good.*

for all the world like/as if exactly like/ as if ▶ *They rode off on their motorcycles, for all the world like a flock of bats.*

have the world at your feet *also* **have the ___ world at your feet** to be very successful and popular (with a particular group) ▶ *The ten-year-old pianist could have the world at his feet, but he's not interested in fame.* ▶ *When she graduated from college she had the corporate world at her feet, with more than 30 job offers to choose from.*

in a world of your own not noticing what is happening around you ▶ *Chris is very sociable, but Ben seems to be living in a world of his own.*

sb is not long for this world someone will not live for very much longer ▶ *Poor old dog – she's not long for this world.*

a man/woman of the world someone who knows a lot about life and is not easily shocked by things ▶ *You can tell us what happened after the party, we're all women of the world.*

mean the world to sb to be extremely important to someone ▶ *This job means the world to her – she'd be shattered to lose it.*

on top of the world extremely happy ▶ *What a beautiful baby – you must be on top of the world!*

out of this world very good, impressive, surprising etc ▶ *The designs for the costumes and stage sets are out of this world.*

won't set the world on fire not to be very exciting, successful, or impressive ▶ *His latest film, although controversial, won't really set the world on fire.*

(it's a) small world said when you are surprised because you have met someone you know in an unlikely place, or when you find out that two people you know from different places know each other ▶ *It's such a small world! I met someone at a party in London recently who used to work with my sister in Singapore!*

think the world of sb to admire, respect, or like someone very much ▶ *She was one of our best employees. The customers thought the world of her.*

watch the world go by to sit somewhere pleasant and see people living their lives around you ▶ *Most of the bars have terraces where you can sip a glass of wine and watch the world go by.*

what is the world coming to? you are

W

surprised and shocked at a situation or action that you do not approve of ▶ *$3 for a grapefruit? What is the world coming to?* ▶ *What's the world coming to if the council won't rehouse you even if you have kids?*

the world is your oyster someone has the chance to do lots of things they want because they are young, well-educated, intelligent etc ▶ *He's got a university degree, two years' experience, and great enthusiasm – the world is his oyster.*

> This idiom comes from a line in Shakespeare's play *The Merry Wives of Windsor*.

a world of difference a big difference ▶ *There's a world of difference between being a great musician and being a great teacher of music.*

(sb thinks) the world revolves around him/her someone thinks that they are more important than anyone else ▶ *I'm so glad I don't work with one of those TV stars who thinks the world revolves around him.* **(sb thinks) the world revolves around sth** ▶ *For me, the world revolves around football.*

the ___s of this world (used with one person's name) people of that type ▶ *We all have to deal with the Dr Smiths of this world – try not to let him upset you.*

WORLDS

(have/get) the best of both worlds to have or get all the advantages and none of the disadvantages of two situations, ways of doing things etc ▶ *Now I work at home, I have the best of both worlds. I can keep up my career and still spend time with my daughter.* **the worst of both worlds**

▶ *This legislation discourages tobacco companies from building factories here, yet allows them to continue advertising, giving us the worst of both worlds.*

be worlds apart to be very different ▶ *Their management styles were worlds apart and we found it difficult to adapt.*

WORM

the worm turns even someone quiet and patient will start to behave differently if they are badly treated for long enough ▶ *He used to bully Joe and he never expected the worm to turn, but eventually Joe landed him in hospital.*

WORST

if the worst comes to the worst even if the worst things happen ▶ *If the worst comes to the worst and we lose the house, we can always move in with my parents.*

WOULDN'T

wouldn't you (just) know it
1 I might have expected that bad luck ▶ *Eventually, we found our way back to the car park, but wouldn't you just know it, the car wouldn't start.*
2 that doesn't surprise me ▶ *"He listens to classical music and reads boring old books." "Wouldn't you know it!"*

WOUNDS

lick your wounds to try and comfort yourself after a defeat, upset, or disappointment ▶ *The team have gone*

W

off to lick their wounds after their disgraceful defeat today.

WRAPS

keep sth under wraps to keep something secret ▶ *The government were hoping to keep the new weapon under wraps for as long as possible.*
be under wraps ▶ *The project is still under wraps – we haven't got authorization for it yet.*
take the wraps off sth to tell people about a new plan, project, product etc for the first time ▶ *The big PC manufacturers will take the wraps off their new models at the trade fair.*

WRECK

be a nervous wreck to be extremely anxious, easily annoyed, sensitive to criticism etc ▶ *If I had to go back and live with my parents again I'd be a nervous wreck by the end of the first week.*

WRINGER

go through the wringer to have a long, unpleasant, and difficult experience ▶ *He's been through the wringer, first with the trial and now with his illness.* **be put through the wringer** ▶ *It is often the children of the divorcing couple who are put through the wringer.*

WRIT

writ large in an extreme form of (a particular thing) ▶ *The experiment demands that seven people live together for a year. This is togetherness writ large.*

WRITING

the writing on the wall something that shows people that a situation will become difficult or unpleasant

▶ *Most of the miners will see the writing on the wall and leave the mines before they are sacked.*

> This idiom comes from a story in the book of Daniel in the Bible, in which the King of Babylon sees a hand writing on the wall. The writing says that an enemy will kill him and take his power.

WRONG

don't get me wrong do not think that I am trying to say something else ▶ *Don't get me wrong – I enjoyed the film, it's just that I expected it to be funnier.*
you can't go wrong (with) it would be sensible to do or use something ▶ *Why don't you get her some flowers? You can't go wrong with flowers!*

WRONGS

two wrongs don't make a right if someone has done something unpleasant to you, you should not do the same type of thing to them ▶ *Starting a fight with him will just cause more resentment, and in any case, two wrongs don't make a right.*

W

X
X number of *also* **X amount of** *or* **X pounds etc** said when you do not know the exact quantity of what you are talking about ▶ *Imagine you have X thousand pounds to invest in something a bit unusual – which of these companies do you think you would choose?*

Yy

YARN

spin a yarn to tell a long and possibly untrue story ▶ *She spun me some yarn about how her neighbour took her to the wrong hospital and then she couldn't get a bus.*

YEAR

it's not my year ➤ it's not my DAY
year in, year out ➤ DAY in, day out

YEARS

never in a million years also ***not in a million years*** never, not at all ▶ *He's a successful author? I would never have guessed in a million years.*

sth puts years on sb also ***sth puts ten etc years on sb*** something makes someone look or seem older ▶ *His daughter's death has put years on him.* ▶ *Don't wear that coat, it puts 20 years on you!* **take years off sb** ▶ *She's lost some weight and it's taken years off her.*

YES

yes and no there is no clear answer to that question ▶ *"Did you enjoy the book?" "Yes and no. I loved her descriptions of local life, but all her characters are so unattractive."*

YESTERDAY

I wasn't born yesterday! also ***do you think I was born yesterday?*** I'm not stupid or easily tricked ▶ *I can tell you've had another row with him. I wasn't born yesterday, you know!*

YONDER

the wide blue yonder far away; the distance ▶ *Don't think you're going to disappear off into the wide blue yonder leaving me to cook dinner again.*

YOU

you gotta do what you gotta do ➤ a MAN's gotta do what a man's gotta do

YOUNG

you're only young once (said to excuse or encourage a young person) take full advantage of being young ▶ *"I'm just going down to the beach with Rob and Phil." "At this time of night? Oh, well, you're only young once, I suppose."*

YOUNGER

you're not getting any younger (said to an old person to stop them doing something too active) be careful now that you are old ▶ *I don't think you should be doing all this gardening. After all, you're not getting any younger.*

Y

Zz

Z'S
catch some Z's to sleep ▶ *"You look tired." "Yeah, I'm going home to catch some Z's."*

ZONE
a ___-free zone a place that has or should have none of a particular thing in it ▶ *We used to argue all the time, so Dad declared the house a politics-free zone.*

> This idiom comes from expressions such as 'military-free zone', 'nuclear-free zone', and 'weapons-free zone' which are often used in agreements between governments or political organizations.

Idioms Quiz

More than meets the eye

Here are 99 ideas for a quiz. Each of the following questions is based on an idiom in the *Longman Pocket Idioms Dictionary*. You will probably know that the answer to all of the questions is "no", but do you know what the idioms mean? If you don't, you can find the answer by looking for the idiom in the main part of the book, at the word that is shown in CAPITAL LETTERS. So, for example, you can find out what "drive someone round the BEND" means by looking at the entry for "BEND".

1. If someone drove you round the BEND, would they use their car?

2. Do you sweep the BOARD when your house is dirty?

3. If you get cold FEET, should you put your socks on?

4. Do you need music to make a SONG and dance about something?

5. If you make a MEAL of something, do you spend a long time in the kitchen?

6. If someone stole your THUNDER, would you tell the police?

7. If someone went APE, would you take them to the zoo?

8. Would you need a brush to paint the TOWN red?

9. If you didn't know which WAY to turn, would it help to look at a map?

10. Do you need long arms to give yourself a pat on the BACK?

11. If someone went through the ROOF, would it leave a hole?

12. Are mice allowed to take part in the rat RACE?

13. Would you need a glass of water to help you swallow your PRIDE?

14. Do you have to be a good swimmer to keep your HEAD above water?

15. If you bit your TONGUE, would it bleed?

16. Can you hear very well if you are all EARS?

17. Do you have to be a magician to do a vanishing ACT?

18. Do you need a knife to have a STAB at something?

19. If you tied the KNOT, would you need a piece of string?

20. Would you eat a red HERRING for breakfast?

21. Do you have to be good at maths to put TWO and two together?

22. If you are going PLACES, do you need a passport?

23. If someone is walking on AIR, are they wearing special shoes?

24. Do you need a spade to make a MOUNTAIN out of a molehill?

25. If you give someone your WORD, will they need to give it back to you later?

26. Do you need a special cloth to wipe the GRIN off someone's face?

27. If someone rained on your PARADE, would you put your mac on?

28. Do you have to be strong to carry the CAN?

29. Do you need a pen to DOT the i's and cross the t's?

30. If something left a bad TASTE in your mouth, would it help to drink a glass of water?

31. If you were digging for DIRT, would you be in the garden?

32. If you drop a CLANGER, does it make a lot of noise?

33. If something goes like a BOMB, does it explode?

34. If you have green FINGERS, do you need to wash your hands?

35. If you TELL someone where to go, are you being helpful?

36. Will FOOD for thought make you put on weight?

37. Do you need a hammer to hit the NAIL on the head?

38. If someone has a sweet TOOTH, should they see a dentist?

39. If you have a lot on your PLATE, is there too much to eat?

40. Is ELBOW grease sold in tins?

41. If you miss the BOAT, will you have to swim?

42. If you have a LUMP in your throat, should you see a doctor?

43. If you got the AXE, could you use it to chop wood?

44. If you were up the CREEK without a paddle, would you be in a boat?

45. Do you need a good voice to sing someone's PRAISES?

46. If you came down on someone like a TON of bricks, would they have to go to hospital?

47. Would you fall over if someone started pulling your LEG?

48. If you brought the HOUSE down, would you need to look for somewhere else to live?

49. Do you have to be in Holland to go DUTCH?

50. Do you need a coat to cover your BACK?

51. Would you need a bicycle to take someone for a RIDE?

52. If you WALK all over someone, will their clothes get dirty?

53. If someone is rolling in the AISLES, are they in church?

54. Would you need a brush to sweep someone off their FEET?

55. Do you need an umbrella for a rainy DAY?

56. If two people are as thick as THIEVES, have they stolen something?

57. If you play with FIRE, will you burn your fingers?

58. If someone stabbed you in the BACK, would it hurt?

59. Do you need wool to spin a YARN?

60. If something were not your CUP of tea, would you have a coffee instead?

61. Do you need a large garden to beat about the BUSH?

62. If something is on the TIP of your tongue, should you swallow it?

63. If you have FRIENDS in high places, do they all live on the top floor?

64. If you hit the ROAD, are you angry?

65. Do very rich criminals wear golden HANDCUFFS?

66. Do you need a gun to kill TIME?

67. If you sent someone to COVENTRY, would they have to pack their suitcase?

68. Do you have to lie down to keep your EAR to the ground?

69. If someone is robbing PETER to pay Paul, should you call the police?

70. Does a fat CAT need to go on a diet?

71. Do you have to be able to swim to leave a sinking SHIP?

72. Do you have to be good at decorating to paper over the CRACKS?

73. If something is on the HOUSE, do you have to climb onto the roof to get it?

74. Do you have to be fast to cut someone to the QUICK?

75. Do you itch a lot if you have ANTS in your pants?

76. If someone drinks like a FISH, do they like water?

77. If you are having a bad HAIR day, should you go to the hairdresser's?

78. Do you need a pencil to draw a LINE under something?

79. If someone has a SCREW loose, do they need some tools?

80. If someone is on CLOUD nine, do they need a parachute?

81. Do you need a hammer to nail your COLOURS to the mast?

82. If you stepped on someone's TOES, would you be dancing with them?

83. If someone is wet behind the EARS, should they use a towel to dry themselves?

84. If you dig your HEELS in, do your feet get dirty?

85. If you lose your MARBLES, are you likely to find them again?

86. Are you asleep if you do something with your EYES shut?

87. If the BALL is in your court, should you try to hit it?

88. Do you need a gun to shoot from the HIP?

89. If someone is over the HILL, do they have a good view?

90. Should you wear dark glasses on a blind DATE?

91. Do you have to be very light to walk on EGGSHELLS?

92. Do you need a knife in order to cut CORNERS?

93. If you cook the BOOKS, do they taste better?

94. If you are in hot WATER, are you having a bath?

95. Do you need bricks to build BRIDGES?

96. Do you take someone to the CLEANERS because their clothes are dirty?

97. If you are tied to someone's APRON STRINGS, do you spend a lot of time with them in the kitchen?

98. If you have your WIRES crossed, would it help to call an electrician?

99. Do you need electricity to recharge your BATTERIES?

In the picture

In order to discover the true meaning of an idiom, you need to understand the words it contains as a group, instead of looking at each word separately. The pictures in the *Longman Pocket Idioms Dictionary* play on the fact that an idiom's actual meaning is different from what the words seem to mean at first sight. This quiz tests whether you know the idioms that are suggested by the pictures on the following pages. Can you match each explanation to one of the pictures on the same page to find the correct idiom?

Here is an example from page 289 to get you started. *To seem silly and be embarrassed* is connected with one of the four pictures you can choose from. These pictures show some socks, a bell, an egg and a trumpet (=the musical instrument in picture D). Do you know an idiom which contains one of these words and which means *to seem silly and be embarrassed*? The answer is 'end up with egg on your face'.

Now look at the other explanations and use the pictures to help you find the idiom. The answers are on page 296.

1.   to seem silly and be embarrassed
2.   to praise yourself in a proud way
3.   to work harder and improve your standard
4.   something sounds familiar

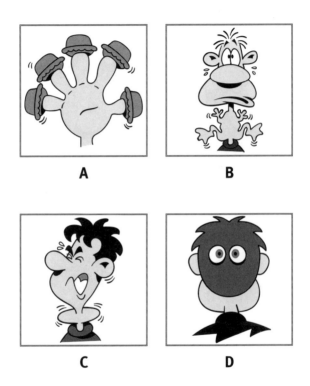

A   **B**

C   **D**

1. to have difficulty speaking because your throat is blocked
2. something is difficult to believe
3. to notice everything that is happening
4. to be involved in many different activities

1. to spoil a situation by criticizing or changing it
2. to be happy because you are making money
3. exactly like each other
4. to keep something a secret

1. a lot of problems
2. someone has the wrong idea
3. to show your true feelings
4. several things happen at the same time

1. to become confident or successful in a new situation
2. to work together to solve a problem
3. to be easily offended
4. to feel very worried or unhappy

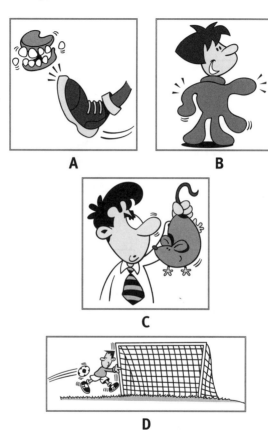

1. to suddenly change your aims
2. to be exactly right for someone
3. to begin to think that something is wrong
4. better than nothing

A

B

C

D

1. to defeat someone completely
2. when you show your approval by clapping
   (=hitting your hands together)
3. to be taking a risk
4. something that shows a situation will become difficult

Page 289:
1C end up with egg on your face
2D blow your own trumpet
3A pull your socks up
4B something rings a bell

Page 290:
1B have a frog in your throat
2C something is hard to swallow
3D have eyes in the back of your head
4A have a finger in every pie

Page 291:
1A rock the boat
2D be laughing all the way to the bank
3C like two peas in a pod
4B keep something under your hat

Page 292:
1A a can of worms
2C somebody is barking up the wrong tree
3B wear your heart on your sleeve
4D it never rains but it pours

Page 293:
1C find your feet
2A put your heads together
3B have a chip on your shoulder
4D have the weight of the world on your shoulders

Page 294:
1D move the goalposts
2B fit somebody like a glove
3C smell a rat
4A better than a kick in the teeth

Page 295:
1B wipe the floor with somebody
2A a big hand
3D be (skating) on thin ice
4C the writing on the wall